BACKROADS
& BYWAYS
OF
IOWA

BACKROADS & BYWAYS OF IOWA

Drives, Daytrips & Weekend Excursions

Michael Ream

THE COUNTRYMAN PRESS
A division of W. W. Norton & Company
Independent Publishers Since 1923

For information about permission to reproduce selections from this book, write to Permissions, The Countryman Press, 500 Fifth Avenue, New York, NY 10110

For information about special discounts for bulk purchases, please contact W. W. Norton Special Sales at specialsales@wwnorton.com or 800-233-4830

Interior photographs by the author
Maps by Erin Greb Cartography, © The Countryman Press
Book design by Susan Livingston
Composition by Chelsea Cloeter

The Countryman Press
www.countrymanpress.com

A division of W. W. Norton & Company, Inc.,
500 Fifth Avenue, New York, NY 10110
www.wwnorton.com

Backroads & Byways of Iowa
978-0-88150-991-5

10 9 8 7 6 5 4 3

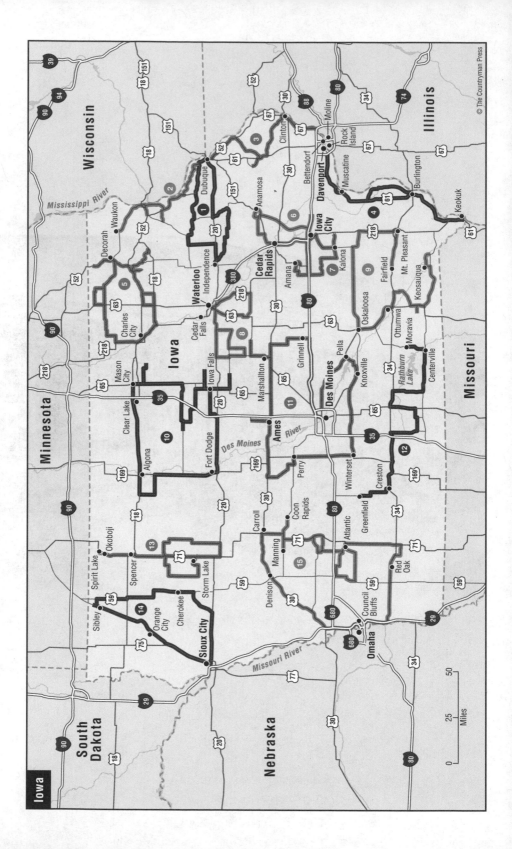

CONTENTS

The Dubuque County Courthouse

INTRODUCTION

I owa is a great place for wandering. A largely rural state with no end of small, unhurried roads off the main highways, it's a place where you can ease back and take life a little slower. Moving across the open landscape and passing by the state's archetypal small towns and farms, there is no end of things to see and do.

While the Mississippi and Missouri Rivers bracket Iowa on the east and west, respectively, with plenty of historic river towns along their lengths, the heart and soul of Iowa is the wide sweep of farmland that covers most of the state with long, thick rows of corn. Driving through rural Iowa is indeed a trip through America's great agricultural empire, motoring along two-lane blacktops and narrow gravel byways past endless farm fields.

But it's not all cornfields and hog pens in Iowa. From the striking bluffs that rise over the Mississippi and Missouri to the Loess Hills, rolling slopes of wind-blown silt that stand along the western edge of Iowa at heights found virtually nowhere else, Iowa's many attractions offer plenty of variety to travelers. Iowa has one of the best preserved pioneer settlements around, the Amana Colonies, where guests can learn about the lives of early immigrants to the state through visits to historic buildings and living history demonstrations, as well as the nearby presidential library and museum of Herbert Hoover, the state's only president. Iowa has the marionettes from *The Sound of Music,* part of the collection of one of the world's most renowned puppeteers, along with one of the greatest concentrations of homes done in the Prairie School style made famous by Frank Lloyd Wright—both in the same place, Mason City. And don't forget the ice cream capital of the world, Le Mars, a town amid the vast empty stretches of northwest Iowa where you can sample yummy goodies at a classic, old-fashioned ice cream parlor.

Iowa City and Ames are all-American college towns, with downtowns and campuses that are perfect for strolling, while the state's "Great Lakes" can be found in the resort area known as Okobokji. They are a bit more modest than their more well-known namesakes, but they're still quintessential summer fun places, as is the nearby town of Storm Lake. All feature nice stretches of water where Iowans head out on boats and water skis to play to their hearts' content.

Escaping to the lakes is a refreshing relief from the summer sun, which can

The old Star Brewery building

get brutal as it beats down on the wide-open landscape. Fortunately, there are plenty of spring and fall days that are like paradise, with moderate temperatures and pleasant breezes blowing across the fields. While winter in Iowa brings subfreezing temperatures and *a lot* of snow, it doesn't stop the fun, as Iowans take to trails with snowmobiles and cross-country skis.

The state capital of Des Moines offers a full slate of attractions and cultural events, as well as a nice selection of restaurants and accommodations. Other urban spots in Iowa include the twin cities of Waterloo and Cedar Falls, which each feature a large complex of downtown museums; the historic railroading center of Council Bluffs; and Dubuque, a classic Mississippi River port whose waterfront has been remade into a showcase of the "Big Muddy."

Rural Iowa has indeed seen its share of struggles over the past few decades, but a road trip through the state's countryside also can be an interesting throwback, with the landscape in some places resembling a Grant Wood painting. You may find yourself in places where it's difficult to find big-box stores and fast food restaurants, and instead discover opportunities to observe artisans working at old-time crafts or have a meal in a historic home or classic country restaurant.

The state's small-town museums frequently focus on the hardships and triumphs of living in an isolated, rural area with an often harsh climate. You'll also see reminders of Germany, Holland, Denmark, Norway, Sweden and other places from which immigrants came to make a new life on the windswept prairie. The list of new arrivals in Iowa continues today, with towns across the state becoming home to immigrants from places like Somalia, Bosnia, Mexico, Ukraine, Vietnam and a host of other far-flung countries.

This points to one of the best parts of a road trip through Iowa: the people. Tradition runs deep in most places across Iowa, particularly the small towns that make up much of the state, and most people are friendly and willing to lend a hand or point you to an undiscovered treasure. It might be an

Dutch dancing at Pella's annual Tulip Time

unheralded museum or a pleasant little country inn where you can fall asleep listening to the chirp of crickets and awake to sunlight streaming over the fields.

Travelers have long made their way across Iowa, beginning with the Ioway Indians who gave the state its name and whose hunting trails stretched across the landscape. In 1846, the Mormons began their great trek west in Iowa, crossing the Mississippi River from Nauvoo, Illinois, and eventually reaching Council Bluffs on the Missouri River, where they camped through the winter before moving on. Visitors continued to crisscross Iowa into the 20th century, with modern roads like the Lincoln Highway bringing hordes through the state's small towns, where many stopped for a bite or to fill up their car and instantly fell in love with the country landscape and friendly people.

So join the long list of travelers who have journeyed through Iowa, but make sure you get off the highways and check out the sights of the Hawkeye State. Meander down the smaller roads; there is history in every small town and country crossroads, and there's always an interesting place to see just around the bend.

Make time during your trip to Iowa to soak up the homespun goodness this most Midwestern of states has to offer. You'll be glad you did.

A NOTE ON THE LISTINGS

Each chapter presents a route to follow along different roads and through towns and cities, with details on attractions you'll find along the way. At the end of each chapter are listings, including those for lodging and dining. These were chosen for their convenience and reliability for the traveler, and sometimes for just plain availability; in Iowa's wide-open rural areas, there are often not many restaurants and hotels from which to choose. The cost codes at the end of these listings break down as follows:

Lodging (standard room for two people)
Inexpensive: Under $75
Moderate: $75–150
Medium: $150–225
Expensive: $225 and over

Dining (price range of dinner entrées)
Inexpensive: $10 or less
Moderate: $11–20
Medium: $21–30
Expensive: $30 and over

Many attractions and some accommodations shutter their doors in winter, opening again only when spring finally arrives and wakens the cornfields from their months of slumber under a blanket of snow. Of course, some places close permanently; it's best to check ahead to see if a place you want to visit is still open for business, particularly in smaller towns and rural areas.

1 Dubuque and Points West:
FROM A CLASSIC RIVER TOWN TO A FAMOUS BASEBALL FIELD

Estimated length: 150 miles from Dubuque west to Strawberry Point and Independence, then east to Dyersville and back to Dubuque.

Estimated time: About three hours to drive the route; at least a weekend to fully explore Dubuque and other places, although you could spend a few days just checking out Dubuque itself.

Getting there: Dubuque lies on the west bank of the Mississippi River at the junction of three main highways: from Cedar Falls/Waterloo, take US 20 about 75 miles east; from Cedar Rapids, take US 151 about 65 miles northeast; and from the Quad Cities, take US 61 about 65 miles north.

Highlights: Dubuque's waterfront, with an aquarium and Mississippi River history. The Fenelon Place Elevator. Field of Dreams in Dyersville. National Farm Toy Museum. The oldest city in Iowa, Dubuque has a colorful history closely tied to the river, which helped turned the city into a prosperous port during the steamboat age in the 19th century. A corresponding lead mining boom, with much of the mineral going to produce ammunition in the years leading up to the Civil War, made Dubuque a rich town indeed, with lead barons and others constructing mansions on the impressive limestone bluffs arching over the city. Downtown streets were lined with grand brick edifices, including a large opera house that still stands.

Things have since quieted down in Dubuque, with the city's harbors long having ceased their frenetic pace of activity, yet the riverfront district in the shadow of the Julien Dubuque Bridge has been transformed into a tourist mecca chock-full of attractions, including a river museum and aquarium, a restored Mississippi River steamboat and a working paddlewheel ferry.

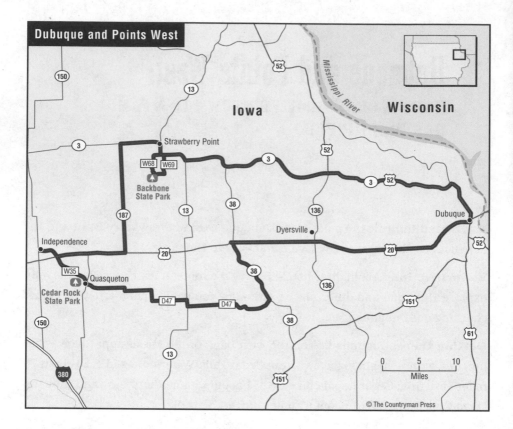

Not far from Dubuque, outside the town of Dyersville, is the *Field of Dreams* movie site, where eager fans make pilgrimages to the legendary baseball diamond. Nearby is Backbone State Park, a mecca for hiking and outdoors enthusiasts, and Strawberry Point, a charming town with a refurbished historic hotel. Architecture buffs can check out Cedar Rock, the classic Frank Lloyd Wright house located in the rolling Iowa countryside.

Begin your visit to Dubuque on the riverfront, just off US 151 and US 61. Along Ice Harbor, the southern of two harbors, lies the **National Mississippi River Museum & Aquarium** (www.mississippirivermuseum .com), a sprawling complex of several buildings devoted to exploring every facet of life along the "Big

One of Dubuque's beautiful brick mansions

Muddy." All sorts of river landscapes are re-created in the museum's buildings, including swamps, ponds, and marshes, with attendant wildlife. Interactive exhibits are found throughout the museum's buildings, including a "wet lab" where kids can get up close and personal with river creatures. Visitors can even pilot a tugboat or explore a river cave. A variety of aquariums located in different museum buildings display all sorts of marine life, among them a 40,000-gallon Gulf of Mexico tank holding sharks, rays and many other fish found at the mouth of the Mississippi. Other tanks feature wildlife such as turtles, otters, frogs, snapping turtles and large alligators. Historic riverboats are on display as well, and there's a 3-D and 4-D theater with a changing selection of films. A boardwalk trail leads to replica dwellings used by Native Americans and frontier fur trappers, and gives visitors the opportunity to spot great blue herons or bald eagles.

Outside on the wharves facing the harbor are the 1934 steamboat *William M. Black* and the towboat *Logsdon,* both of which are open to visitors. Radio-controlled boats are available for kids to pilot here, too. If you want to take a spin on the river, **Dubuque River Rides** offers cruises on both a paddle-wheeler and an 80-foot-long motor yacht.

North of the museums and aquarium, closer to Dove Harbor, sits the large **Diamond Jo Casino** complex (www.diamondjo.com) as well as the old **Star Brewery** building. The latter's impressive brick structure features a Romanesque design and was one of the first Iowa breweries to establish itself after the end of Prohibition in 1933. It continued to brew beer

The old Star Brewery building

through the 1990s. Today, the building is home to **Stone Cliff Winery** (www.stone cliffwinery.com) as well as **Star Restaurant and Ultra Lounge** (www.dbqstar .com), a hip eatery and watering hole.

Just past the brewery is the **Shot Tower**, which was built in 1856 and produced lead shot up until the Civil War. It later served as a fire watchtower until 1911, when it caught fire and was completely gutted. The tall, slim, stone structure was extensively renovated in 2010 and is a nice landmark for strollers and joggers following the nearby path along the riverfront. Nearby trails provide splendid views of the river and surrounding woodlands—you may even see a bald eagle or great blue heron hiding among the trees. Before leaving the riverfront area, you can also check out Dubuque's **restored train depot**, tucked away between the museum and US 61/151.

Just west of this main road is downtown Dubuque, where streets march uphill to bluffs high above the river. To get

Dubuque's Shot Tower

a blufftop view of the city, head for the **Fenelon Place Elevator** (www.dbq.com /fenplco), a unique cable car that goes uphill from its station at the western end of Fourth Street. Built by a former mayor and prominent citizen of Dubuque looking for a way to save time on the trip from his home high on the bluffs to his downtown office (and work in a nap at lunchtime), the elevator's cars climb 189 vertical feet on nearly 300 feet of track, making it perhaps the world's shortest and steepest scenic railway. The cars and track have been improved and rebuilt over the years, and a round-trip will set you back $2.

After completing the elevator ride, you find yourself back in downtown

The Grand Opera House

Dubuque, which despite the surrounding hills actually has fairly flat streets and is well suited for walking. Downtown's many interesting buildings include the **Five Flags Center** (www.fiveflagscenter.com), a historic theater across the street from the city's visitors center, and the **Grand Opera House** (www.thegrandoperahouse.com), built in 1890 and still used for local productions following a nearly $5 million renovation.

The **Dubuque Museum of Art** (www.dbqart.com) stands at Seventh and Locust Streets across from Washington Square Park. The museum has several works by Grant Wood and other regional artists, as well as changing exhibitions in a variety of styles.

Your walk around the riverfront and downtown may leave you a little worn out and wanting a break—take a rest at one of the many coffee bars that have sprouted up downtown. **Manna Java World Café** (www.mannajava.com), located at 700 Locust Street in the old Roshek's Department Store building, has a full menu and offers a relaxing atmosphere to kick back and people-watch, while **Jitterz** sits just a few blocks from a large outdoor clock that stands in the middle of Main Street.

If you're up for more local history, check out the **Old Jail Museum** (www.mississippiriver museum.com/features_historic sites_jail.cfm), an Egyptian Revivalist structure adjacent to the

Fenelon Place Elevator climbs 189 vertical feet.

The Dubuque County Courthouse and Old Jail Museum

Dubuque County Courthouse, with lots of historic artifacts housed inside and a replica dungeon in the basement. There's also the **Four Mounds Estate** (www.fourmounds.org), a historic 1908 gentleman's farm and mansion on a bluff above the river, with trails that take in the extensive grounds and many farm buildings. The **Mathias Ham House** (www.mississippiriver museum.com/features_historicsites_ ham.cfm) is a mansion with elegant furnishings and design from the golden age of steamboating. It too sits atop a bluff, befitting a prosperous resident of Dubuque. A short film illustrates the 19th-century lead boom in Dubuque and the surrounding area, while costumed guides give tours of the house throughout the summer—you may even hear the tales of ghosts who are said to haunt the house.

The Ham House is located by **Eagle Point Park** (www.cityofdubuque.org /index.aspx?NID=573), perhaps the nicest of Dubuque's parks, with spectacular

---

HISTORY COMES ALIVE IN DUBUQUE

For those who wish to learn more about Dubuque's rich past, the city's **Historic House Tour and Progressive Dinner** (www.river museum.com/features_historicsites_tours.cfm) visits notable homes and sites, including the Ham House and Star Brewery, with guides who take visitors back to the late 19th century, when steamboat traffic had made Dubuque into a bustling and prosperous city of the Victorian era. At each stop on the tour, visitors dine on one course of a multicourse meal and period entertainment is provided.

Dinners are available only for groups of 20 or more. Cost is $50 per person, and dinners can be booked through the **Dubuque County Historical Society** by calling 563-557-9545 or 1-800-226-3369.

views of the river and into nearby Illinois and Wisconsin. Both history and the outdoors are on display at **Mines of Spain Recreation Area** (www.minesof spain.org). Located on the southern edge of Dubuque, the area was the site of a Meskwaki Indian village, also serving as a trading post for fur trappers and a center for lead mining operations. It was eventually settled in 1788 by Julien Dubuque, who is believed to be the first permanent European settler in Iowa. A castlelike monument pays tribute to the city's namesake. Numerous nature trails cross the area, passing through landscapes that include the rare bur oak savanna and providing excellent spots for bird-watching. An on-site interpretive center has displays on local geology and ecology.

In addition to Mines of Spain, Dubuque maintains a comprehensive network of walking and hiking trails. The **Dubuque Arboretum and Botanical Gardens** (www.dubuquearboretum.com) has many different species of plant life laid out in numerous gardens, including a formal English garden, water and shade gardens, a Japanese garden and an herb garden. It's also home to thousands of hostas that represent hundreds of varieties of the popular garden plant.

Exploration of another kind can be found at **Crystal Lake Cave** (www.crystal lakecave.com) a few miles south of Dubuque on US 52. The large complex of caves and passageways was discovered in 1868 by lead miners who stumbled upon a veritable treasure trove of underground wonders. You could easily spend many hours here, following pathways past stalactites and stalagmites and marveling at rock formations with names like "The Chandelier," "St. Peter's Dome" and "The Pipe Organ." Keep your eyes peeled for cave pools as well. Perhaps the most awe-inspiring sight of all is in "The Chapel," a room within the cave complex that features walls covered with colorful crystal rock.

Heading out of Dubuque on IA 3, you soon leave the city and find yourself in rambling countryside where farm fields climb the terraced hillsides. After about an hour's drive through the pastoral scene, you reach the turnoff that leads you to **Backbone State Park** (www.iowadnr.gov), the oldest state park in Iowa. Named for a bedrock ridge that runs through the park—although local lore has it that the devil lost his backbone here as he slithered east toward the Mississippi—the park has a popular swimming beach and numerous hiking trails, as well as kayaks and canoes for rent. There's also a museum that pays tribute to the Civilian Conservation Corps, which built most of the park, including the stone lodge by the beach.

After some rugged outdoor activity, you'll be ready for a night in one of the park's cabins. Or head for the nearby town of **Strawberry Point**, instantly recognizable by the large strawberry mounted in front of City Hall, and check in to the **Franklin Hotel** (http://franklin-hotel.net). Built in 1902, the hotel retains its old-fashioned charm, while the dining room serves a hearty menu of all-American favorites, including strawberry pie and shortcake for dessert.

After taking a look around Strawberry Point, which also features an antique soda fountain in the town drugstore and an impressive collection of heirloom dolls and Victorian lamps in the **Wilder Memorial Museum** (www.strawberry pt.com/wilder_memorial_museum.htm), head west on IA 3 and south on IA 187 before turning west at the town of **Lamont** to reach the **Richardson-Jakway Historic Site** (www.east-buc.k12.ia.us/bccb/jakway.htm). Located in the Jakway Forest, the 1851 home gives visitors a look at rural Iowa life in the 19th century.

Continue south on IA 187 to pick up US 20 West to **Independence**, where you can visit **Wapsipinicon Mill** (www.buchanancountyhistory.com/mill.php). Completed in 1870, the six-story mill includes displays of original milling stones and machines, letting visitors see how the mill progressed from manual to steam and electric-powered milling. Outside, the Wapsipinicon River flows by, making for a nice spot for a stroll along its banks or to downtown Independence. Grind some corn yourself on a hand crank or sift some ground corn to make cornmeal. Independence's **Visitors Center** is housed in a restored redbrick train depot, which was moved two blocks to its current location and features a 1926 steam engine and a coal car on the grounds.

Following W35 southeast of Independence and parallel to the river soon brings you to **Cedar Rock** (www.stateparks.com/cedar_rock.html), a unique residence outside the town of **Quasqueton**. Also known as the Walter House, the Frank Lloyd Wright–designed home sits on a limestone bluff overlooking the river. Completed in 1950, it was the first and most elaborate of 10 houses that Wright designed in Iowa after World War II, and like the nearby mill, it is listed on the National Register of Historic Places. It's a simple Wright design known as Usonian, a straight, largely compact structure with a bedroom at one end and a living and dining room at the other that cover nearly 1,000 square feet. Wright was involved in nearly every design aspect of the house, including the furniture, carpets and draperies. The picturesque view looks out over the wooded river valley. Look closely to see Wright's signature on the tile outside the entrance.

THE DRIFTLESS AREA

Dubuque lies near the heart of the "Driftless Area," a wide swath of countryside whose name comes from the fact that prehistoric glaciers that flattened the landscape farther north stopped here before reaching the area where Wisconsin, Illinois and Iowa meet. Driftless topography is thus marked by rolling hills, steep river valleys and mounds that form some of the highest points amid flat farmland, including Charles Mound, at 1,235 feet the highest point in Illinois, located about 25 miles east of Dubuque.

The Driftless Area also grew into a major lead mining center in the 19th century: the metal was fairly easy to extract, as the glaciers had not buried it under tons of rock and debris, and many fortune seekers arrived and set up small claims. A lot of the mined lead ended up shaped into bullets at Dubuque's old shot tower and other factories, thus boosting Dubuque's wealth and status. Across the river in Illinois, the city of Galena, whose name comes from the natural form of lead, also prospered. Both cities retain a whiff of their faded glory and wealth, with historic downtowns and old mansions standing atop the hills that characterize the landscape.

If you're interested in learning even more about lead mining, take the short drive up to Platteville, Wisconsin, home of The Mining Museum (www.mining.jamison.museum), which includes numerous mining artifacts, displays and photographs, along with a guided tour into an 1845 lead mine. The museum also offers rides in old ore cars pulled by a vintage locomotive. Numerous other historical artifacts are on display in the adjacent Rollo Jamison Museum, which focuses on local history. Contact the museum at 405 East Main Street, Platteville, WI 53818; or 608-348-3301.

Back on the road, you may want to take a scenic drive around the countryside of Buchanan County, which is known for its barn quilts—tour maps of area barns are available at the Wapsipinicon Mill or the Independence Visitors Center. To the east in Hopkinton is the Delaware County Historical Museum Complex on the site of an old college campus. The complex features several historic buildings, including a depot and one-room school, a collection of old farm machinery and a large Civil War monument.

You can also just head back toward Dubuque, either by taking US 20, which shoots straight east toward Dubuque and the Mississippi River, or by opting for a more meandering country drive along D47. If you choose the latter, you'll eventually pick up IA 136 and head up to **Dyersville,** home of one of the most popular and iconic attractions in all of Iowa: the *Field of Dreams* movie site (http://field ofdreamsmoviesite.com).

It's difficult to overstate the impact this movie had on perceptions of Iowa—or the interest it sparked in the baseball field carved out of a sweep of corn. Hollywood arrived in the summer of 1988, building the field in just three days and filming the movie throughout the hot, dry summer. What most of the hordes of tourists who descend on the field don't realize, however, is that for many years it sprawled over the farms of two families who maintained separate gift shops out past the foul lines. Eventually, the field became the property of just one of the families, and baseball purists and movie fans continue to arrive daily from spring through fall, taking in the diamond standing among the cornfields—a perfect spot to take a seat on the simple wooden bleachers and watch the sun slowly set on a warm summer's day. However, if you plan to knock a few balls into the outfield or play some catch along the base paths, you'll have to get in line—plenty of visitors come prepared with bats, balls and gloves. As of 2011, the field was up for sale, but it's a safe bet that tourists will continue to make the pilgrimage for years to come. Dyersville is also home to a unique collection of toys and collectibles at the **National Farm Toy Museum** (www.nationalfarmtoymuseum.com), where tons of miniature tractors and other agricultural keepsakes line shelves on two floors. Dioramas depict typical Iowa farms over the years, moving from pioneer times to the modern age. A small room upstairs has toys that children can actually play with. If seeing all these toys makes you want to pick up one or more of your own, at least three area stores offer farm toys for sale (plus the museum gift shop, of course).

There's still more to see in Dyersville: the **Basilica of St. Francis Xavier** (www.xavierbasilica.com), one of only 52 basilicas in the United States, stands over downtown. (A basilica is a church with special ceremonial rites conveyed by the Pope.) The striking Gothic architecture stands out amid the typical small town surroundings. If you're still up for more, check out the **Dyer-Botsford Historical**

GALENA

Worth a side trip or longer visit for its scenic views and pleasant downtown, Galena sits across the Mississippi and about 15 miles east of Dubuque, among the scenic rolling hills and valleys of the Driftless Area, which was untouched by the glaciers that rolled over the Midwest and created wide swaths of flat prairie. Like Dubuque, Galena prospered in the steamboat era and from local lead mining. The Galena History Museum (211 South Bench Street; 815-777-9129; www.galena historymuseum.org) is a good place to get started in learning about the area's history. Another popular spot is the Ulysses S. Grant Home State Historic Site (500 Bouthillier Street; 815-777-3310; www.granthome.org), dedicated to the president and Civil War general who briefly lived in Galena prior to the war, one of nine Civil War generals who called Galena home. Main Street is perfect for strolling among its many small shops and art galleries, while charming bed & breakfasts are found in town and the surrounding countryside. The area also features some 10 golf courses. Contact the Galena/Jo Daviess County Convention & Visitors Bureau (101 Bouthillier St.; 1-877-464-2536; www.galena.org) for more information.

House & Doll Museum in a restored Victorian home, one of the first houses built in Dyersville. The museum showcases authentic Victorian furnishings, an antique Christmas tree and more than 1,000 dolls, including dolls depicting numerous famous individuals, displayed among vintage dollhouses and accessories.

The Becker Woodcarving Museum is located a few miles outside of town, while nearby New Vienna is the site of the Heritage House Museum, which features 23 rooms of antiques, quilts and other period items. Guided tours take visitors through the house, which originally served as the rectory for St. Boniface Church, a gothic structure located across the street and built in 1887 from local limestone.

Heading east, it's not a very long ride back to Dubuque, where you can have dinner in one of the nice restaurants that have cropped up in downtown storefronts and old mansions, or take a rest in one of the many historic inns or bed & breakfasts around town.

IN THE AREA

ACCOMMODATIONS

The Barn House, 13527 Gun Club Road, Epworth. Call 563-876-3337. An old, rambling barn between Dubuque and Dyersville, reborn as a country home for rent, The Barn House accommodates large family groups with six bedrooms, five bathrooms, a full-size kitchen and dining area, and a handsome great room with a stone fireplace. The property sits amid peaceful rolling countryside, with lots of quiet nooks and crannies around the spacious, high-ceilinged, restored barn. Requires a two-night minimum stay, with rates based on the number of people. Website: www.thecountrybarnhouse.com.

Black Horse Inn, 5259 South Mound Road, Sherrill. Call 563-552-1800. About 10 miles north of Dubuque along the scenic Great River Road sits this bed & breakfast, originally constructed of native limestone in 1856 as a stop on the stagecoach route that ran along the Mississippi. Each of the five suites has its own unique furnishings, including comfortable king- and queen-sized beds. Modern amenities include wireless Internet access. In addition to breakfast, the inn can provide other meals, and the on-site restaurant serves Friday and Saturday dinners and a Sunday brunch. Inexpensive to Moderate. Website: www.blackhorse-inn.com.

Clarke Manor, 216 Clarke Drive, Dubuque. Call 563-588-1182. An elegant home that has stood in Dubuque since the 1850s, this bed & breakfast has four themed suites named for glamorous destinations like Italy, San Francisco and Paris. The inn is located atop Seminary Hill, with a yard, cupola and rooftop deck that overlook the city and river, along with pleasant gardens for strolling. For many years the home was occupied by the Roshek family, who owned and operated Dubuque's much-beloved department store. (You can still see the building downtown at Seventh and Locust Streets.) Inexpensive to Moderate. Website: www.clarkemanor.com.

Four Mounds Inn, 4900 Peru Road, Dubuque. Call 563-556-1908. Located in the mansion on the grounds of a sweeping historic farm overlooking the Mississippi River, this bed & breakfast has five guest rooms with private baths and fireplaces, as well as a nearby guest cottage with rustic touches. Many of the rooms in the main house have views of the gardens and surrounding countryside, including some river views. A perfect choice for those looking for some peace and quiet. Moderate. Website: www.fourmounds.org.

The Hancock House, 1105 Grove Terrace, Dubuque. Call 563-557-8989. One of several grand old Victorian houses in town converted to overnight accommodations, this

Queen Anne-style home has nine rooms, all with private baths and some with whirlpool tubs. Very comfortable and a good spot for a relaxing weekend. Inexpensive to Moderate. Website: www.thehancock house.com.

Hotel Canfield, 36 West Fourth Street, Dubuque. Call 563-556-4331. An old-school hotel, definitely for those who prefer retro-style accommodations. Very modestly priced and conveniently located just a short distance from both riverfront and downtown attractions. Inexpensive.

Hotel Julien, 200 Main Street, Dubuque. Call 563-556-4200. Dubuque's downtown luxury hotel has benefited from a $30 million renovation, with a sumptuous lobby and full slate of guest amenities, including an indoor pool and whirlpool, spa and fitness center. Rooms have granite countertops and vanities, refrigerators, flat-panel televisions, WiFi access and mini-bars. The top-of-the-line Al Capone suite pays homage to one of Dubuque's most (in)famous visitors. A restaurant and lounge are located on-site. Downtown is right outside the front door, and it's just a short drive to riverfront attractions. Moderate to Expensive. Website: www.hoteljuliendubuqe.com.

Mandolin Inn, 199 Loras Boulevard, Dubuque. Call 563-556-0069. Another grand mansion converted to a bed & breakfast, this one was built by a

A trolley awaits passengers outside the Hotel Julien

prominent local banker in the early 20th century. The stately Edwardian home offers fantastic accommodations with touches like private porches in some rooms and antique furniture. The centerpiece of the home is its opulent dining room, where an elaborate mural of a forest flows above oak paneling. On the landing of the grand oak staircase is a leaded and painted glass window depicting Saint Cecelia, patron saint of musicians, holding a mandolin. Inexpensive to Moderate. Website: www.mandolinninn.com.

Quiet Walker Lodge, 18132 Paradise Valley Trail, Durango. Call 1-800-388-0942. This secluded bed & breakfast sits amid a lush forest a short drive from Dubuque and is perfect for a quiet romantic getaway. Suites feature queen-sized beds, kitchenettes and fireplaces; some have whirlpool tubs. Breakfast includes a plethora of fresh fruit and homemade breads, as well as gourmet quiches and fresh-brewed coffee. Inexpensive to Moderate. Website: www.quietwalkerlodge.com.

Redstone Inn & Suites, 504 Bluff Street, Dubuque. Call 563-582-1894. This large and ornate Victorian bed & breakfast has elegant touches like marble fireplaces and intricate wood-work, as well as private baths for each room. The Fenelon Place elevator is just a couple blocks away, and the inn is perfectly located for a stroll over to the art museum or Grand Opera House. There is a wide range of room sizes and corresponding prices. Inexpensive to Expensive. Website: www.theredstoneinn.com.

The Richards House, 1492 Locust Street, Dubuque. Call 563-557-1492 or 1-888-557-1492. The Richards House is a huge old mansion that retains much of its original interior, including working fireplaces in many of the eight guest rooms and stained-glass windows throughout the four-story house. Breakfasts include lots of yummy homemade breads and sweet items. Inexpensive to Moderate. Website: www.therichardshouse.com.

DINING

The Bridge Restaurant & Lounge, 31 Locust Street, Dubuque. Call 563-557-7280. This no-frills restaurant (look for the large neon signs by the entrance) offers up some honest, simple grub like steaks, chicken, and broiled and fried fish, with a variety of choices on the menu. It's a popular spot with locals, who stop off for drinks and dinner. The Sunday breakfast buffet is a good deal, with more selections than you'll find at a typical hotel breakfast. Moderate. Website: http://bridgerest.com.

L. May Eatery, 1072 Main Street, Dubuque. Call 563-556-0505. This downtown restaurant is sort of a hip, modern take on a bar and grill that still manages to be friendly and welcoming. The menu features old standbys like meat loaf, lasagna and New York strip steak alongside more intriguing choices like Chilean sea bass and osso buco. A long list of specialty cocktails, wine and beer, including selections from the nearby Potosi brewery, draws crowds around the bar at the front of the narrow room. Moderate to Medium. Website: www.lmayeatery.com.

Mario's, 1298 Main Street, Dubuque. Call 563-556-9424. An old-school Italian joint established by a family patriarch who arrived in New York from Italy and then made his way to Dubuque. Expect plenty of red sauce on the pastas, and perfectly tender veal scaloppine and parmigiana. The extensive menu also has pizza, antipasti and seafood options. There are even some Midwest-influenced dishes like fettuccine à la lumberjack and daily specials such as a pork chop sautéed in red wine and banana peppers. Inexpensive to Moderate. Website: http://mariosdubuque.com.

Pepper Sprout, 378 Main Street, Dubuque. Call 563-556-2167. A truly enticing dining experience, this modest storefront near the Hotel Julien at the south end of downtown has a changing menu that emphasizes fresh, seasonal ingredients and innovative preparations. Entrées may include vodka chicken penne, grilled bison with a balsamic onion jam or stuffed quail with cornbread andouille sausage. Be sure to have a taste of their decadent desserts. Vegetarian choices are available. Extensive wine list. Medium. Website: www.peppersprout.com.

Shot Tower Inn, 390 Locust Street, Dubuque. Call 563-556-1061. Locals swear by the pizza at this unassuming downtown restaurant, which has specialty pies like the blanco with olive oil, garlic and marinated tomatoes, or the hot taco with jalapeños, onions and red pepper. Plenty of sandwiches, salads and pasta dishes available as well. Inexpensive to Moderate.

Victory Cafe, 756 Main Street, Dubuque. Call 563-556-4407. Nothing fancy here, just good, all-American food like burgers and catfish, as well as a full slate of subs, including a delicious meatball with marinara sauce and provolone. A good choice

A clock on Dubuque's Main Street

for breakfast as well, with eggs, omelets and hash hot off the grill. Inexpensive. Website: http://victory cafes.com/index_files/VictoryCafe DubuqueIA.htm.

RECREATION

Diamond Jo Casino, 301 Bell Street, Dubuque. Call 563-690-4800. A huge gambling facility adjacent to other riverfront attractions, featuring nearly 1,000 slot machines. The onsite **Mississippi Moon Bar** books plenty of name entertainers in all genres of music and is a fun hangout, with regular comedy nights and dueling pianos. Website: www.diamondjo .com.

Dubuque's American Lady, 1630 East 16th Street, Dubuque. Call 563-557-9700. And **Dubuque River Rides,** 500 East Third Street, Dubuque. Call 563-583-8093. Website: www.dubuqueriverrides.com. Both offer cruises on the Mississippi, with Dubuque River Rides setting off on an authentic paddle-wheeler as well as a more modern motor yacht. Plenty of theme trips are available, as well as sunset, dinner and happy hour cruises. Website: www.american ladycruises.com.

Dubuque Fighting Saints, 1800 Admiral Sheehy Drive, Dubuque. Call 563-583-6880. Dubuque's team in the United States Hockey League, the Saints take to the ice at Mystique Community Ice Center, facing off

The *Spirit of Dubuque* riverboat

against opponents from around the Midwest. Website: http://dubuque fightingsaints.com.

Dubuque Greyhound Park at Mystique Casino, 1855 Greyhound Park Road, Dubuque. Call 563-582-2970. The dogs hit the track from May through October, while the adjacent casino offers slot machines and table games, including poker tables, as well as live entertainment. Website: www .mystiquedbq.com.

Heritage Trail, 13768 Swiss Valley Road, Peosta. Call 563-556-6745. Stretching more than 25 miles from Dubuque to Dyersville, this former rail corridor is a well-maintained trail for hiking and biking in the summer and snowmobiling and cross-country skiing in the winter. Passing by some excellent scenic views, it's a good trail even for novices, with only a few steep climbs. Website: www.dubuquecounty.org /Conservation/HeritageTrail/tabid/19

3/Default.aspx. In Peosta, about 10 miles west of the Dubuque riverfront, is the **Swiss Valley Park,** which includes the **Swiss Valley Nature Preserve and Center** (www.dubuque county.org/Conservation/SwissValley Park/tabid/59/Default.aspx) with some excellent trails of its own.

OTHER CONTACTS

Dubuque Area Convention & Visitors Bureau/Iowa Welcome Center, 300 Main Street, Dubuque, 52001. Call 563-557-9200 or 1-800-798-8844. Website: www.traveldubuque.com.

Buchanan County Tourism Visitors Center, 1111 Fifth Avenue Northeast, Independence, 50644. Call 319-334-3439. Website: www.buchanancounty .com

Dyersville Area Chamber of Commerce, 1100 16th Avenue Court Southeast, Dyersville, 52040. Call 563-875-2311. Website: www.dyers ville.org.

Eastern Iowa Tourism Association, P.O. Box 189, Dyersville, 52040. Call 563-875-7269 or 1-800-891-3482. Website: www.easterniowatourism .org.

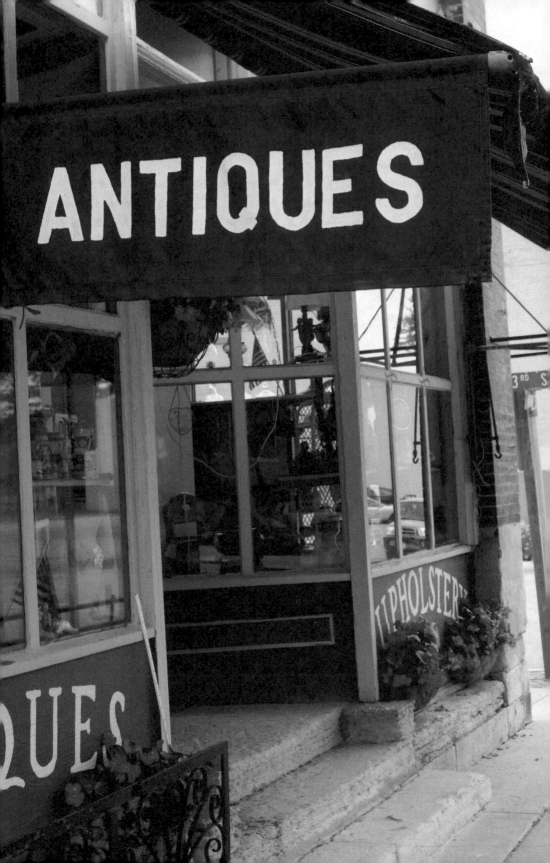

2 Great River Road North:
SCENERY & SHOPPING IN HISTORIC RIVER TOWNS

Estimated length: About 150 miles from Dubuque to McGregor and back.

Estimated time: You can do the trip in a long weekend; add a few days if you want to relax and really take in the river.

Getting there: The trip begins in Dubuque and heads north, following the Mississippi River in some places and moving inland in others.

Highlights: An acclaimed restaurant in Balltown that has been serving diners for more than 150 years. An impressive lock and dam and corresponding historic lockmaster's house in Guttenberg. Lots of shopping opportunities along McGregor's Main Street and some excellent nature trails at nearby Pikes Peak State Park. Elkader's historic buildings and museums and a canoe trip on the nearby Turkey River. Plus, of course, the striking views over the bluffs along the Mississippi.

Starting out in **Dubuque,** head north out of the city, following smaller county roads that climb up the bluffs over the Mississippi—you may occasionally catch a glimpse of the river below, but often it's too far in the distance.

The "Great River Road" isn't a single road, but rather a selection of roads ranging from two-lane blacktops to main highways. This trip at times follows the officially designated Great River Road, and at other times meanders onto other routes, occasionally cutting away from the river.

Your first stop should definitely be in the small hamlet of **Balltown,** where you can fuel up for the journey ahead at one of Iowa's great gustatory palaces: **Breitbach's Country Restaurant** (www.breitbachscountrydining.com), which has been serving diners since 1852 and continues to turn out some fine down-

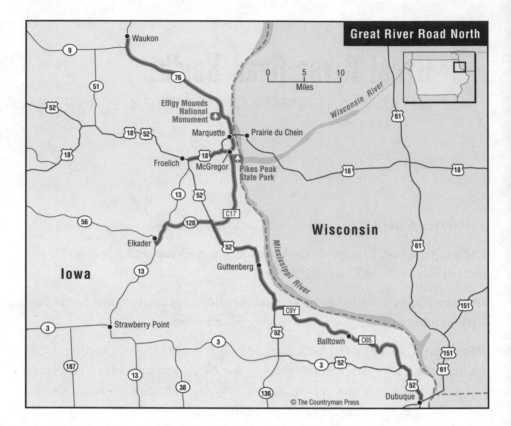

home cooking in a rambling house on Balltown's narrow main drag. Simple favorites like steaks, chicken and prime rib, as well as delicious homemade pies, come hot and fresh from the kitchen. The restaurant is open for breakfast, lunch and dinner, and has a full bar.

Opened under a federal permit from President Millard Fillmore and run by the Breitbach family since 1862, Breitbach's survived fires in 2007 and 2008 to continue drawing both faithful regulars and travelers who make the pilgrimage down country roads. Celebrities and politicians have stopped by as well. After your meal, take a stroll around the back of the building for a look at the farmland rolling on the surrounding bluffs toward the Mississippi. (There's also a scenic overlook just down the road.)

Back behind the wheel, follow the winding roads parallel to the river until you reach US 52, where you turn north and head just over 5 miles to **Guttenberg** (GUT-en-berg, like a stomach). Perched on a limestone bluff high above the Mississippi, Guttenberg has one of the most dramatic views ever of the river where torrents of water pour through historic **Lock & Dam #10** (www.mvp.usace.army .mil/navigation/default.asp?pageid=145&subpageid=182). Operating since 1937, the facility has a nearly 800-foot-long concrete dam spanning the river, with two locks and a dozen gates that regularly open to allow towboats to pass through.

Stick around to see the lock in action—it's well worth it. Moving the towboats and their barges through the lock requires navigating a space that allows just 2½ feet on each side before being raised up to the level of the river on the other side.

Once you've seen the lock do its thing, take a stroll to Guttenberg's other at- tractions, which are conveniently clus-

tered along a strip of green parkland atop the bluff. Overlooking the lock is the old **Lockmaster's House,** a simple white frame structure. The last remaining lockmaster's house along the Mississippi still on its original site, it's chock-full of historical memorabilia relating to Guttenberg and the Mississippi, and the staff is more than happy to fill you in on details of life on the river. The basement has numerous photos detailing the construction of the lock and dam, while upstairs is a re-

The old Lockmaster's House in Guttenberg

creation of the office of a longtime local physician.

Just down the street is the **Guttenberg Aquarium and Fish Management Station** (www.guttenbergiowa.net/ThingsToDo.html), a modest building that contains Mississippi River fish in naturalistic habitats. Like the lock and dam, it dates from the 1930s. Operated by the Iowa Department of Natural Resources in conjunction with a local fish hatchery, the aquarium has catfish, pike and other river fish. A popular Saturday farmers' market is held adjacent to the aquarium from spring through fall.

Outside, a stroll along the 2-mile riverfront boardwalk gives you another look at the lock and dam, and confirms that Guttenberg is very much a river town, with marinas that fill up with recreational boats in the summer.

Leaving Guttenberg, you'll swing away from the river, following US 52 about

---

PLAGMAN BARN

If you're in the area in late September, swing by this rambling old barn (www.plagmanbarn.com) on C7X, about 10 miles west of Guttenberg and just east of the town of Garber, for a full-blown extravaganza of historic rural life. Antique tractor demonstrations and all sorts of crafts, including brickmaking, butter churning and blacksmithing take place, and numerous antique items are on display.

---

12 miles until you reach its intersection with IA 128 and head west. Another dozen miles brings you to Elkader, a charming and historic town on the banks of the Turkey River. There are nine buildings here on the National Register of Historic Places, but the jewel in the crown is the town's Opera House (www.elkaderoperahouse.com), a solid redbrick structure built in 1903 that hosted shows for nearly 50 years. Since then, it has been everything from a roller rink to a library to a fire station, and has housed city government offices as well. Upon its centennial in 2003, the building was completely renovated, and it is now once again used for shows, including both community theater and touring productions. Tours are available by contacting City Hall.

Interestingly, Elkader's name comes from Abd al-Qadir al-Jaza'iri, an Algerian national hero who led his people against a French invasion in the 19th century. Today, Elkader maintains a sister city program with Algeria.

A nice walking tour in Elkader (www.elkader-iowa.com/Historic-Sites.html) starts at the Clayton County Court House at High and Bridge Streets, then takes a short stroll over to Carter House Museum (www.carterhousemuseum.com), an 18-room Greek Revival mansion built by two pioneer brothers in 1855. The home is a "mirror duplex," or double house. It is the site of the local historical museum and includes large collections of artifacts and a photo history of Elkader. Next, step onto the Keystone Bridge, a picturesque span that is the longest bridge of its kind west of the Mississippi River, and take in the view of the Turkey River.

On the opposite side of the bridge are many more historic homes, including the Becker House, a fine example of Victorian architecture, and the Stemmer House, built in the Queen Anne style. (Brochures detailing Elkader's many historic homes and other structures are available through the Chamber of Commerce.) Or, you may prefer to simply meander up and down the banks of the river: the historic river walk goes south from the courthouse, following the route the town's original boardwalk took to the train depot, and eventually reaches the city park, where dedicated hikers can continue on the Pony Hollow Trail and walk nearly 5 miles into surrounding countryside on the site of former railroad tracks.

Also in the city park is the **Rural Heritage Museum** (www.iowabeautiful.com /northeast-iowa-tourism/george-maier-rural-heritage-center-elkhader-iowa .html). Built from scratch by a World War II veteran who followed his dream of showcasing Midwest rural life, the museum is housed in a restored 1919 sales barn and features large collections of household items, automobiles and all sorts of miscellaneous bric-a-brac, as well as a small-town general store interior completely re-created on the premises. New items are frequently moved into the museum.

If you're looking for more rural Iowa history, take a short drive to the **Motor Mill** (www.motormill.org), a complex of historic structures on the Turkey River about 7 miles from Elkader. The 90-foot-tall mill itself dates from the late 1860s and was built with stone quarried from surrounding bluffs. Water power came from a nearby dam, enabling the mill to crank out bag after bag of flour using wheat from the surrounding fields. Unfortunately, the mill was soon beset by a flood and an infestation of insects that destroyed the area's wheat crop.

Today, the mill tells the story of those hardscrabble years of carving a living from the land. Adjacent structures include a cooperage, stable, an ice house that stored blocks of ice harvested from the river, and an inn used by farmers who stayed overnight while waiting for their grain to be ground into flour.

You can also explore the area via canoe. Riverside Park in the shadow of the Keystone Arch Bridge in Elkader is a good spot for setting off on a paddling trip on the Turkey River, which flows past limestone bluffs and other scenic views as it winds through the countryside before reaching the mill. (See *Recreation* for information on canoe outfitters.)

Eager to get back to the mighty Mississippi? Fear not—from Elkader, head back the way you came on IA 128 and US 52, then continue south, back toward Guttenberg. You'll only go about a mile on US 52, however, before you veer left on C17, which you'll follow back to the junction with 56, where you turn left and head north, rejoining the official Great River Road. Soon, the river looms in sight

Bridal Veil Falls in Pikes Peak State Park

and after several miles you come to the turnoff for **Pikes Peak State Park** (www .iowadnr.gov), one of Iowa's true natural gems.

Several hiking trails begin just past the parking area, near an open observation deck that provides a splendid view of the confluence of the Mississippi and Wisconsin Rivers from 500 feet up, the highest bluff on the Mississippi. Trails wind their way down the wooded bluffs, passing occasional exposed faces of limestone, with one trail going past Bridal Veil Falls, a modest yet picturesque waterfall. It's a lovely spot to spend an hour or an afternoon, with a large picnic shelter just past the parking area. Campsites are available for overnight stays.

There are also parking areas and trailheads closer to **McGregor**, just a few miles up the road. A thriving river port during the steamboat era, McGregor is nestled in a picturesque valley marked by soaring limestone and sandstone bluffs. Early residents cut into the bluffs to create storage spaces for various items, including refrigerated goods: a local brewery built a large complex of "caves" to keep its beer cool.

Since the decline of steamboats and then railroads, the town has remade itself as a shopper's paradise: sellers of antiques and other funky goods stretch up and down Main Street. Many historic buildings have been restored and renovated, giving McGregor a definite "old-time" feel and making for a nice stroll around downtown's compact streets. Walking guides can be picked up at the Chamber of Commerce, 146 Main Street.

Connoisseurs of kitsch should be sure to make a stop at **McGregorville Specialty Mall** (www.mc gregorville.com), which has all sorts of retro goodies—including vintage

McGregor's Main Street

clothing and jewelry and lots of kids' items—crammed into multiple buildings. Take a break from shopping at the authentic 1950s soda fountain, which has food as well as ice cream treats.

The shopping whirl continues at **River Junction Trade Company** (www .riverjunction.com), which specializes in historic period clothing, including items used in historic re-enactments. If you've been looking for an authentic frontiersman getup, including accessories like guns and knives, or perhaps

McGregorville Specialty Mall on McGregor's Main Street

a handmade Stetson hat out of the Old West, this is the place to find it. The inventory is truly massive and impressive, and the proprietor is happy to discuss whatever items strike your fancy. Check out their full selection of Civil War memorabilia, too.

Continuing your stroll along Main Street brings you to the **McGregor Historical Museum.** Learn about the history of McGregor, which grew from a ferry landing to one of the most bustling ports along the Mississippi, as well as the works of a local artist who used sand gathered at nearby Pikes Peak to create exquisite "sand paintings" in glass bottles. The museum has somewhat limited hours—it's a good idea to check ahead with the Chamber of Commerce to see when it's open.

McGregor is also a nice spot for a boat ride on the Mississippi, which is very wide and scenic as it flows past the town. **Maiden Voyage Tours** (www.maiden voyagetours.com) offers river tours seven days a week on a 50-foot-long, open-air sight-seeing vessel that docks right by the city park. The boat captain gives a good local history lesson, touching on the heritage of boating and fishing as well as noting local flora and fauna. Custom trips focusing on fishing, swimming from sandbars and learning about river history are also available if arranged in advance. Across the river, **Mississippi Explorer Cruises** (www.mississippiexplorer .com) offers similar trips out of nearby Prairie Du Chien, Wisconsin, as well as Lansing, Iowa, with plenty of opportunities to spot bald eagles soaring overhead and other river wildlife.

Those who really want to spend some time on the river should look into renting a houseboat. **Boatels** (boatelshouseboatrentals.com) operates a marina and rental service in McGregor and offers a variety of different sized houseboats for a weekend or longer.

In nearby **Marquette**, the **Marquette Depot Museum** (www.mcgreg-marq .org/community.htm) is a worthwhile stop for train buffs, with model steam engines and other railroadiana. It's also a good spot for picking up brochures and information on other local sights. In between Marquette and McGregor is the district headquarters of the **Upper Mississippi River National Wildlife & Fish Refuge** (www.fws.gov/Midwest/uppermississippiRiver). Covering 260 miles from Wabasha, Minnesota, to Rock Island, Illinois, the refuge is composed of islands and swampy areas in the river and is home to a plethora of wildlife, with more than 300 species of birds, including half the world's canvasback ducks and some 5,000 heron and egret nests. Bald eagles are also prevalent along this stretch of the river, which offers numerous opportunities for bird-watching and outdoor activities, including fishing and hunting.

Leaving McGregor and moving away from the river once again leads to some more interesting spots. Spelunkers looking for a caving trip with a twist should head to **Spook Cave** (www.spookcave.com) about 7 miles west of McGregor by the intersection of US 18 and US 52. Even non-cave fans may appreciate this attraction, which involves riding through the underground chambers in a boat (watch your head!). The boat driver motors the boat past lots of stalactites and other fea-

---

PRAIRIE DU CHIEN, WISCONSIN

C rossing the river to Prairie Du Chien (Doo-SHEEN) gives you the opportunity to see another historic river town, with attractions that include the **Fort Crawford Museum** (www.forcrawfordmuseum.com) and its exhibits detailing local history. The fort was established as an American military post after a local battle of the War of 1812. Also in town is **Villa Louis** (http://villalouis.wisconsinhistory.org), a Victorian home furnished with period items.

Prairie Du Chien is also known as Wisconsin's second-oldest city, home to an annual June rendezvous that re-creates life in the early 1800s, complete with fur trappers, settlers and Native Americans.

tures of the limestone cavern while keeping up a steady patter of lore about the cave. It's a fun trip; a classic, old-school roadside attraction.

Continuing west on US 18/52, keep your eyes peeled for the turnoff to **Froelich.** A blink-and-you'll-miss-it hamlet, Froelich (www.froelichtractor .com) was once a thriving town with an important contribution to Iowa history: in 1892, town namesake John Froelich created a gasoline-powered tractor engine that could go both forward and backward, thus offering an alternative to the steam engines then in use, which

Burlingame's General Merchandise store in Froelich

were difficult to maneuver and prone to breakdowns and explosions that threatened to spark huge fires in the fields. Froelich's engine was eventually picked up by a group of investors in Waterloo, Iowa. The company that developed from such humble beginnings was eventually sold to John Deere, which at the time was on its way to becoming the world's most dominant farm equipment company and had a massive tractor works and other manufacturing plants in Waterloo, Iowa, not far from Froelich. Today, a general store in Froelich is preserved to look much as it did in the town's heyday, and there's a small tractor museum next door.

From Froelich, US 18/52 continues west into the cornfields toward **Monona,** where the **Monona Historical Museum** (www.mononahistoricalmuseum.org) displays lots of artifacts, like an old telephone switchboard and phone booth and a cell from the old town jail. Return to Marquette and head north on IA 76. Just 4 miles north of Marquette is **Effigy Mounds National Monument** (www.nps.gov /efmo), where more than 200 prehistoric mounds have been found, including several built to resemble birds and bears. The mounds' origins remain a mystery, although scholars believe they were religious sites or tribal symbols used in sacred ceremonies. The mounds were constructed roughly 1,400 to 850 years ago by Indians of the Woodland Period, who were unique among the native peoples of North America in that they regularly built mounds in the shapes of animals, including turtles, lizards and bison.

The monument is divided into north and south areas separated by the Yellow River, with trails ranging in length from 2 to 7 miles leading to different clusters of mounds. One trail leads 3½ miles from the visitors center to Hanging Rock, a limestone outcrop with a nice view of the Mississippi. Other overlooks also provide views across the Wisconsin River, as well as of the bald eagles and other birds that soar overhead.

An even larger group of mounds is located 12 miles south of the monument— ask for directions and information at the visitor center. There's also a boat launch available. A more extensive slate of outdoor options can be found a few miles from the mounds on IA 76 at **Yellow River State Forest** (www.iowadnr.gov /Destinations/StateForests/YellowRiverStateForest.aspx), which covers more than 8,000 acres and is home to more than 60 species of birds and numerous opportunities for hiking, camping, hunting and fishing.

Twenty miles past Effigy Mounds on IA 76 is **Waukon,** home to the **Allamakee County Historical Center** (www.allamakeehistory.org). Housed in the town's original brick and limestone courthouse, the museum features plenty of local history, including a piano and organ from a historic church, medical and legal exhibits, and the building's original second-floor courtroom. A log cabin that was once home to Norwegian immigrants is on the museum grounds and is furnished with period items, while a historic red schoolhouse can be found nearby at the county fairgrounds.

IN THE AREA

ACCOMMODATIONS

American House Inn, 116 Main Street, McGregor. Call 563-873-3364. After a day antiquing in McGregor, take in the view of Mississippi River from your expansive suite in this historic hotel, which was built in 1854 and harkens back to McGregor's glory days—Mark Twain is said to have spent a night here. The upstairs Steamboat Landing Suite has a full kitchen and four bedrooms and sleeps up to nine, while the lower level's Stagecoach Stop Suite has two bedrooms and a small kitchenette. Moderate. Website: www.american houseinn.com.

The Claytonian, 100 South Front Street, Clayton. Call 563-964-2776. Nestled just off the Great River Road in the small riverside hamlet of Clayton, this bed & breakfast is nicely situated between Guttenberg and McGregor and is just a short drive from Pikes Peak State Park. All suites have river views. A nice spot if you're looking for plenty of peace and quiet. Inexpensive to Moderate. Website: www.jphilarnold.com/claytonian/first page.htm.

The Court House Inn, 618 South River Park Drive, Guttenberg. Call 1-888-224-2188. Located right across from Guttenberg's River Park on a bluff over the Mississippi, this restored historic inn has 2 two-bedroom suites and a separate three-bedroom house, all of which are equipped with kitchens and full baths. There's a back deck and patio with a gas grill for guest use. Inexpensive to Moderate (suites), Moderate to Expensive (house). Website: www.thecourthouseinn.biz.

Eagles Landing Winery and Bed & Breakfast, 82 North Street, Marquette. Call 563-873-2509. A cedar-log sided country retreat perched on the banks of the Mississippi, Eagles Landing offers striking views of the tree-covered surrounding bluffs that are especially notable during fall. A choice of single rooms with private baths and larger suites are good for families. The inn serves delicious four-course breakfasts with either an American, German or Norwegian menu, and includes complimentary wine from the winery, which is just down the street. Rates vary depending on room. Website: www.halvorson .org/eagleslanding.

Elkader Jailhouse Inn, 601 East Bridge Street, Elkader. Call 563-245-1159. Yes, this squat stone structure served as the county jail and housed offenders until 2006. While a few decorative touches of its former life remain—look for the metal cagework in the lounge area—this is first and foremost a charming and airy historic inn with three guest suites, including a two-room family suite. Inexpensive to Moderate. Website: http://elkader jailhouseinn.com/default.aspx.

Elkader Pines Bed and Breakfast, 22624 IA 128, Elkader. Call 563-245-2387. Country lodging three miles outside of Elkader at this moderately priced home with two guest rooms. Take a stroll through the garden and the namesake pine trees. Website: www.elkaderpines.com.

Goshawk Farm Bed and Breakfast, 27596 Ironwood Road, Elkader. Call 563-964-9321. This rustic, two-story limestone farmhouse is nestled among towering maples. There are three guest rooms on the property and a hearty country breakfast waiting in the morning. Inexpensive. Website: www.alpinecom.net/~nikgosh.

The Lamp Post Inn & Gallery, 424 Main Street, McGregor. Call 563-873-1849. A charming Victorian home with leaded glass windows and original woodwork, The Lamp Post Inn also includes a gallery with works by local artists. Its three rooms include two with private bath. Inexpensive. Website: www.innandgallery.com.

The Landing, 703 South River Park Drive, Guttenberg. Call 563-252-1615. A restored stone warehouse and button factory that sits right on the river, The Landing has 10 unique rooms featuring exposed limestone and beams. Some suites have balconies that are perfect for watching the waters of the Mississippi. Inexpensive to Moderate. Website: www.thelanding 615.com.

Little Switzerland Inn, 126 Main Street, McGregor. Call 563-873-2057. Right in the middle of Main Street's shopping and strolling, this charming historic building is now a bed & breakfast with four spacious rooms, including a log cabin with fireplace next door to the main building. Guests may choose from options including private deck, balcony and screened porch, which provide plenty of open-air spaces perfect for relaxing with your favorite beverage. The second floor has nice views of the Mississippi. Inexpensive to Moderate. Website: www.littleswitzerlandinn.com.

McGregor Lodging Guest Suites, 214 Main Street/214 A Street, McGregor. Call 563-873-3112. A trio of unique apartment-style lodgings clustered around the north end of downtown: the Suite on Main sleeps up to six people in two bedrooms on the second floor of a historic bank building, while the Loft & Found and the Courtyard Studio are adjacent to each other on A Street in a building

that housed McGregor's original city hall, jail and fire department. Each sleeps up to four on a queen bed and sleeper sofa. A courtyard leads to the "caves" that were cut into the bluffs soaring above the town and used for storage by early residents and businesses. Moderate (Suite on Main), Inexpensive to Moderate (Loft & Found and Courtyard Studio). There's also a larger loft property a mile outside of town, but it's available only for monthly rentals. Website: www .mcgregorlodging.com.

McGregor's Landing Bed & Bath, 111 First Street, McGregor. Call 563-873-3150. Looking for a true old-time lodging experience? This place may be for you: each guest room in the rambling old building by Triangle Park at the north end of downtown is stocked with antique furnishings, including vintage iron bed frames and clawfoot tubs. (Don't worry—rooms have modern heating and cooling.) Put your feet up on the wraparound porch that runs outside each room and take in the surrounding scene, including views of the river. Note that it's a "bed & bath"—there's no breakfast served here, although you can have a cold one at Uncle Sam's Saloon, an authentic Old West–style drinking den with hardwood floors. The owners also operate River Junction Trade Company, a downtown shop with all sorts of period clothing and accessories. Inexpensive to Mod-

erate. Website: www.mcgregorlanding
bedandbath.com.

River Park Place, 302 River Park
Drive, Guttenberg. Call 563-880-5856.
If you're looking to spend more time
in the area, this facility has three furnished apartments for rent by the
week or the month. There's a two-
bedroom apartment and two studio
apartments. All have a washer and
dryer, and the studios have whirlpool
bath and shower combos as well as
kitchenettes. Website: www.river-park
-place.com/default.html.

DINING

Doug's Pub & Grill, 7 Schiller Street,
Guttenberg. Call 563-252-3301. This
narrow room on Guttenberg's main
drag is a nice place to stop and relax
while making the Great River Road
Drive. Dig into a steak or plate of ribs,
or have a chicken pesto or portobello
sandwich. Afterward, take a stroll
through Guttenberg's hilltop park,
which stretches along the Mississippi. Moderate. Website:
www.dougsguttenberg.com.

Fennelly's Irish Pub, 105 First
Street Northwest, Elkader. Call 563-
245-3663. Casual bar and grill with
steaks, sandwiches and salads, as
well as some nods on the menu to the
old country, including Irish stew,
bangers and mash, and fish and
chips, as well as local favorites like
fried catfish. There's also a full slate
of chicken wings from mild all the
way to extreme. Inexpensive to Moderate. Website: www.fennellysirish
pub.com.

The Irish Shanti, 17455 Gunder
Road, Gunder. Call 563-864-9289. Le-
gions of hungry diners make the trek
down country roads to this crossroads town 10 miles outside of Elkader largely for one reason: the
Gunderburger, a massive patty made
with at least a pound of ground beef.
Hardcore eaters dig in wearing a hat
shaped like the burger. There are
plenty of other items on the menu,
but the Gunderburger is the real
draw, spilling out of the bun and
available with all manner of toppings.
Good selection of beers and Irish
whiskeys as well. Inexpensive to
Moderate. Website: www.thegunder
burger.com.

Johnson's Restaurant, 916 High
Street, Elkader. Call 563-245-2371. A
no-frills roadside place with ample
portions of tasty homestyle food.
There's a popular lunch buffet and a
menu with steaks, seafood, chicken
and other choices. The buffet is also
served on weekends, including a Friday night seafood buffet. Breakfast is
available all day. Don't leave without
trying a slice of the homemade pie.
Inexpensive to Moderate. Website:
www.johnsonsrestaurantelkader.com.

**Old Man River Restaurant & Brew-
ery,** 123 A Street, McGregor. Call 563-
873-1999. Located in a building listed
on the National Register of Historic

Places that formerly housed the office of steamboat tycoon Joseph "Diamond Jo" Reynolds, this high-ceilinged, exposed brick bar and grill serves up a variety of tasty offerings like pork tenderloin, New York Strip steak and a variety of pasta dishes. Good burgers, too, as well as lighter choices like Cobb and Thai salads. Handcrafted beers range from lagers and pale ales to Scottish and German dark brews. Moderate to Medium. Website: www .oldmanriverbrewery.com.

Rausch's Café, 123 North US 52 (Fifth Street), Guttenberg. Call 563-252-2102. Look for the sign outside with the large coffee cup advertising this simple small-town diner adjacent to a garage. While inside, look for the photos of Barack Obama, who stopped in for breakfast in 2011. A good choice—it's a great spot to fuel up for a day on the road. In addition to breakfast, which is served all day, Rausch's is known for its roast beef dinners and hot beef sandwiches. Inexpensive.

Riverview Restaurant, 102 US 18, McGregor. Call 563-873-9667. An unpretentious bar and grill with a simple menu of hamburgers, chicken and its specialty, spaghetti and meatballs. A nice spot for a lazy late afternoon, when you can watch the sun over the Mississippi. Inexpensive.

Schera's Restaurant & Bar, 107 South Main Street, Elkader. Call 563-245-1992. Perhaps your only chance to dine on authentic Middle Eastern–style cuisine in small-town Iowa (makes sense in a town named after an Algerian hero, no?), Schera's serves up North African–inspired dishes like couscous royale, chicken with apricots and seafood with Algerian spices. The menu also has many American-style dishes like steaks, pasta and vegetarian choices, as well as an extensive list of beer and specialty cocktails. Moderate. Website: www.scheras.com.

RECREATION

Big Foot Canoe Rental, 419 Big Foot Road, Monona. Call 563-539-4972. Rents canoes, kayaks and tubes for exploring the nearby Yellow River. Also offers shuttle service for boaters. Located about 15 miles west of McGregor and Marquette.

Lady Luck Casino, US 18, Marquette. Call 1-800-4-YOU-BET. Offers slots, video poker and table games, including blackjack, craps and poker seven days a week. Website: http://marquette.isleofcapricasinos.com /index.aspx.

Paint Creek Riding Stables, 1948 Sandhill Road, Waukon. Call 563-568-4722. Supervised trail rides as well as hayrides and pony rides for kid are available here. There's also a pond for paddleboating and a nearby trout stream.

Turkey River Canoe Rental, 117 South Main Street, Elkader. Call 563-245-1559. Canoe rentals for float trips on the Turkey River, as well as guided

McGregor offers many shopping opportunities.

trips that can last anywhere from a few hours to overnight.

OTHER CONTACTS

Allamakee County Economic Development, 101 West Main Street, Waukon, 52172. Call 563-268 2624 or 1-800-824-1424. Website: www.allamakeecounty.com.

Clayton County Development Group, 132 South Main Street, P.O. Box 778, Elkader, 52043. Call 563-245-2201 or 1-800-488-7572. Website: www.claytoncountyiowa.com.

Guttenberg Development and Tourism, 323 South River Park Drive, Guttenberg, 52052. Call 1-877-252-2323. Website: www.guttenbergiowa.net.

Elkader Area Chamber of Commerce, 207 North Main Street, Elkader, 52043. Call 563-245-2857. Website: www.elkader-iowa.com.

Clayton County Visitor Center, 29862 Osborne Road, Elkader, 52043. Call 563-245-1516.

Marquette-McGregor Chamber of Commerce, 146 Main Street, McGregor, 52157. Call 1-800-896-0910. Website: www.mcgreg-marq.org.

Waukon Chamber of Commerce, 101 West Main Street, Waukon, 52172. Call 563-568-4110. Website: www.waukon.org.

3 Great River Road South from Dubuque to the Quad Cities:

JAZZ AND JOHN DEERE ON THE MISSISSIPPI

Estimated length: Close to 220 miles round-trip, Dubuque to Davenport and back.

Estimated time: You really need several days to take advantage of all there is to see in the towns along the way. Alternately, you can pick and choose from the towns on the route and have a weekend getaway.

Getting there: The trip begins in Dubuque, which is easily accessible from US 61, 20 and 151. You can also begin the trip at its other end in Davenport, which is right on I-80 and just west of the northern end of I-74 in Illinois.

Highlights: A plethora of shopping opportunities and excellent river views in LeClaire, as well as a museum devoted to native son Buffalo Bill Cody. Numerous historical attractions in the Quad Cities, including sites devoted to John Deere, jazz musician Bix Beiderbecke, and Native American warrior Black Hawk. Impressive caves in Maquoketa. A gem of an arboretum in Clinton.

This trip, like the one heading north from Dubuque along the Great River Road, takes in a dizzying sweep of scenery and history, visiting more classic river towns where the spirit of old riverboat captains and bustling ports lives on.

The route runs for many miles inland before cutting briefly over to the river at Bellevue, then once again moving away to stop at Maquoketa, home of famous caves, before shooting down to Clinton, where it hugs the river's shoreline all the way to the Quad Cities.

Leaving Dubuque, head south on US 61/151, then swing south onto US 52, following it as it passes by the Mines of Spain Recreational Area (see the Dubuque chapter). After only about 5 miles, you reach **Czipar's Apple Orchard,**

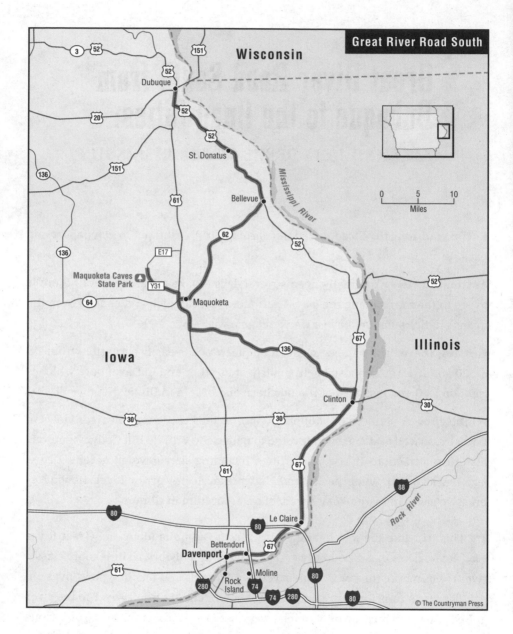

a family-run operation for nearly 50 years, with 1,000 trees. You can pick your own apples, selecting from the wide variety that grows in the orchard, and there are all sorts of yummy goodies for sale, including pies and apple bread. The fourth weekend in September is the orchard's Apple Festival, with a flea market, children's games and all sorts of arts and crafts displays.

After about another 10 miles on US 52, you will come to **St. Donatus** (Do-NAY-tus), a tiny village with a fascinating history. Nestled among rolling lime-stone hills, it was settled largely by immigrants from Luxembourg beginning in the 1830s, and grew to resemble a village in the old country, including a Catholic chapel modeled after one in Luxembourg. The chapel is open to visitors, as is an outdoor Way of the Cross built in 1861 and said to be the first of its kind in America. There is also a Lutheran church and numerous historic homes which were built with limestone blocks quarried from the surrounding hills and then covered with stucco, in the European fashion. Many local residents are descended from the original settlers and continue to speak the language of their forefathers, which you may hear if you stop in for a meal at Kalmes Restaurant, a popular eatery serving Continental cuisine (see *Dining*).

Back on US 52, continue to drive south, following the road as it curves and descends to the Mississippi at **Bellevue,** a sleepy little town in the shadow of river bluffs that is home to **Bellevue State Park** (www.iowadnr.gov). The park, which is located south of town and divided into two units, has scenic river views along its winding trails, as well as a nature center and adjoining butterfly garden set among cottonwood and willow trees. It's easy to spot many different species of the winged creatures. In winter months you may spot bald eagles soaring overhead. Nearby is a large spread of prairie, and numerous native plants crop up along the paths.

From Bellevue, the routes shifts onto IA 62, which moves away from the river and heads 20 miles southwest to **Maquoketa,** jumping-off point for **Maquoketa Caves State Park** (www.iowadnr.gov) to the west of town, which is considered to have the finest accessible caves in Iowa. The park has close to a dozen caves reached by a trail that winds through the rocky landscape, including the spectacular Dancehall Cave and plenty of smaller ones. (You'll need rugged clothes and a flashlight to explore some of the more cramped passages.) Unfortunately, many of the stalactites, stalagmites and other cave features were scavenged by earlier visitors, but it's still a neat place to visit. (*Note:* The caves were closed in 2011 due to the threat of a disease that could kill off the bat population. Call ahead to see if they have reopened. The rest of the park was not affected by the closure.) In addition to the caves, there's a natural bridge that soars 50 feet above a creek and a 17-ton rock balanced precipitously along the path. The park's interpretive center does a good job explaining the geology and history of the area. Spring wildflowers and fall leaf colors further enhance a visit to the park.

More outdoor beauty can be seen at **Hurstville Interpretive Center** (www .jacksonccb.com/HIC.html) located north of Maquoketa just off US 61. Built next to a nearly 20-acre wetland, the center has a nice diorama depicting local wildlife and water fauna in their natural habitats. After viewing the exhibits inside, step out onto the deck and scan the wetland for the actual animals, or take a stroll on the trails while watching for butterflies and native wildflowers. There's a fishing pond and a butterfly garden on-site as well. Nearby are the remains of the **Hurstville Lime Kilns,** which heated limestone from the surrounding hills into mortar that was used in the construction of area buildings.

After you've had your fill of nature and spelunking, it's time to hop onto US 61 to head south out of Maquoketa, then onto IA 136 for the drive down to **Clinton,** whose riverfront is one of the more impressive along the Mississippi. The city sits at the widest point of the river, which stretches nearly 2 miles across just above a large lock and dam. Tugboats continue to push barges underneath the city's two bridges, while a long, extensively landscaped riverwalk winds lazily along the banks of the "Big Muddy." The paved path is a popular spot for both locals and visitors to take a stroll. Along the riverwalk you'll find both the stadium of Clinton's minor league baseball team (see *Recreation*) and the **Clinton Area Showboat Theatre** (www.clintonshowboat.org), a restored paddle-wheeler that presents everything from musicals to comedy to children's shows.

Also on the riverfront is the **Clinton Historical Society Museum** (www.iowa beautiful.com/east-iowa-tourism/372-clinton-county-historical-society-museum -clinton-iowa.html), where you can learn about Clinton's long connection with both steamboats and railroads. Numerous rooms are full of artifacts and photographs of the town's history.

A former lumbering center whose many sawmills cut up logs floated down the Mississippi from Minnesota and Wisconsin, Clinton counted several millionaires among its residents in the second half of the 19th century. Many built mansions in town, the most notable being the **Curtis Mansion** (www.clintonia .com/dpculturalhist.html), which sits a few blocks from the riverfront on Fifth Avenue, a broad street running west from downtown, and offers tours by appointment or on Wednesday after-

Clinton Area Showboat Theatre

noons in the summer. The large brick Queen Anne home features terra-cotta accents and still has its original Tiffany glass windows as well as some impressive fireplaces and intricately carved woodwork. The dining room is done exclusively in cherry wood, including a ceiling with different depictions of cherries carved into it.

There are opportunities to get out into the great outdoors in Clinton as well: **Bickelhaupt Arboretum** (www .bick-arb.org) is a botanical wonderland with 14 acres of trees, shrubs,

Curtis Mansion, one of Clinton's most notable structures

perennials and annuals. The gardens have reached maturity since being planted in 1970, and they include a hosta display garden and one of the nation's top conifer collections. Lots of ornamental shrubs, native prairie plants and flowering trees like crab apples, magnolias and redbuds make this a very pleasant place to wander around.

The outdoor tour continues at **Eagle Point Park**, which stretches along the bluffs above the Mississippi and provides some spectacular views and plenty of places for kids to play, including a "castle" built from native stone. There's also a rustic lodge that can be rented out for events. The nearby **Soaring Eagle Nature Center** hosts occasional classes and sits among hiking trails and restored prairie landscapes.

One other place to check out in Clinton is the **Felix Adler Children's Discovery Center** (http://adlerdiscoverycenter.org). Kids will love playing with the many hands-on exhibits, including a huge Brio train engine, as well as interactive play spaces like a grocery store, hospital and tree house. Youngsters can even simulate space travel at several exhibits that teach different principles of science. There's a small miniature golf course and a separate area for toddlers, too.

Moving on, hop onto US 67 for the 25-mile drive down to **LeClaire**, which proclaims itself the "fastest growing town in Iowa" and is yet another fine example of a river town that provides a look at life on the Mississippi both past and present. While Clinton boasts the widest spot on the Mississippi, LeClaire's claim to fame is quite different: located at a sharp bend, this was considered one of the trickiest stretches along the river to navigate due to the rocks, sandbars and other debris that could sabotage a steamboat and possibly rip it apart. As a result, riverboat pilots who could navigate the area, known as the "upper rapids," were in demand, and LeClaire came to be the home of more pilots per capita than any other city on the Mississippi. Pilots would wait in the shade of a large

Downtown LeClaire

elm tree to be picked up by passing steamboats and maneuver through the tricky course, taking the boat safely down to Davenport, where they would return by wagon or boat and do it again.

The water level was raised after locks and dams were built on the river in the 1920s, and the steamboat era ended long before that, but its spirit lives on in the many homes of steamboat pilots that line LeClaire's hilly streets, as well as several on Cody Road, the main drag of town, which runs parallel to the river. A brochure with a self-guided tour of the homes is available at the Mississippi Valley Welcome Center, located about a mile south of downtown on a street that winds adjacent to I-80.

Down a short, steep hill from Cody Road is the riverfront itself, including the steamboat *Lone Star,* the oldest surviving wooden-hulled workboat, which saw duty beginning in the 1860s as both a water taxi and a towboat, moving logs along the river. Today, it sits in dry dock next to the dock for **Twilight River Boat Cruises** (www.riverboattwilight.com), a replica steamboat that offers overnight cruises to Dubuque (see *Recreation*).

Next to the boat docks is the **Buffalo Bill Museum** (www.buffalobillmuseum leclaire.com), a tribute to the legendary frontiersman who was born in a log cabin outside LeClaire in 1846. The museum includes displays and memorabilia related to Buffalo Bill's long and colorful life, which included stints as a Pony Express rider, a U.S. Army scout and, of course, an impresario famous for his "Wild West Show." Other displays focus on the local Sauk and Fox Native American tribes, pioneer settlers in the area and lesser-known native sons of LeClaire. These include James Ryan, who invented the flight data recorder known as the "black box" used as standard equipment on commercial flights, and James Eads, an engineer who built gunboats during the Civil War that were a precursor to the submarine and later designed a steel bridge that spans the Mississippi at St. Louis.

BUFFALO BILL: AN AMERICAN ORIGINAL

One of the most colorful characters to emerge from the American Old West, Buffalo Bill is as responsible as anyone for creating the image of life on the frontier. His elaborate productions showcased cowboys and Indians demonstrating their skills at horseback riding and reenactments of famous events like train robberies and cavalry battles across windswept terrain.

After spending his early years on a homestead in rural Scott County, Iowa, near LeClaire, William Cody left home at age 14 to become a Pony Express rider. He served with a cavalry unit during the Civil War, and after the war served as an Army scout, keeping watch for hostile tribes and hunting buffalo meat for both soldiers and railroad workers. It was his skill as a buffalo hunter that earned him his famous nickname.

In 1872, he was awarded the Medal of Honor, and soon thereafter began performing in the wild west shows that were becoming popular in America. Eventually, he developed his own show, which featured many performers who would go on to become household names, including Sitting Bull and Annie Oakley. The show was wildly popular, touring in both America and overseas and making Buffalo Bill one of the most recognizable celebrities of his day.

Buffalo Bill continued performing for many years and was instrumental in developing the town of Cody, Wyoming, where he settled on a sprawling ranch. He died in Denver, Colorado, in 1917, and his grave sits on nearby Lookout Mountain.

In addition to the museum in LeClaire and his nearby preserved homestead, Cody is commemorated with the Scott County Cody Trail, which winds through the rolling countryside, stopping off at the homestead, pioneer village and other sites, including a marker outside LeClaire designating Buffalo Bill's birthplace.

A section of a famous elm tree known as the "Green Tree Hotel" is also on display—it stood for many years along the riverbank and was the spot where pilots congregated as they waited to be picked up by steamboats that needed assistance steering through LeClaire's treacherous channels.

More Buffalo Bill nostalgia is found at the **Buffalo Bill Cody Homestead** (www.scottcountyiowa.com/conservation/buffalobill.php), located several miles northwest of LeClaire in a rural area near the Wapsi River. Bill lived briefly in the 1847 farmhouse, built by his father, Isaac Cody, and situated among the rolling hillsides that were once part of the wide sweep of prairie that covered Iowa. The homestead has been restored and is stocked with 19th-century furnishings and other items. The carpet in the living room has been handwoven from rags, which was typical at the time, while the bedroom was added after the Cody family had moved on, eventually settling in Kansas Territory, where Bill began his long love affair with the frontier. There's also a replica log cabin schoolhouse and actual buffalo grazing in the surrounding fields.

Not far from the homestead is **Dan Nagle Walnut Grove Pioneer Village**, located on the site of an early Scott County settlement that thrived as a stagecoach stop in the 1860s and today contains 18 historic buildings, including a blacksmith shop, saloon, barbershop, schoolhouse and 1870 train depot. Many of the storefronts are found along a replica boardwalk, while the old-fashioned soda shop, open summer weekends, offers thirsty visitors a chance to sip a variety of ice cream treats.

In addition to its historic attractions, LeClaire is also very popular as a shopping destination, with antique and gift shops lining five blocks of Cody Drive. Perhaps the most famous of these is **Antique Archaeology** (http://antiquearchaeology.com), featured on the television program *American Pickers*, shoehorned in an alley behind a gas station. You may visit on a lucky day when one of the hosts is in the shop—they really do have an impressive and varied assortment of goodies, notably a selection of vintage bicycles and motorcycles.

A short drive down US 67 brings you to Iowa's largest city on the Missis-

Leading the way to Antique Archaeology, star of the *American Pickers* TV show

sippi: Davenport, third largest city in Iowa, with a population of 100,000. It is also the largest of the Quad Cities, which straddle the river in both Illinois and Iowa and include Bettendorf in Iowa and Moline, East Moline and Rock Island in Illinois. Together, they have a population of close to 400,000.

Inundated during the epic 1993 floods that submerged communities along the upper Mississippi, Davenport has for years resisted building a flood-wall or levee to protect the city, prefer-ring to leave its riverfront area open and accessible. (Houses and other structures are required to be built so that they stand above the flood plain.)

LeClaire Park is along the river, as are paved walkways and bike paths. Bi-cycles are available for rent at the Union Station Visitor Center, where you can also obtain maps of area bike paths. Also out of the visitor center, **Iowa Segway** (www.iasegway.com) offers guided tours of the riverfront and area historical sites. The nearby **Centennial Bridge** crosses the river and has a walkway designated for pedestrians and cy-clists. Also nearby is the **Skybridge**, a pedestrian bridge located a couple blocks from the downtown visitor center. It arches over River Drive between Brady and Main Streets, with great views of the Mississippi.

Downtown is also home to the **Putnam Museum** (www.putnam.org), a nat-ural history and science museum with exhibits such as a Mississippi River cave, large animal dioramas, Egyptian mummies and multimedia astronomy displays, as well as Iowa's largest IMAX theater. It also features numerous national trav-eling exhibits. The **Figge Art Museum** (http://figgeart.org) occupies a sleek glass structure, and its collection includes works from the Renaissance to modern art, including a large number of pieces by American artists and galleries devoted to

THE MISSISSIPPI RIVER TUG-OF-WAR

Every August, LeClaire participates in arguably the longest tug-of-war in the world: a rope is stretched some 2,500 feet across the Mississippi to Port Byron, Illi-nois, and teams on either side of the river proceed to pull their way to victory. Men's, women's and children's teams all compete. As of 2011, Illi-nois held the edge in victories. It's the highlight of LeClaire's weekend-long Tug Fest, which also includes a parade, fire-works over the river, musical entertainment and all sorts of food and craft vendors.

Frank Lloyd Wright and the American West. There are touring and temporary exhibits, too.

More art can be found at **Bucktown Center for the Arts** (www.bucktown arts.com), a restored warehouse with numerous studios of artists working in a variety of media. **River Music Experience** brings to life the sounds of the Mississippi, from blues to jazz to rock 'n' roll, with exhibits and a live music venue. In Bettendorf, the **Family Museum** (www.familymuseum.org) has all kinds of neat exhibits for kids, including a weather center with an interactive tornado, a place to make music and an outdoor play area with plenty of stuff to climb on, swing from and slide down. There are many educational exhibits as well as an area for smaller children.

Like the rest of Iowa, Davenport experienced a wave of immigration in the 19th century from central and northern Europe, especially Germany: by the 1850s, approximately 3,000 residents—some 20 percent of the city's population—were German immigrants, with their own schools, newspapers and a thriving community. That heritage is commemorated at downtown's **German American Heritage Center** (http://gahc.org), which was originally a *gast haus,* or hotel, for German immigrants. It has permanent exhibits that follow the journey of immigrants from the old country to America. Across the river in Moline, the **Center for Belgian Culture** (www.belgianmusuemquadcities.org) preserves the history of what was the largest Belgian community in the United States.

Among the local notables of German descent was legendary jazz cornetist Bix Beiderbecke, who is honored with an annual jazz festival and whose childhood home still stands at 1934 Grand Avenue. Another famous home is that of Antoine LeClaire, founder of Davenport and namesake of the river town to the north, at 630 East Seventh Street. Yet another famous resident was Ronald Reagan, who, after graduating from college in Illinois, briefly worked as a radio announcer in Davenport and lived in an apartment overlooking the Mississippi before moving on to Des Moines and, ultimately, Hollywood.

Davenport and the Quad Cities developed thanks to their ideal location at the spot where the Rock River flows into the Mississippi from Illinois, as well as the rich farmland that spread out from the river into the surrounding countryside. Mills sprung up along the river, harnessing its power to grind wheat and saw wood, and Davenport soon became an important stopping point for steamboats and later for railroads, leading to a showdown between the two powerful trans-

THE BLACK HAWK WAR: AN EXPLOSION ON THE FRONTIER

The Quad Cities were the flashpoint of one of the more notable confrontations between Native Americans and the U.S. government in the push westward across the North American continent. Following the Louisiana Purchase in 1804, which included all of present-day Iowa, settlers began moving into the area. Tensions increased with the Sauk and Fox tribes, who had been living along the Mississippi for many years, including a large settlement near where the Rock River flows into the Mississippi at present-day Rock Island.

Many tribal chiefs signed treaties, turned over land to the government and led their people out of the area to settle farther west of the river. However, the Sauk warrior Black Hawk resisted the turnovers and by 1830 had rallied many others to take up the fight with him against the government troops. Tensions and skirmishes escalated until 1832, when Black Hawk led more than 1,000 of his followers back across the Mississippi and into Illinois. A force of federal troops was assembled to track down Black Hawk and his party, and skirmishes exploded into full-blown war.

After unsuccessful attempts at surrender, Black Hawk led his party north into Wisconsin, where the war climaxed at the Battle of Bad Axe along the Wisconsin River. The last battle of the Indian Wars to take place east of the Mississippi, it ended with the massacre of hundreds of Indians; more died there than at the other famous massacre sites of Sand Creek or Wounded Knee. Black Hawk himself was imprisoned and eventually returned to Iowa, where he died in 1838. His autobiography remains in print to this day, providing an important historical account of an often overlooked chapter of the Indian Wars and westward expansion.

Following the end of the war, the Sauk Chieftain Keokuk signed a treaty giving the U.S. all the tribe's land in Illinois as well as a 50-mile-wide strip on the west bank of the Mississippi. The 6 million acres of land came to be known as the Black Hawk Purchase.

Black Hawk is commemorated in Rock Island with a three-story mural downtown, and at the Black Hawk State Historic Site (http://blackhawk park.org), which includes a museum with life-size replicas of Sauk summer and winter homes as well as numerous artifacts and an 18-ton granite statue of the Sauk warrior. Trails wind through the surrounding woods.

portation industries that culminated with a steamboat ramming the first railroad bridge across the Mississippi in 1856, just weeks after it was completed. The railroad hired a young lawyer named Abraham Lincoln to argue their side in a subsequent lawsuit, which went all the way to the Supreme Court, where the railroad won the case, establishing a precedent that lead to three main rail lines coming to the Quad Cities.

The area's development accelerated further after a blacksmith named John Deere established a plow factory in Moline in 1848, using a new design that kept soil from clinging to the plow's blade. This revolution in plowing helped Deere's factory grow into the world's foremost agricultural equipment manufacturer and helped turn the Midwest into the breadbasket of the world.

Deere's legacy is everywhere in the Quad Cities, with plants on both sides of the river, and especially in Moline, still home to **Deere & Company World Headquarters,** which is open to visitors. Nearby is the **John Deere Pavilion** (www.John DeerePavilion.com), which includes a huge collection of vintage and modern tractors and interactive displays on new technologies being used in agriculture. The **John Deere Harvester Works** has a visitors center and also offers tours by appointment of the company's largest combine factory.

For those looking for an even bigger John Deere fix, the **John Deere Historic Site** (www.JohnDeereHistoricSite.com), located about an hour east of the Quad Cities off I-88 in Grand Detour, Illinois, has a replica of Deere's original blacksmith shop. It's open from May through October.

Back in Moline, the **Deere-Wiman House** sits on a hill overlooking the site of the original plow factory. It and the nearby **Butterworth Center** were homes of the Deere family. Both have beautiful gardens and offer guided tours by appointment. John Deere is buried in **Riverside Cemetery,** perched on a bluff above the Mississippi. The grave sits at the crest of the cemetery, which is open to the public.

As with Deere, the Quad Cities have been long wedded to heavy industry, including at the **Rock Island Arsenal,** historically the largest government-owned weapons manufacturing facility, which began producing gear for the military during the Spanish-American War and continued through World War II, when some 20,000 workers assembled weaponry and heavy equipment, including tanks. It sits on Arsenal Island, the largest island in the upper Mississippi.

The island was originally the site of Fort Armstrong, built following the War of 1812 in order to assert U.S. claims to the frontier, as well as to provide a military presence for settlers who were moving into lands where Native Americans were already living and insure passage of vessels on the river.

The arsenal is a national historic site, with many areas open to the public. These include **Rock Island Arsenal Museum** (http://riamwr.com), which has a large collection of firearms, including several rare weapons, along with military vehicles and other displays. Farther down the island are both the **Rock Island National Cemetery** and the **Rock Island Confederate Cemetery**, resting place of nearly 2,000 Confederate prisoners of war, some of the 12,000 who were held in a prison camp at the island.

Also on the island is the **Colonel Davenport House** (www.davenporthouse .org), home of Davenport's namesake, George Davenport, a native of England who served in the Black Hawk War and made a fortune in fur trading. He also cultivated friendships with both local Native American tribes and the most prominent individuals in the area. Tragically, he was murdered in his own home in 1845. Guided tours of the house take visitors past period furniture and decorations, as well as displays related to Davenport's prolific life.

A replica of a Fort Armstrong blockhouse from 1816 sits just past the end of the bridge that connects the island to Davenport. The nearby **Mississippi River Visitor Center** (www.missriver.org) has detailed exhibits on the locks and dams built by the Army Corps of Engineers to tame and control the river, as well as displays on barge and boat traffic.

Finally, no visit to Davenport would be complete without taking a spin over to the **Village of East Davenport** (www.VillageofEastDavenport.com), a former logging settlement reborn as a hip shopping and nightlife destination. The **11th Street Bar and Grill** and **Mound Street Landing** both offer live music, but the real highlight is a visit to **Lagomarcino's,** an old-fashioned ice cream shop founded in 1908 as a confectionary by an Italian immigrant. All sorts of scrumptious sundaes are served up, with some big enough to share. There are also sandwiches and salads for light meals. (Be sure to save room for the ice cream!)

One last attraction requires you to hop on I-80 and head a few miles west to Exit 284 and the **World's Largest Truckstop** (www.iowa80truckstop.com). This place lives up to its name, with a sit-down restaurant and numerous fast-food eateries, a massive travel store, barbershop, dentist, movie theater and, best of all, the **Iowa 80 Trucking Museum** (http://iowa80truckingmuseum.com) with its showroom full of vintage trucks and other highway artifacts. Every July there's a truckers' jamboree.

IN THE AREA

ACCOMMODATIONS

Decker Hotel & Restaurant, 128 Main Street, Maquoketa. Call 563-652-6654. From the lobby on up its impressive staircase and bannister, this hotel reflects its long history dating to 1875. Eight guest rooms and six suites have period furniture and also include private bathrooms and individual heating and air-conditioning. The restaurant has plenty of all-American choices like steak, fried catfish and grilled chicken, while the lounge is a nice spot to ease back over a beer or a game of pool. Website: http://deckerhotel.us.

Gehlen Inn Guest House, 101 Main Street, St. Donatus. Call 563-773-2480 or 1-800-280-1177. This is a simple country inn housed in a historic former tavern in Iowa's Luxembourg village. There are six rooms available, including some with whirlpool tubs and a suite with a private entrance and deck. Some rooms have private baths. Guests receive a discount breakfast in Kalmes Restaurant across the street. Inexpensive. Website: www.gehlenhouse.com.

Hotel Blackhawk, 200 East Third Street, Davenport. Call 563-322-5000 or 1-888-525-4455. Modern rooms are featured in this historic hotel near the riverfront and downtown attractions. The airy, high-ceilinged lobby and mezzanine are a nice contrast to hip rooms stocked with amenities like flat-screen televisions and stylish bathrooms. There's a large indoor pool, day spa and even a bowling alley, as well as a restaurant and lounge. Moderate to Expensive. Website: http://hotelblackhawk.com.

Mont Rest Inn, 300 Spring Street, Bellevue. Call 563-872-4220 or 1-877-872-4220. Sitting regally on a wooded bluff with striking views of the river flowing before it, Mont Rest dates from the Victorian era. Note the unique round room atop the front of the house—it was built to host high-stakes card games, enticing riverboat gamblers to lay down their money when they came to town. There are numerous rooms ranging in size and price, with all having working fireplaces and whirlpool tubs. The owners will even arrange for a tee time on the local links or a canoe trip down the Mississippi. Moderate to Expensive. Website: www.montrest.com.

Squiers Manor Bed and Breakfast, 418 West Pleasant Street, Maquoketa. Call 563-652-6961. A beautiful Queen Anne mansion restored to its original Victorian grandeur, Squiers Manor has eight rooms and suites throughout the house. At the top is the loft suite, which has exposed brick walls and occupies nearly 500 square feet. The ballroom suite is twice as big and has a 24-foot-high ceiling soaring over the king-sized bed and whirlpool tub. The food selection is varied and eclectic and includes plenty of decadent desserts. A perfect spot to hide out for a weekend—the staff will deliver breakfast to your room if you want. Room prices vary widely depending on size. Website: www.squiersmanor.com.

Stoney Creek Inn, 101 18th Street, Moline, Illinois. Call 309-743-0101 or 1-800-659-2220. This Quad Cities outpost of a Midwest chain is done up with decor that evokes a north-woods hunting lodge, with touches like knotty pine and a large lobby fireplace. Rooms are comfortable and include theme suites focused on hunting, fishing and the great out-doors. There's a swim-through pool with whirlpool and sauna. This is an ideal location for those visiting John Deere attractions, and it's also near the Rock Island Arsenal. Inexpensive to Moderate. Website: www.stoney creekinn.com.

DINING

Crane and Pelican Café, 127 Second Street South, LeClaire. Call 563-289-8774. In a restored Italianate home built by a steamboat pilot in a resi-dential section of LeClaire, this restaurant retains historic touches, including elaborate chandeliers and intricate metal fireplaces. The food, however, is thoroughly contemporary and includes pan-seared Atlantic salmon, grilled chicken breast in gar-lic cream sauce and a classic Iowa pork chop. Pastas and entrée salads are also found on the menu along

with some innovative sandwiches, in-cluding an asparagus and roasted red pepper combination and a three-cheese grilled cheese, as well as the hearty and popular meat loaf sand-wich. Moderate. Website: www.crane-andpelican.com.

Faithful Pilot Café, 117 North Cody Road, LeClaire. Call 563-289-4156. An intimate little bistro with some ad-venturous selections: try the feta-and garlic-stuffed roast chicken or the Dijon walnut-crusted salmon with sugar snap peas and cauliflower purée. There's an extensive wine list and an impressive selection of marti-nis. Perfect for a relaxing lunch after a morning spent perusing LeClaire's antiques shops, and a nice change from the typical small-town cafés found along the Great River Road. Nice Sunday brunch, too. Moderate to Expensive. Website: www.faithfulpilot .com.

Front Street Brewery, 208 East River Drive, Davenport. Call 563-322-1569. Great river views are a bonus at this casual downtown brew pub. Choose from among the many beers brewed

Crane and Pelican Café, a former riverboat pilot's house in LeClaire

Downtown Clinton

in-house to accompany favorites like steak, ribs, chicken, or seared or blackened fish. Their most popular offering is bangers and mash, with a choice of either bratwurst or polish sausage garnished with sauerkraut, grilled onions and horseradish sour cream. Plenty of salads on the menu as well. Moderate. Website: http:// frontstreetbrew.com.

Kalmes Restaurant, 100 Main Street, St. Donatus. Call 563-773-2480 or 1-800-280-1177. Both the decor and the menu invoke the old country at this popular spot in Iowa's Luxembourg village: pictures of castles and other European scenes cover the half-timbered walls, while the kitchen turns out dishes like Wiener schnitzel, blood sausage and sauerkraut, as well as plenty of all-American favorites like steaks, chicken and seafood. There's a Friday seafood buffet and a Sunday breakfast buffet, too. Inex-

pensive to Moderate. Website: www .gehlenhouse.com.

Machine Shed, 7250 Northwest Boulevard, Davenport. Call 563-391-2427. Down-home country cooking in a big, rambling restaurant just off I-80, one of several Midwest locations. The lengthy menu specializes in farmers' favorites like fried chicken, chicken-fried steak and meat loaf, all served in generous portions. Also known for its massive cinnamon rolls, which can easily feed two people. Moderate. Website: www.machine shed.com.

Patrick's Steakhouse and Brewery, 132 Sixth Avenue South, Clinton. Call 563-243-5539. A sports bar and grill near the riverfront with a relaxing atmosphere and a rustic touch: the restaurant is located in an old paper company building, and the brick and glass block exterior exudes historic charm. Nothing very fancy from the kitchen, just substantial and tasty burgers, steaks and other stuff cooked on a grill. Delicious rotisserie chicken, too. Stick around to watch the game. Moderate. Website: http:// steakhousebrewery.com.

Rastrelli's, 238 Main Ave., Clinton. Call 563-242-7441. A classic Italian place, passed down in the family from its founders, with an extensive menu of favorites like chicken cacciatore, tortellini and lasagna, as well as steaks, chops and seafood. Also has pizzas, salads, burgers and sandwiches. The decor is Tuscan country villa and the portions are generous. Moderate to Expensive. Website: http://rastrellis.com.

Ross' Restaurant, 430 14th Street, Bettendorf. Call 563-355-7573. A classic diner, open 24 hours a day, with an impressive phone book of a menu. Breakfast is always served (of course!) and their signature item is the "Magic Mountain": Texas Toast topped with a heaping helping of ground beef, french fries and cheese sauce—it's not for the squeamish eater. (There's also a meatless version with green pepper, onion and tomato.) Good burgers and sandwiches, as well as numerous salads and wraps. Inexpensive. Website: www.rossrestaurant.com.

Sippi's Restaurant, 406 West Second Street, Davenport. Call 563-323-3911. Simple yet tasty dishes are the rule at this casual bar and grill in a historic downtown building. The burgers are big and meaty, as are the ribs and the massive 14-ounce rib eye. Lighter choices include grilled tilapia or salmon, as well as several wraps and salads. Appetizers like BBQ nachos and chicken wings with a selection of sauces can be a meal in themselves. Moderate. Website: www.sippis.biz.

SHOPPING

Banowetz Antique Mall & Showroom, 122 McKinsey Drive, Maquoketa. Call 563-652-2359. A huge antiques emporium, with more than 150 dealers in 50,000 square feet of showroom space. Expect to spend a *lot* of time poring over furniture, accessories, glassware, decorative items and other antique pieces. Fortunately, the sellers and staff can help you navigate the huge number of offerings. Website: www.banowetz antiques.com.

The Book Worm, 110 South Riverview Street, Bellevue. Call 563-872-4802. A huge selection of books in all sorts of genres is available at this shop along Bellevue's riverfront. Check out the shelves devoted to state and local history—you can find plenty of books about Iowa here. There are also knickknacks and accessories for sale. Website: www.belle vuebookworm.com.

Mississippi Cottage Antiques, 606 North Cody Road, LeClaire. Call 563-289-1515. Find everything from vintage glassware to carved wooden bowls, fine art to jewelry at this shop in a rambling old house on LeClaire's antique row, with its many rooms ideal for spending an hour or more perusing the items on display. Website: www.mississippicottageantiques.net.

Mississippi River Distilling Company, 303 North Cody Road, LeClaire. Call 563-484-4342. For a change of pace from the many small wineries that dot Iowa, check this out: handcrafted vodka and gin are distilled at this modest structure just off the

LeClaire waterfront. Tours take visitors through the distilling process "from grain to glass," and conclude in the tasting room, where guests can sample the different spirits. There's a retail shop on-site as well. Website: www.mrdistilling.com.

Off the Wall & Great River Gallery, 116–124 North Riverview Street, Bellevue. Call 563-872-3388. Representing more than 70 artists, this pair of galleries just off the river offers changing exhibitions and regular educational programs as part of an effort to maintain and enrich the local art scene. Website: www.offthewallartgallery.biz.

Old City Hall Art Gallery, 121 South Olive Street, Maquoketa. Call 563-652-3405. A long-standing gallery owned by a local husband and wife who showcase their works alongside pieces by other artists. Many of their creations are portraits, including a series depicting local residents, as well as larger multimedia works, installation art and ethereal portraits that are depicted as allegories. Website: http://oldcityhallgallery.com.

RECREATION AND ENTERTAINMENT

Celebration River Cruises, 2501 River Drive, Moline, Illinois. Call 309-764-1952 or 1-800-297-0034. Cruise the Mississippi on a replica paddlewheeler while learning about local history and life on the river. Half- and full-day trips are available, and include lunch and dinner options. Website: www.celebrationbelle.com.

Channel Cat Water Taxi. Call 309-788-3360. Ride along the river on this open-air pontoon boat, part of the Quad Cities mass transit system, with regular stops in Davenport, Bettendorf and Moline. It runs from Memorial Day through Labor Day. Website: www.visitquadcities.com/company.php?id=107.

Clinton Lumber Kings, 537 Ballpark Drive, Clinton. Call 563-242-0727. Clinton's minor-league affiliate of the Seattle Mariners take to the field at Alliant Energy Stadium on the Clinton riverfront, the perfect place to be on a warm summer evening when a soft breeze blows off the Mississippi. Look for ticket deals and promotions throughout the season. Website: www.minorleaguebaseball.com/index.jsp?sid=t500.

Isle Casino Hotel Bettendorf, 1777 Isle Parkway, Bettendorf. Call 563-441-7000 or 1-800-724-5825. More than 40,000 square feet of slots and table games along the riverfront, as well as three restaurants and an on-site marina. Website: http://bettendorf.isleofcapricasinos.com/index.aspx.

Jumer's Casino and Hotel, 777 Jumer Drive, Rock Island, Illinois. Call 309-756-4600 or 1-800-477-7747. This all-on-one-floor casino with more than 1,000 slot machines has a sleek nightclub and hotel with indoor pool and day spa. Website: www.jumerscri.com.

Michael's Fun World, 354 West 76th Street, Davenport. Call 563-386-3826. This family fun center near the Davenport airport offers everything from go-carts to rock climbing to odder games like jousting and "trampoline basketball." It's easy to spend all day here—there are also batting cages, miniature golf and concessions. Website: http://michaelsfunworld.com.

Quad Cities River Bandits, 209 South Gaines Street, Davenport. Call 563-3-BANDIT. The Bandits draw fans to Modern Woodmen Park, which has stood on the same site on the banks of the Mississippi since 1931. In the shadow of the Centennial Bridge, it's a great spot to kick back and take in a game. Website: www.minorleaguebaseball.com/index.jsp?sid=t565.

Twilight River Boat Cruises, 406 Franklin Street, Scales Mound, Illinois. Call 815-845-2333 or 1-800-331-1467. Setting off from LeClaire's historic riverfront, this replica steamboat chugs up the Mississippi, passing by the striking limestone bluffs that line the river and the many locks and dams that define the channel, before docking in Dubuque for an overnight stay at a local hotel. The boat returns to LeClaire the next day. Meals and snacks are available onboard and entertainment is provided as well. Website: www.riverboat twilight.com.

Wild Rose Casino, 777 Wild Rose Drive, Clinton. Call 563-243-9000 or 1-800-457-9975. Blackjack, poker, craps, roulette and slots are all offered at this casino on the south side of Clinton. There are two restaurants on-site, too. Website: www.wildrose resorts.com.

OTHER CONTACTS

Bellevue Area Chamber of Commerce, 210 North Riverview, Bellevue, 52031. Call 563-872-5830. Website: www.bellevueia.com.

Clinton Convention & Visitors Bureau, 721 South Second Street, Clinton, 52732. Call 563-242-5702. Website: www.clintoniowatourism.com.

Maquoketa Area Chamber of Commerce, 117 South Main Street, Maquoketa, 52060. Call 563-652-4602 or 1-800-989-4602. Website: www.maquoketachamber.com.

Mississippi Valley Welcome Center, 900 Eagle Ridge Road, LeClaire, 52753. Call 563-322-3911 or 1-800-747-7800. Website: www.iowawelcome center.com.

St. Donatus Historical Society, P.O. Box 66, St. Donatus, 52071. Call 563-773-2480. Website: www.gehlenhouse .com.

Union Station Visitor Center/Quad Cities Convention & Visitors Bureau, 102 South Harrison Street, Davenport, 52801. Call 563-322-3911. Website: www.visitquadcities.com.

4 Rollin' on the River:

MUSCATINE, BURLINGTON, FORT MADISON AND KEOKUK

Estimated length: About 120 miles each way from Davenport to Keokuk and back.

Estimated time: Could be done in a weekend or even as a long day trip from the Quad Cities, stopping off at a selection of the listed sights and towns.

Getting there: Start in Davenport/Quad Cities, which lie along I-80 and US 61, the main road of this trip.

Highlights: Spotting bald eagles in Keokuk. Seeing an entire restored pioneer fortification in Fort Madison. Learning about Muscatine's history as the pearl button capital of the world and Burlington's heritage as a railroad center. Strolling some of the charming riverfronts and hopping across the Mississippi to Nauvoo for a look at historic Mormon sites.

This is a more leisurely trip paralleling the Mississippi; much of it follows the old "Blues Highway," US 61, which in some spots makes up the Great River Road. Populated areas are fewer along this route, and the larger cities are sleepy places that stretch like a necklace of faded jewels along the river. You can almost feel the history here—the days when steamboats plied the currents and stopped off in bustling river ports to unload goods and passengers. Today, they're worthwhile places to stop for a meal or a stroll along the banks of the river, as well as home to some unique attractions.

Heading out of Davenport, follow US 61 about 20 miles south to **Muscatine**, which has one of the more pleasant riverfronts, marked by a soaring bridge that lights up the area at night. The city was home to Iowa's largest black population in the 1840s and '50s, including many residents who escaped slavery and followed

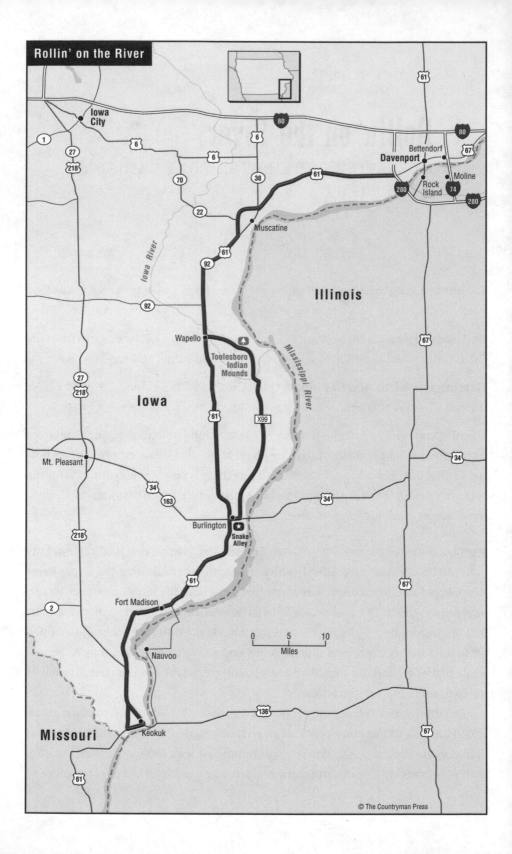

Rollin' on the River

the Underground Railroad north to Iowa. Mark Twain also lived here briefly in the 1850s, working as a journalist and forming his picture of the great river as it flowed past the bustling river town.

Muscatine's downtown is remarkably well preserved. Sitting among the many charming shops on Second Street, near the river, is the **Muscatine History and Industry Center** (www.muscatinehistory.org), a storefront museum with some very neat displays on the area's long heyday as a button-making center. Beginning in the 1890s, the manufacturing of pearl buttons dominated life in Muscatine, earning it the nickname "Pearl City." The buttons came from clams harvested from the Mississippi, and "cutting shops" and related businesses sprang up all over town.

At its peak, more than half of the buttons in the world were made in Muscatine and half the town's population was employed in the button industry. Unfortunately, changes in the industry wiped out Muscatine's button factories by the 1960s. Visitors can spend quite a bit of time checking out the museum's displays of photographs featuring mountains of clamshells outside the factories, as well as replicas of a clamming boat, button machines and recorded histories of veteran button makers.

Close by is the **Muscatine Art Center** (www.muscatineartcenter.org), which is composed of two facilities: a gallery with works in a variety of media and a historic mansion that displays pieces from the family whose efforts helped found the center. The collection includes a selection of works focused on the Mississippi River and the communities and people that live along it. There are works by great artists such as Matisse, Degas, Renoir and Iowa's own Grant Wood.

Farther away from the river, near the intersection of US 61 and IA 22, is the **Muscatine Arboretum** (www.neighborhoodlink.com/Muscatine_Arboretum _Association), with more than 1,000 trees and shrubs. The arboretum and an **Environmental Learning Center** are located in **Discovery Park,** which also has some nice trails for walking. Moving back toward Davenport on IA 22 brings you to **Pine Creek Grist Mill** (http://pinecreekgristmill.com), a restored working mill that dates from 1848, making it one of the oldest operating gristmills in the nation. Watch the three millstones grind out buckwheat and corn flour and check out the adjacent **Melpine School,** which has mementos of one-room schoolhouse days, including photos, old schoolbooks, desks and other period items. Both structures are located in **Wildcat Den State Park,** which has an extensive system of trails leading to sights like Devil's Punch Bowl and Steamboat Rock. There are some breathtaking views of the surrounding bluffs and the nearby Mississippi River.

Moving on from Muscatine, US 61 shoots due south, moving several miles west of the river and passing through vast acres of farmland. Outside the town of **Wapello,** closer to the Mississippi, is **Port Louisa National Wildlife Refuge** (www.fws.gov/midwest/portlouisa), nearly 9,000 acres that are home to more than 270 species of birds, with millions of the winged creatures passing through on annual migrations. Look for the red-bellied woodpecker and white pelican, as well as bald eagles and other wildlife.

From Wapello, veer onto X-99 and follow it a few miles to **Toolesboro Indian Mounds.** The seven burial mounds, situated on a bluff near the Mississippi, were built between about 100 B.C. and A.D. 200 by native peoples known as the Hopewell, prolific mound builders who used a variety of burial techniques in their mounds, giving archaeologists a wealth of material to study. The largest of the mounds measures about 100 feet wide and 8 feet high and is one of the largest mounds in Iowa. Numerous artifacts have been found at the site. An on-site educational center has exhibits related to the mound builders.

From Toolesboro, head south on either US 61, which shoots through wide open farm fields, or cut over to the more scenic Great River Road. There are virtually no populated areas until you reach **Burlington,** which has a picturesque downtown that slopes down to the banks of the Mississippi. The visitors center, located in the city's historic port building, is well stocked with information.

Burlington's steep hills from the riverfront and downtown up to its residential neighborhoods give it a unique look among river towns and also contribute to one of the odder sights you'll see anywhere: **Snake Alley** (www.snakealley .com), a winding stretch of serpentine built early on in the city's history to deal with the challenge of moving goods from the waterfront up the steep inclines. It vies with Lombard Street in San Francisco for being the most crooked street in the world.

At the top end of Snake Alley stands **Phelps House** (www.dmchs.org), a handsome Victorian mansion from the 1850s furnished with period antiques. The third floor is dedicated to local medical history and a ballroom showcasing vintage outfits. Numerous other Victorians dot the surrounding streets, including some charming bed & breakfasts. The nearby **Des Moines County Heritage Center** is

Burlington's Snake Alley

housed in the old library, and its displays include a large diorama depicting life among the area's native inhabitants and a re-creation of a 19th-century pioneer settlement, which is great for kids. Visitors also can learn about the area's notable natives, including preeminent conservationist and naturalist Aldo Leopold and Bart Howard, an entertainer and composer responsible for the 1960s hit, *Fly Me to the Moon.*

Burlington's other main draw is its many parks. In addition to Riverwalk Park near the visitors center—which can provide walking guides to the park and other scenic downtown routes—there are several other interesting spots in the countryside, including **Starr's Cave Nature Center** (www.dmcconservation.com). Starr's Cave is one of only two state geological preserves in Iowa, and its rock formations are found nowhere else in the world. Numerous hiking trails crisscross the park, visiting sites with names like Devil's Kitchen. Unfortunately, the cave itself was closed in 2010 and will likely remain closed for several years, as will all caves in Iowa, due to the threat of a disease that could kill off the bat population. It's worth calling to see if the cave has reopened.

The park is also considered an excellent spot for bird-watching—you may catch a glimpse of hawks, herons or songbirds, as well as deer, wild turkeys, beavers, foxes and other wildlife. The park's nature center has exhibits that include a full-size replica beaver pond.

Other Burlington-area parks include **Big Hollow**, which has an observatory for stargazing and several shooting ranges, **Crapo Park**; a riverside park that includes a renowned arboretum and a log cabin located on the spot where Zebulon Pike first raised the American flag while exploring the area for the U.S. government; and **Geode State Park**, located about 10 miles west of Burlington, which features a display of quartz formed in local limestone. The sparkling crystals are neat to look at, even as geologists puzzle over their origins.

Bangert Gardens (www.bangertgardens.com) is a botanical wonderland with more than 200 different species of trees and flowers, as well as a pleasant stream and a nice cactus garden. The private gardens offer tours based on time availability. **Zion Schoolhouse** has been preserved from its days as a working one-room school. And don't avoid **Mosquito Park**—despite its name, it has an ideal location, atop a bluff just outside of downtown, for watching the river flow by.

Back on US 61 heading south, it's about 20 miles to **Fort Madison**, a city brimming with history of the river, the railroad, and westward expansion. It was the site of a stockade built in 1808 following the Louisiana Purchase to guard settlers moving into the area; the first U.S. military fortification on the upper Mississippi; and the site where the first white child was born in Iowa, in 1810.

The fort became the site of numerous skirmishes with the local Sauk Indians, and was evacuated and burned in 1813 by retreating troops, who slipped through a secret trench in the night to waiting boats on the river.

A monument marks the site of the original fort, while a short distance away on the banks of the Mississippi, **Old Fort Madison** (www.fortmadison-ia.com/old fort.htm) is a replica of the original fort and the site of interactive programs led by costumed historical interpreters. Try your hand at dipping a candle, shouldering an authentic musket, and learning about the hardscrabble lives of pioneers on the frontier.

A territorial prison was established here in 1839, and the city eventually grew into a thriving river port, prospering further after it gained railroads in 1857 and 1887. Eventually, a large complex of train yards and maintenance shops sprang up just outside the city. The Santa Fe Swing Span Bridge, completed in 1927, carries both railroad cars and automobiles across the Mississippi. It is the longest double-decker swing span bridge in the world.

Trains still rumble day and night along the tracks that run between the river and downtown, passing by a pair of depots, one of which is the Old Santa Fe Depot, a handsome brick structure built in Mission Revival style and including a bell tower. It is home of both Fort Madison's visitors center and to the North Lee County Historical Museum (http://fortmadisonhistory.org), with exhibits on the railroad, Native American culture, the Civil War and the epic 1993 flood of the Mississippi. There's a vintage caboose parked outside.

Interestingly, Fort Madison has had a Mexican community since the early 20th century, with many coming to work on the railroad. The city has hosted a Mexican Independence Day celebration every September for nearly 100 years.

Across the tracks from the Santa Fe depot is the Burlington Northern Depot, which houses the Fort Madison Area Arts Association (www.fmaaa

---

NAUVOO, ILLINOIS:
WELLSPRING OF THE MORMON TREK

The starting point for one of the most epic migrations in American history, the movement of Mormon pioneers across the harsh landscapes and weather of the Great Plains and Rocky Mountains to their eventual destination on the shores of the Great Salt Lake, Nauvoo sits on the Illinois side of the Mississippi, about halfway between Fort Madison and Keokuk. It was home to the largest community of Mormons, including founder Joseph Smith, for several years. Mormons were forced out of town in 1846, two years after Smith was murdered by a mob, and began trekking west.

There are numerous historic sites in the Nauvoo area, including the Joseph Smith Historic Site (www.rlds.org/js) and the Nauvoo Temple (www.nauvootemple.com). The town's visitors center has information on these and other sights.

.com). Its gallery includes works by both local and national artists in a variety of media. Ask at the visitors center for a brochure on Artsippi, an annual "art crawl" that features the studios of local artists both in Fort Madison and across the river in Galena, Illinois.

The legacy of the "iron horse" continues at **Riverview Park,** adjacent to the depots, where an impressive steam engine is displayed. Opposite the depots, downtown buildings, including some interesting shops and restaurants, stretch along the length of the park.

The coming of the railroads led to building booms in the city, resulting in close to 100 grand Victorian homes. The visitors center can provide a brochure describing a self-guided tour that travels past many fine old homes, Fort Madison's first hospital and a museum dedicated to the **Sheaffer Pen Company,** which emerged from humble beginnings in Fort Madison to become one of the world's preeminent manufacturers of fountain pens.

The tour also includes the **Fort Madison Community Mural,** an intricate scene depicting famous historical figures of the area, including Sauk warrior Black Hawk, an early chief justice of the Iowa Supreme Court and a local resident

The George M. Verity River Museum

BALD EAGLES ALONG THE MISSISSIPPI

Keokuk is a prime spot for viewing bald eagles, which congregate in large numbers in the area during their winter migration and can be seen from December through February, with spectators arriving en masse during the city's Bald Eagle Appreciation Days in January (www .keokukiowatourism.org/eagledays.htm).

The magnificent birds soar above the Mississippi and can be seen from Victory Park along the riverfront. Activities include presentations on local ecology and wildlife and Native American history.

who spoke out against slavery. Also depicted are scenes such as the great flood of 1993, a bald eagle soaring over the Mississippi and Fort Madison's annual Mexican Fiesta.

Two miles north of Fort Madison off X-32 is a restored one-room school known as Brush College (http://fortmadisonhistory.org/home/brush_college), which has been stocked with replica items from the 1880s, including kerosene lamps and a wood-burning stove. North of the city on US 61 is the Daniel Mc-Conn Barn, the only Pennsylvania Dutch double-decker barn in Iowa, with a foundation of hand-laid stone and three cupolas atop the roof. The large structure spreads out over three levels inside.

Swinging back south onto US 61, follow the road as it hugs a long bend in the river, then unkinks and descends into Keokuk, down at the southeastern tip of the state, at a bend in the river where Iowa, Illinois and Missouri come together.

Like many other cities along the Mississippi, Keokuk is a faded river town with the remnants of once-grand structures lining its streets. It's named for a Native American chief who led his people even as they were expelled from the area. A monument to the chief stands in the city's Rand Park, which also has a performance pavilion and a flower garden.

Keokuk's riverfront is not quite as accessible as those in other river towns. It is home to the George M. Verity River Museum (www.keokukiowatourism.org /verity.htm), located on an authentic paddle-wheel steamboat that saw heavy service pushing barges on the river in the 1920s and '30s, with exhibits on Mississippi River life and history.

The boat sits in the shadow of the Keokuk-Hamilton Bridge, which has an observation deck that provides nice views of the river and a nearby lock and dam. Heading back into town, you may want to take a short tour of the Grand Avenue District, which stretches for many city blocks along a bluff overlooking a bend in the river and includes many notable historic homes. Also check out the Grand Theatre downtown, which has been restored and hosts a variety of events.

Near downtown and the Grand Avenue District, the Miller House Museum (www.keokukiowatourism.org/millerhouse.htm) has been preserved to look as it did in its days as an elegant 19th-century residence. It also houses many artifacts of Keokuk's history, including a portrait of its namesake. The city is also home to the Keokuk National Cemetery (www.cem.va.gov/cems/nchp/keokuk.asp), the only national cemetery in Iowa and the resting place of more than 4,000 soldiers. Keokuk also hosts an annual Civil War re-enactment that draws enthusiasts from many states.

IN THE AREA

ACCOMMODATIONS

Candelight Manor Bed and Breakfast, 303 South Sixth Street, Burlington. Call 319-758-0428. An elegant home in Burlington's historic residential district, with oak and maple floors and period furnishings in the rooms and common areas, including a grand piano and staircase with carved bannister. Nice views of the Mississippi River, too. Inexpensive to Moderate. Website: www.candle manor.net.

The Grand Anne, 816 Grand Avenue, Keokuk. Call 319-524-6310. Another Queen Anne mansion on Grand Avenue, dating from Keokuk's days as a booming river port and reborn as a bed & breakfast. There are five guest rooms with features like oak and walnut beds and magnificent views of the Mississippi from some rooms. One guest room is located on the top level of the home's turret. Moderate to Medium. Website: www.bbonline .com/ia/grandanne.

Kingsley Inn, 707 Avenue H, Fort Madison. Call 319-372-7074. Eleven rooms and seven suites house guests in this historic hotel reborn as a bed & breakfast overlooking the riverfront. The lobby has Persian rugs, vintage lighting fixtures and other striking touches. Rooms are named after historical figures and have been lovingly restored. The adjoining **Alpha's Restaurant** (see *Dining*) serves up some yummy grub. Moderate. Website: www.kingsleyinn.com.

The Manor Bed & Breakfast Inn, 804 Avenue F, Fort Madison. Call 319-372-7994. Covered with ivy, this charming redbrick Victorian home features two guest rooms, a screened porch with wicker furniture perfect for relaxing and even a swimming pool. It's adjacent to downtown and a short walk from riverfront attractions. Website: www.themanorbedand breakfast.com.

Mississippi Manor, 809 North Fourth Street, Burlington. Call 319-753-2218. Another Victorian Italianate home on the bluffs overlooking downtown Burlington and the Mississippi, this bed & breakfast embraces a river theme, with rooms named after Mark Twain and his characters. The Twain suite has a large bay window with splendid views. All rooms have private baths. Inexpensive to Moderate. Website: www.mississippimanorbnb.com.

Victoria Bed & Breakfast Inn & Studios, 422 Avenue F, Fort Madison. Call 319-372-6842. Run by a local artist, this Federal-style home dates from the 1850s and has a choice of rooms with king, queen and double beds, including several canopy beds, as well as private and shared baths. Ask about the room with tower access, which provides a three-sided view of the nearby Mississippi River. The home faces Settlers Park, a nice green space. Inexpensive to Moderate. Website: www.VictoriaBedand BreakfastInnandStudios.com.

Wild Rose Manor Guest House, 100 North Eighth Street, Burlington. Call 319-758-9756. The ornate rooms in this historic home near Snake Alley and downtown Burlington include antique chandeliers and furnishings. Hallway decor tends more toward the eclectic, with both a deer head and wreaths of flowers. A choice of breakfasts is available. Inexpensive. Website: www.wildrosemanorguesthouse.com.

DINING

Alpha's Restaurant, 709 Avenue H, Fort Madison. Call 319-372-3779. Tasty food in an unpretentious grill room on Fort Madison's main drag, with the Mississippi just across the street by Riverview Park. You can't go wrong with the steaks, including a massive rib eye, or the meaty, bone-in Iowa pork chop, but just about everything on the menu is nicely cooked, including pasta and seafood dishes and dinner salads. Stick around for dessert and watch the river roll by. Full bar and decent wine list. Moderate. Website: http://alphasontheriverfront.com.

Ogo's Restaurant & Buffet, 3753 Main Street, Keokuk. Call 319-524-6467. A no-frills eatery with a buffet groaning with comfort foods like fried chicken, baked ham and roast beef; seafood items including shrimp and catfish; and salad and dessert bars. A great value if you're looking for some real all-American food; brings in crowds on Friday and Sat-

urday nights. Website: www.ogos
restaurant.com.

Port City Underground, 208 West
Second Street, Muscatine. Call 563-
263-4743. An unassuming restaurant
in the heart of downtown Muscatine
with Italian standbys like pastas and
pizzas, including specialty pies such
as a Californian with Alfredo sauce
and fresh vegetables, and an authentic Margherita. A large selection of
soups, sandwiches and salads fill out
the menu, and there's an impressive
choice of beer, wine and cocktails.
Moderate. Website: www.portcity
pizzas.com.

Wild Whisk Bistro, 807 Avenue G,
Fort Madison. Call 319-372-1711. A
simple yet snazzy breakfast and
lunch joint, with a full slate of eggs
and other morning options, sandwiches and salads. Try the grilled rib-
eye sandwich with caramelized
onions or the Mediterranean wrap
with hummus, Kalamata olives and
feta. Wild Whisk also has a few pizza
and pasta offerings, and there's a
long list of coffee drinks. It's a perfect
spot to fuel up before taking a stroll
around town or hitting the road. Inexpensive. Website: www.wildwhisk
.com.

SHOPPING

Pearl Plaza, 208 West Second Street,
Muscatine. A collection of shops spe-
cializing in everything from stylish
clothing to chocolates to gifts and
home accessories. There's also a
restaurant housed in a former button
factory, recalling Muscatine's long
history as the button capital of the
world, as well as a coffeehouse that
has sandwiches and snacks. Website:
www.pearlplaza.com.

Pendemonium, 619 Avenue G, Fort
Madison. Call 319-372-0881. Perhaps
only in a city whose history is so in-
tertwined with fountain pens could
you find a shop dedicated to the fine
writing instruments. Located in a vintage storefront downtown, it stocks
high-quality and antique pens and
accessories, including many items
you've never heard of or you thought
were extinct, like blotters and ink-
wells. Pendemonium also has a full
line of stationery and inks in more
colors than you could possibly imagine. Website: www.pendemonium
.com.

RECREATION AND
ENTERTAINMENT

Catfish Bend Casino, 3001 Winegard
Drive, Burlington. Call 1-866-792-
9948. More than 1,000 slots fill this
huge casino along with table games
and numerous dining options and
fun stuff in the adjoining entertainment complex. Website: www.the
pzazz.com.

FunCity, 3001 Winegard Drive,
Burlington. Call 1-866-792-9948. Lo-
cated in the same complex as Catfish
Bend Casino, this family entertain-

ment center has an indoor/outdoor water park, go-carts, laser tag, video arcades and other ways to keep kids preoccupied for a couple hours or the entire day. There's also an on-site hotel and day spa. Website: www.the pzazz.com/funcity/funcity.asp.

OTHER CONTACTS

Port of Burlington Welcome Center, 400 North Front Street, Burlington, 52655. Call 319-752-8731. Website: www.greaterburlington.com.

Fort Madison Area Convention & Visitors Bureau, 709 Ninth Street, Fort Madison, 52627. Call 1-800-210-8687. Website: www.fortmadison.com

Keokuk Area Convention & Tourism Bureau, 329 Main Street, Keokuk, 52632. Call 1-800-383-1219. Website: www.keokukiowatourism .org.

Muscatine Convention and Visitors Bureau, 319 East Second Street, Muscatine, 52761. Call 563-263-8895. Website: www.muscatine.com.

5 Northeast Iowa:
NATURE TRAILS AND A TOUCH OF NORWAY

Estimated length: About 200 miles, looping from Decorah west to Charles City, then north and east to Cresco before returning to Decorah.

Estimated time: Weekend.

Getting there: You can reach Decorah by taking US 18 from the Mississippi River roads and then switching to US 52, or by taking US 63, then IA 24 and finally US 52 from Waterloo/Cedar Falls.

Highlights: Norwegian culture and lots of outdoor recreation in and around Decorah. The all-American town of Charles City, with some fine historic buildings. A first-rate miniature circus in New Hampton.

Begin the trip in **Decorah.** Known as a jumping-off point for canoeing and kayaking trips down the upper Iowa River, which runs right past downtown, as well as scenic driving routes and mountain biking trails, Decorah sits among a rugged landscape of high bluffs. It is famous for its Norwegian heritage, seen in everything from the largest museum in America devoted to a single ethnic group, to an annual festival that brings the food, dances and culture of Norway to town every July.

There's also a smorgasbord of dining and lodging options in Decorah, including a grand, historic hotel, making the town a nice spot to put your feet up and relax.

Begin your visit to Decorah at the **Vesterheim Norwegian-American Museum** (http://vesterheim.org) on downtown's main drag. The impressive collection of exhibits covers four floors and begins with murals in the lobby depicting scenes from Norway in the mid-1800s, the period of heaviest immigration to

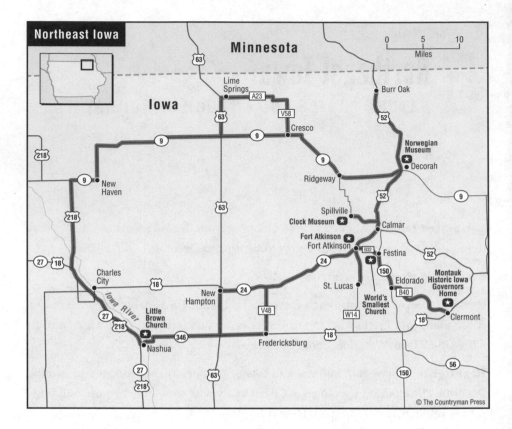

North America. The museum collection includes nearly 25,000 objects, including a Norwegian fishing boat and a ship used to cross the Atlantic. Other rooms have period home furnishings and religious and military displays, as well as a great selection of sleds and skis fashioned by early immigrants to deal with the harsh Midwestern winters.

Outside are 16 historic buildings spread across the museum grounds and downtown Decorah, including replica log cabins used by early settlers, a stone mill, a one-room schoolhouse and an impressive Lutheran church. Guides explain each structure and are happy to answer questions. Allow plenty of time for your visit—there's a lot to see!

Down the street from the Vesterheim, the **Hotel Winneshiek** (www.hotel winn.com), Decorah's fanciest lodging (Barack Obama spent a night here in 2012), is worth a visit in its own right to take in the opulent lobby, with its Waterford crystal chandelier, grand staircase with mural, and detailed millwork. The historic hotel once housed an opera house on its upper level, where you can still see the lavish, scenic stage curtain, and has emerged dazzling from a multimillion-dollar restoration with sumptuous guest rooms and an acclaimed restaurant.

Close to downtown is the **Porter House Museum** (www.porterhousemuseum .com), an Italianate mansion that was home to an inveterate collector: there's a large display of mounted butterflies, rocks and postage stamps, as well as artwork and historic artifacts. The house has an unusual feature you'll spot before you even step inside: the wall in front of the house is encrusted with stones and crystals, and also features representations of aquatic creatures like a whale and a giant turtle. There are plenty of fountains and birdbaths in the grounds around the house, too, and even a water garden. Altogether it's quite a collection of stuff.

The house sits in the **Broadway-Phelps Park Historic District**, which has many historic homes in various styles, including Queen Anne and Gothic Revival, and is listed on the National Register of Historic Places. Of special note is the **Octagon House** at 408 West Broadway, a style popular in the 18th and 19th centuries yet almost never seen today. (There's also a small octagon garage next to the house.) Phelps Park still has a kiln used to make bricks for many of Decorah's original buildings, as well as a bandstand and gazebo. Contact the Winneshiek

Hotel Winneshiek in Decorah

County Convention and Visitors Bureau for information about a self-guided tour through the neighborhood.

Decorah goes all out for Nordic Fest (www.nordicfest.com), which kicks off near the end of July. Featured events include a parade, Norwegian dancing and music, and ethnic costumes from throughout Scandinavia. Don't miss the rock-throwing competition—it's quite a sight. Hotels and other lodgings can fill up during the festival, but it's not too far to make a day trip from other towns and cities on and near the Mississippi.

Before heading out on the main route, try a side trip: to the north, drive out of Decorah on US 52 and go about 15 miles to Burr Oak, site of the Laura Ingalls Wilder Park & Museum (www.lauraingallswilder.us). This childhood home of Laura Ingalls Wilder is, interestingly, one that she never wrote about in her series of books about growing up on the frontier. The Ingalls family moved here in 1876, when Laura was 9 years old, after a plague of grasshoppers devastated their home in Minnesota. They stayed in Burr Oak for only a year, during which time Charles Ingalls managed a small hotel, and then returned to Minnesota. Burr Oak is the only home of Laura Ingalls still on its original site. Guided tours of the hotel are available, and the town celebrates "Laura Days" the fourth weekend of June.

Moving along to another pioneer site, take winding country roads east of Burr Oak to reach the Locust School Museum. Built in 1854, the one-room schoolhouse was in operation for more than 100 years. Since closing, it has been pre-

AN EAGLE SOARS IN DECORAH

Decorah became the focus of wildlife biologists and bald eagle lovers all over the world in the spring of 2011, when a camera trained on a nest broadcast the live hatching of three eaglets on the Internet.

Millions watched the eaglets hatch in their aerie, located 80 feet up in a cottonwood tree near Decorah's fish hatchery. After the hatching, the camera continued to broadcast from the nest as the eaglets matured and eventually spread their wings to fly away. (You can still see the archived videos on YouTube.) One of the three was fitted with a satellite transmitter, which has been sending back pictures as the eagle travels throughout the region, visiting several neighboring states.

DECORAH'S AGRICULTURAL ATTRACTIONS

Numerous farming-related sites are open to visitors in and around Decorah. **Northeast Iowa's Dairy Center** (www.iowadairycenter .com) in nearby Calmar is a working dairy farm that offers the chance to see cows being milked in a modern facility, as well as a "hall of breeds" and dairy-related items in the farm's museum. **Seed Savers Exchange Heritage Farm** (www.seedsavers.org) is a unique farming operation dedicated to saving all sorts of rare and offbeat seed varieties—more than 8 miles of trails wind through the orchard and gardens of the farm, which has preserved thousands of varieties of fruits and vegetables. You may do a double take when you spot the farm's herd of rare white cattle. **Pinter's Gardens & Pumpkins** (www.pintersgardensandpumpkins) is perfect for a visit in the fall, when visitors can walk through the corn maze, take a hayride and peruse the pumpkin patch for a perfect Halloween jack-o'-lantern. **Winneshiek Wildberry Winery** (www.wwwinery.com) has 3 acres of vineyards interspersed with hiking paths, a good place for a stroll before settling in at the tasting room to check out some Iowa wines, including more offbeat vintages like raspberry and blackberry. **Peake's Apple Orchard** is 12 miles east of Decorah, but worth the trip, both for its many types of apples and its caramel apple sundaes on Sundays! The **Decorah Fish Hatchery** (www.iowadnr.gov/InsideDNR/DNR StaffOffices/FishHatcheries/DecorahFishHatchery.aspx) is the central trout raising facility for streams and lakes across Iowa, producing both rainbow and brook trout, and is located in a beautiful park that includes picnic areas, a waterfall and its own trout stream for fishing.

served as it was, with vintage desks, seats and blackboard. The museum hosts living history demonstrations for area schoolchildren and is open to visitors.

Going south from Decorah, take US 52 about 10 miles and you will reach **Calmar**, home of **The Dairy Center** (see "Decorah's Agricultural Attractions"). Moving onto smaller rural roads, head west to **Spillville**. This tiny country village has a large number of residents of Czech descent as well as an intriguing attraction: the **Bily Clocks Museum** (www.bilyclocks.org). The huge, ornate clocks housed in a modest structure are the life's work of two brothers, Frank and Joseph Bily,

DVOŘÁK IN IOWA: CLASSICAL MUSIC IN THE CORNFIELDS

Spillville, a typical Iowa rural town, was home not just to the Bily brothers and their intricately carved clocks, but also briefly to internationally renowned composer Antonin Dvořák. Burned out on his work as director of the National Conservatory of Music in New York City, Dvořák escaped to Spillville in the summer of 1893, settling down among many fellow Czechs who had immigrated to the rural village. Contrary to popular belief, Dvořák did not compose the "New World Symphony" while in Spillville; it was already written, and he made some corrections before premiering it after returning to New York. He did, however, compose his String Quartet in F, popularly known as the "American Quartet," as well as his Quintet in E-flat in Spillville. On Sundays he played the organ at St. Wenceslaus Church in town. In addition to his home, Dvořák is commemorated with a memorial in Spillville's Riverside Park.

Spillville natives who began their intricate carvings as a hobby when not busy farming. Eventually their work grew in size and scope, honed on long winter days and evenings. The clocks, some of which stand more than 8 feet tall, are built of native woods like walnut, butternut, hard maple and oak, as well as imported woods like cherry and mahogany. The 12 apostles clock includes each of the apostles, one per hour. Other clocks commemorate American history, Charles Lindbergh's trans-Atlantic flight, the book of Genesis and other historic events. The brothers never sold a single clock, even refusing an offer of $1 million from Henry Ford, and actually considered having the clocks burned upon their death. Fortunately, the clocks were preserved along with the brothers' tools and some additional carvings. Spillville also has an 1854 Czech schoolhouse and St. Wenceslaus Church, an impressive stone structure with a prominent tower and several wings of rooms.

The next stop is about 5 miles to the west of Calmar on IA 24. Fort Atkinson is a tiny settlement established as a military garrison to watch over the Winnebago Indians after they were removed from Wisconsin in 1840. It included 24 buildings inside a stockade wall and 14 more buildings outside. Troops at Fort Atkinson were crowded into a relatively small space, and the fort played no role in any battles or other military activities. Its importance further decreased after the troops were pulled out in 1846 to fight in the Mexican-American War. Local volunteers carried on with staffing the fort, but it no longer had any reason to exist and was soon abandoned.

Today, the fort is arguably more active than it was during its heyday: an annual "rendezvous" is held every September and features demonstrations of daily pioneer life and military activities at the fort, including cannon shoots.

From Fort Atkinson, jog south to **Festina,** where you can stop and visit the **World's Smallest Church.** St. Anthony of Padua Church measures a mere 12 by 16 feet and can hold barely eight people. (The steeple however, rises 40 feet.) The surrounding parkland on the Turkey River is a nice spot for a picnic. Continue on IA 150 and more country roads, following the Turkey River to **Clermont.** The main attraction here is **Montauk** (http://montaukiowa.com), the historic home of Iowa's 12th governor, William Larrabee. The brick and limestone mansion sits on a hill outside town and was named after a lighthouse on the Atlantic Ocean— both Larrabee and his wife were East Coast natives.

A successful banker and businessman who owned a mill in Clermont, Larrabee returned to Montauk after serving two terms as governor. Tours of the home include a look at some of the family's extensive art collection as well as statues on the front lawn of Civil War generals. (Larrabee also commissioned a statue of Abraham Lincoln that stands in Clermont.)

Retrace your way back to Festina and then Fort Atkinson, where you can either head west on IA 24 or take a detour south to **St. Lucas,** home to the **German-American Museum** and its numerous displays detailing the area's German heritage as well as local history. The town also hosts an annual Oktoberfest in September.

From either St. Lucas or Fort Atkinson, you'll head west and cruise through the cornfields to **New Hampton.** Like countless other Iowa towns, it prospered with the coming of the railroad in the 19th century, and like so many others it has a local museum in the town's old **Carnegie Library** (www.carnegiecultural center.org). But this is no ordinary small-town museum: it contains one of the finest displays of circus miniatures you'll see anywhere.

The displays are housed in large glass cases, with vintage circus posters hanging on the walls. One depicts a circus parade down New Hampton's Main Street, with wagons full of animals moving past the sidewalks. You can practically smell the peanuts and sawdust!

Others show performers executing tricks under the big top, and there's also a sideshow. All the pieces are meticulously detailed and were created by a local circus fan. An impressive miniature train set and a scale model of an early Iowa farm can be found in the basement. There are also numerous historic artifacts throughout the museum, and the staff is very knowledgeable about local history. It's well worth the trip.

Before moving on, you may want to take a slight detour down to **Fredericks-burg**, home of the **Hawkeye Buffalo Ranch** (www.hawkeyebuffalo.com). This family farm offers guided tours to view a buffalo herd that grazes in a pasture. Tours begin with an informative presentation of facts about buffalo before heading out in the back of a pickup. Along the way, you may spot some of the rest of the farm's menagerie, including llamas and burros.

Once you reach the buffalo, you'll have the opportunity to feed the bulls, cows and calves whole ears of corn. Don't freak out—it's actually a lot of fun, and the family knows how to keep things safe. Back at the farm, there are buffalo skulls and hides for sale, as well as steaks, roasts, burgers and jerky. Separately, the ranch also organizes buffalo hunts.

From Fredericksburg you can head due west to **Nashua,** home to the **Little Brown Church in the Vale** (www.littlebrownchurch.org). Made famous by a song dedicated to a church on the frontier, the brown exterior actually came about out of economic necessity: the completion of the church was slowed by the outbreak

---

CHARLES CITY: TRACTORVILLE, U.S.A.

O ther communities may lay claim to inventing the tractor, but it was Charles City that gave this Iowa silhouette its name: the term "tractor" was first used here about 1900, when the first Hart-Parr gasoline-powered tractor engine was developed in town. It was the first production-model tractor in the United States. The company grew steadily and by the 1970s employed nearly 3,000 workers at a sprawling local factory. But it was pummeled by the farm crisis in the 1980s and closed for good in 1993.

Today, the only reminder of Charles City's long history of tractor-making is found at the Floyd County Museum, which displays some of the town's earliest models.

of the Civil War, which also made white paint expensive, so the church was given the brown coat it retains to this day.

While the church maintains an active congregation, it also has become a popular spot to get married and has hosted nearly 75,000 weddings to date. So many couples have been married here that the church has begun hosting a "marriage reunion," where those who attend renew their vows. Tours can be arranged in advance.

Adjacent to the church is **Old Bradford Pioneer Village**. Run by the local historical society, it includes authentic

The Charles City Art Center is housed in the city's old Carnegie Library.

log cabins, an incredibly small doctor's office and two one-room schools, one of which holds historic artifacts. An old railroad depot contains train memorabilia.

From here, it's not far to one of Iowa's best small towns, **Charles City**, which has made a concerted effort to not only preserve but enhance its historic downtown. Unfolding from the banks of the Cedar River, it features a nice town green, known as **Central Park**. It's the perfect setting for the town's Fourth of July celebration, which features, of course, a parade, as well as lots of kids' activities and other events spread over several days.

The park fronts Charles City's old Carnegie Library, which now serves as the **Charles City Art Center** (www.CharlesCityArts.com). The center's galleries mainly showcase local and regional works. Meanwhile, the current public library houses the **Mooney Collection**, which is an impressive assortment of prints, woodcuts, lithographs and engravings from around the world. The collection includes many originals, among them works by Picasso, Matisse, Rembrandt, Salvador Dali and Grant Wood.

The art connection continues with Charles City's numerous works of public art ranging from realistic statues to more abstract works sprinkled around downtown and in residential neighborhoods. The greatest number can be seen along the riverfront—look for the "bicycle benches" at the southern end.

TENNIS, ANYONE?

Tennis fans may want to drop by the All Iowa Lawn Tennis Club, a single grass court that is a nice counterpart to Iowa's much more famous field of dreams. The court sits on a family farm outside Charles City and does justice to its inspiration at Wimbledon, right down to the strawberries and cream that are served after matches, with the fruit grown in a patch right next to the court.

A labor of love built by a lifelong tennis fan, the court hosts occasional tournaments, but has also been open to anyone who wants to play. Still, check with the owner before you unzip your racket cover.

Another attraction worth checking out is the **Floyd County Historical Museum** (www.floydcountymuseum.org) located across the river from downtown. There are thousands of items in the large facility, including a fully stocked replica drugstore from the early 20th century, a pioneer log cabin, a one-room schoolhouse and horse-drawn farm machinery, as well as its successor, the gasoline-powered tractor.

History continues at the **Carrie Chapman Catt Girlhood Home** (www.catt .org), dedicated to the memory of the pioneering suffragette who founded the League of Women Voters in 1920. Her consciousness was sparked early in this idyllic town, when at age 13 she openly questioned why her mother was not voting in the presidential election.

The house, which sits next to a restored prairie landscape, has many permanent exhibits related to Catt's life and work, including, of course, the fight for women's right to vote, as well as displays on pioneer settlement. It is also headquarters to the National 19th Amendment Society, which works on current issues related to Catt's interests.

Even more history can be seen on a self-guided **Historic Homes Tour**, with maps available through the Charles City Area Chamber of Commerce (ask about an audio tour as well). The tour begins at the **Charles Theatre**, a wonderfully preserved art deco movie house that dates from 1935 and still shows movies for just a few dollars a ticket.

The tour then weaves to the river and back through town, taking in more than 25 structures, including the art center in the Carnegie Library and a couple houses on Central Park, notably a stylized mansion with Ionic columns. There are also several nice parks in town, including **Andres Memorial Park,** with a bell tower and gazebo, and **Flora Ellis Park,** which has a long stone retaining wall.

After taking a stroll around Charles City, you may be ready to hit the road again, and the route offers some nice scenery in the form of several **barn quilts** found on area byways. Or, if you're just eager to move on, take a long loop north and then east, stopping in the town of **Cresco.**

The town boasts a popular farmers' market and, like Decorah, is popular for its year-round outdoor recreation. There are many historic buildings, including the **Cresco Opera House,** which opened in 1915, still shows live performances and also serves as the town's movie theater. The beautiful interior includes winged cherubs and an impressive archway framing the stage.

Other downtown structures include a log cabin furnished with period items, a vintage diesel train engine and Cresco's original public library, built in 1914. The **Kellow House** is a Second Empire–style home that is also the location of the **Howard County Museum.**

Check at the **Cresco Welcome Center** for a brochure listing the town's historic buildings. The welcome center also houses the **Iowa Wrestling Hall of**

The art deco Charles Theatre in Charles City

Fame, which has displays honoring famous grapplers. There's another display honoring Ellen Church Marshall, a Cresco native who founded the forerunners of today's flight attendants and also served in the Army Nurse Corps during World War II. The Folsom Museum, south of Cresco, has antique toys and other items.

The countryside surrounding Cresco is a worthwhile spot for a scenic drive, especially around the nearby Turkey River. At this point, you are moving out of farmland and back into the more rugged bluffs and valleys that define the northeast corner of the state. You can also tour the countryside by bicycle: there are several trails here, including the Prairie Farmer Recreational Trail, which runs for nearly 20 miles from Cresco all the way to Calmar, skirting Spillville along the way.

If you're not quite ready to finish the trip, you can take a little side trip to Lime Springs, home to Lidtke Mill, which ground grain for 100 years. Many artifacts are on display, and the adjacent mill house has been restored to the way it looked in the early years of the mill.

IN THE AREA

ACCOMMODATIONS

B&B on Broadway, 305 West Broadway, Decorah. Call 563-382-1420. Just two blocks from downtown, this red-brick home with a tower has five guest rooms with antiques and comfortable beds. Persian rugs cover the hardwood floors. All rooms have a private bath. The King's Chambers features a private balcony, while the spacious Royal Suite sits under the eaves at the top of the house. Moderate to Medium. Website: www.bandb onbroadway.com.

Bluffs Inn Resort, 1101 IA 9 East, Decorah. Call 563-382-8600 or 1-877-382-8600. A modest hotel on the edge of Decorah with basic rooms and an on-site restaurant. The hotel also has a pool, fitness center and indoor walking track. Inexpensive to Moderate. Website: www.bluffsinn.net.

Cedar Dreams Inn, 521 West Water Street, Decorah. Call 563-387-6185. Tucked away behind a brick storefront across the street from the Vesterheim Museum, this inn has hardwood floors and is done up in rich earth tones, a nice accent to the wooded bluffs that surround Decorah. Many of the materials used in the inn were salvaged from other area buildings. Two guest rooms are each furnished with a queen-sized bed. There's a shared bath down the hall and a common kitchen area and living room. Moderate. Website: http://cedardreamsinn.com.

Dee Dee's Bed & Breakfast, 201 Riverside Avenue, Decorah. Call 563-382-2778. This petite Queen Anne cottage is within walking distance of many Decorah attractions. There's a pair of guest rooms, each with a private bath. A good value for accommodations in town. Inexpensive.

Dug Road Inn, 601 West Main Street, Decorah. Call 563-382-9355. Sitting under a canopy of tall pines, this Italianate home is conveniently located near downtown attractions and the riverfront. Six guest rooms include three with private bath. The top-floor suite has a light, airy feel, with windows all around, as well as a fireplace. Breakfast includes tasty baked goods. Moderate to Expensive. Website: www.dugroadinn.com.

Hotel Winneshiek, 104 East Water Street, Decorah. Call 563-382-4164 or 1-800-998-4164. Decorah's grand old hotel and one of the more impressive lodgings in Iowa, with well-appointed rooms clustered around an open atrium, where light shines through a stained-glass skylight. The building dates to 1870 and was previously home to an opera hall erected by a prominent local saloonkeeper. Restored with modern amenities, the hotel still retains its marble fireplace, crystal chandelier and exquisite cherry wood millwork in the lobby. The hotel's restaurant serves innovative all-American fare in a relaxed atmosphere with a full bar. Moderate to Expensive. Website: www.hotel winn.com.

Leytze's Corner Bed & Bath, 704 West Water Street, Decorah. Call 563-382-5856. A former church converted to an English Tudor home, this cozy lodging has modest, comfortable rooms with twin-, full- or queen-sized beds and is furnished with antiques from the 1920s. No breakfast, but there's a kitchenette and eating area. Sit with a cup of coffee or tea around the fireplace after a day of hiking the nearby bluffs or soaking up Decorah's historic downtown. Inexpensive to Moderate. Website: www .leytzescorner.com.

The Loft on Water Street, 106 East Water Street, Decorah. Call 563-380-9189. A hip walk-up apartment that provides a taste of urban style in the heart of Decorah. There are two bedrooms (each with a queen-sized bed), a small bathroom, living room and a modest eat-in kitchen, as well as laundry facilities and indoor parking. It's right next to the Hotel Winneshiek and the adjoining Agora Arts gallery. Medium. Website: www.agora arts.com/loft/index.html.

Old Hospital Lodge, 3484 Highlandville Road, Decorah. Call 563-546-7847. This historic former hospital is located in the countryside about 15 miles north of Decorah, and makes a good backwoods base for fishing or hunting trips. There are four separate units, each furnished in basic style and including two queen beds, full bath and kitchen. The decor should appeal to outdoorsmen, with scenes of different game animals on the walls. Inexpensive to Moderate. Website: www.oldhospitallodge.com.

Palisades Inn, 2566 Ice Cave Road, Decorah. Call 563-382-5258 or 563-387-7110. On the outskirts of Decorah by Palisades and Van Peenen Parks, this is an ideal spot to set out on a hiking or canoeing trip through the surrounding countryside. The separate one-bedroom, apartment-style suite has a full kitchen, full bath and private deck where you can kick back and soak up the relaxing country air. There are also two additional rooms in the main house with double beds and a shared bathroom. No breakfast. Moderate. Website: www .palisadesinn.com.

River's Bluff Getaway, 3301 Chimney Rock Road, Decorah. Call 563-382-5075 or 563-379-3013. This rustic, two-bedroom cabin north of Decorah also has a loft that sleeps up to six people and comes complete with cooking and eating utensils, bedding and towels. A woodpile provides logs for campfires in the adjoining fire pit. There's also a cozy stove in the living room. Perfect for a quiet weekend retreat. Moderate to Medium. Website: http://riversbluffgetaway.com.

The Roundhouse Retreat, 903 Vernon Street, Decorah. Call 563-382-2194 or 563-380-5597. An authentic geodesic dome nestled in the woods 5 miles north of Decorah and overlooking the upper Iowa River valley, this guesthouse has three bedrooms plus a sleeping loft and two bathrooms, including one with a sauna. There's also a pool table and foosball table. No television reception, so you'll have to use the set to watch movies— that is, when you're not exploring the surrounding countryside. Relax on the deck, which has a gas grill, picnic table and fire ring supplied with firewood. Medium. Website: www.the roundhouseretreat.com.

Sherman House Bed and Breakfast, 800 Gilbert Street, Charles City. Call 641-228-3826 or 1-888-528-3826. A unique collection of rooms in a home marked by a large wraparound porch. Rooms have names like the Blue Danube and the No Kai Oi, which has a Hawaiian theme. There are whirlpool tubs in some rooms and fireplaces in all but one. It's within walking distance of the art and history museums. Moderate.

Taylor-Made Bed & Breakfast, 330 Main Street, Spillville. Call 563-562-3958. Several cozy, well-appointed rooms in a rambling historic home. All rooms have private baths, and there are also rooms in two outbuildings, including the Woodshed, which is actually a very handsome, rustic yet comfortable lodging with front porch and kitchen nook. (Guests in the outbuildings may eat breakfast in the main house.) Breakfast is a hearty country feast with fresh baked goods. Moderate. Website: www.taylor madebandb.com.

Whispering Pines Cabin, 1824 Canoe Ridge Road, Decorah. Call 563-380-2285 or 563-380-0136. Another woodland retreat, this log cabin has a good-sized living room and sleeps up to four people on a queen-sized bed and a hide-a-bed. The fully equipped kitchen includes cooking and eating utensils, and there's a two-person whirlpool tub in the bathroom. A nice spot in both warm and cool months. Moderate. Website: www.whisperingpinesdecorah.com.

DINING

Family Table Restaurant, 817 Mechanic Street, Decorah. Call 563-382-2964. A longtime Decorah favorite in a converted drive-in, with burgers, sandwiches and entrées like broasted chicken and country-fried steak. Breakfast is a big draw as well, with crisp Belgian waffles and good eggs Benedict. There's also lighter fare like soups and salads. Inexpensive. Website: www.familytabledecorah.com.

Hart's Tea & Tarts, 113 West Water Street, Decorah. Call 563-382-3795. Guests will discover a touch of the British Isles at this narrow room in downtown Decorah, where scones come with jam and Devon cream. Light lunches include sandwiches and salads, as well as a soup of the day served with homemade bread. There are usually a few flavors of tarts to choose from. Inexpensive. Website: www.hartsteaandtarts.com.

La Rana Bistro, 120 Washington Street, Decorah. Call 563-382-3067. The cooking has touches of the Mediterranean and features fresh ingredients in this minimalist space with warm woods and exposed brick walls. The à la menu includes dishes like hanger steak, pork tenderloin braised with fennel and butter-poached sea bass, as well as an upscale mac and cheese and the old standby chicken Marsala. Or just have a selection of appetizers like the tapas plate and bruschetta with a glass of wine or mixed drink from the bar. Moderate to Medium. Website: http://laranabistro.com.

Mabe's Pizza, 110 East Water Street, Decorah. Call 563-382-4297. A long-standing, family-run pizza parlor popular with locals and Luther College students. All kinds of toppings are available, as are combinations like taco and bacon cheeseburger pizza. There's also a full assortment of burgers, sandwiches, pastas and salads. Moderate. Website: www.mabespizza.com.

McCaffey's Dolce Vita, 2149 Twin Springs Road, Decorah. Call 563-382-4723. Piping hot pizzas emerge from the wood-fired oven at this rustic spot just past the Decorah city limits. The menu has several specialty pies and numerous toppings, all served on McCaffey's signature sourdough crust. The restaurant also serves a mélange of entrées and sandwiches, including New Orleans po' boys and pasta dishes. Moderate. Website: www.mcdolcevita.com.

The Pub at the Pinicon, 2205 South Linn Avenue, New Hampton. Call 641-394-4430. A casual bar and grill on the outskirts of town, with brass rails, dark wood and some simple, tasty fare: steaks, chops and seafood are the mainstays. There are some good salads as well. The small dining room sometimes fills up, but there are high tables in the bar area. Moderate.

Rubaiyat, 117 West Water Street, Decorah. Call 563-582-9463. "Food for Thought" is the motto at this restaurant in a former mercantile building, which means lots of fresh and seasonal ingredients in dishes like pan-seared duck breast, grilled seafood and summer sausage scaloppine. A separate "happy hour menu" offers specials on appetizers to nibble on while you sip a glass from the extensive wine and beer list. Medium. Website: www.rubaiyatrestaurant .com.

Stone Hearth Inn, 811 Commerce Drive, Decorah. Call 563-382-4614. Casual family restaurant with favorites like steaks, seafood, pasta and broasted chicken. There is indeed a fireplace, adding to the down-home atmosphere. Moderate. Website:

www.decorahdining.com/stonehearth /index.htm.

Three C Bistro, 510 Hildreth Street, Charles City. Call 641-228-3544. One of the nicer places to eat in Charles City, with a menu of simple favorites like grilled salmon, beef stew, and lemon and herb chicken. There's even prime rib and, of course, an Iowa pork chop, as well as pastas and burgers. Wine and cocktails are available, too. Moderate. Website: http:// threecbistro.com.

SHOPPING

Agora Arts, 104 East Water Street, Decorah. Call 563-382-8786. A contemporary art gallery located at the Hotel Winneshiek, with an impressive selection of handcrafted jewelry, pottery, prints, sculpture and other items. The works of more than 200 American artists are represented here. Website: www.agoraarts.com.

Vanberia, 217 West Water Street, Decorah. Call 563-382-4982. This shop on Decorah's main drag specializes in Scandinavian imports (look for the Scandinavian countries' flags out front), including gifts, crafts, jewelry and household items. Website: www.vanberiadecorah.com.

RECREATION AND ENTERTAINMENT

Hruska's Canoe Livery, 3233 347th Street, Kendallville. Call 563-547-4566. This outfitter on the Iowa River can provide everything you need for a fun trip through some of the best paddling country in Iowa. Canoes, kayaks and tubes are all for rent, and they can transport you to the most popular put-in and take-out points along the river, including at Decorah. A great way to spend a day on the river, floating past scenic bluffs. Website: www.bluffcountry.com/hruska's .htm.

River & Trail Outfitters, 212 Pulpit Rock Road, Decorah. Call 563-382-6552. A full-service bicycle, canoe and kayak rental shop with shuttle service and a knowledgeable staff that can set you up with maps and suggestions on where to go on the trails or the river. Website: www .canoedecorah.com.

OTHER CONTACTS

Winneshiek County Convention and Visitors Bureau, 507 West Water Street, Decorah, 52101. Call 563-382-3990 or 1-800-463-4692. Website: www.decoraharea.com.

Chicakasaw County Tourism, 10 Amherst Boulevard, Nashua, 50658. Call 641-435-4187. Website: www .chickasawtrails.com.

Charles City Area Chamber of Commerce, 401 North Main Street, Charles City, 50616. Call 641-228-4234. Website: www.charlescity chamber.com.

Howard County Business and Tourism, 101 Second Avenue Southwest, Cresco, 52136. Call 563-547-3434. Website: www.howard-county .com.

6 Iowa City and Cedar Rapids:
A CLASSIC COLLEGE TOWN AND A TASTE OF CZECH AND SLOVAK CULTURE

Estimated length: A roughly 80-mile loop between the two cities, plus a few short side trips.

Estimated time: You could do a day trip, picking and choosing from the attractions, or a weekend or even longer—really, both Iowa City and Cedar Rapids each have enough to keep a visitor occupied for a few days.

Getting there: Begin in Iowa City, at the intersection of I-80 and I-380, then continue up I-380 to Cedar Rapids and surrounding areas.

Highlights: A classic college-town atmosphere in Iowa City, including an excellent natural history museum. An eye-popping collection of motorcycles in Anamosa. Roaming the Iowa countryside that inspired Grant Wood and seeing his studio in Cedar Rapids. A memorable meal at the Lincoln Café in Mount Vernon. The library and reconstructed boyhood home of Herbert Hoover, Iowa's only president.

B oth cities were hard hit by the 2008 flooding of the Cedar and Iowa Rivers, which destroyed thousands of homes and businesses. Many tourist attractions are still in the slow process of recovering—it's best to call ahead before visiting.

An archetypal university town, **Iowa City** hosts some 30,000 University of Iowa students on a campus that sprawls over rolling hills along the Iowa River. The compact downtown is perfect for walking, with lots of interesting restaurants and shops along with a pedestrian-only mall where you can hang out and watch the parade of students and professors on their way to and from classes. (The only drawback is that parking spaces downtown can be at a premium.)

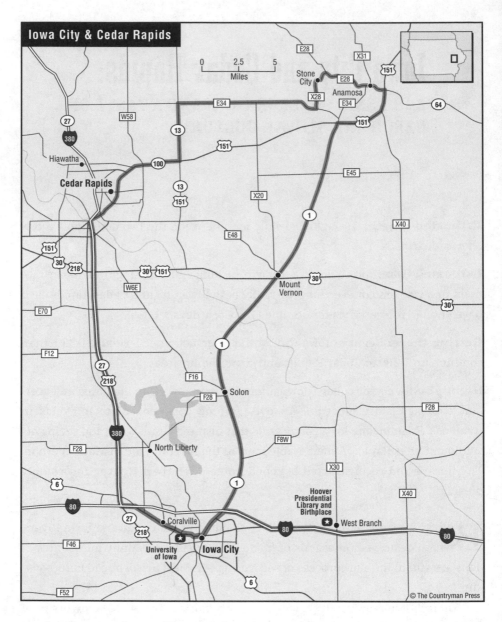

Iowa City & Cedar Rapids

Another popular strolling and shopping area is on Linn Street, past Van Allen Hall, while a popular farmers' market is held by City Hall out past the edge of downtown. Check out the sidewalks as you stroll around the downtown area and campus: the city's **Literary Walk** (www.icgov.org/default/?id=1585) honors authors of note with brass plaques embedded in the pavement. The university is renowned for its creative writing program, which has produced many acclaimed scribes. Since 2009 the town has hosted the **Iowa City Book Festival** (www.iowacitybookfestival.org) in July, with a large book sale and numerous panel discussions and readings, including several by nationally famous authors.

One of the most notable sites in Iowa City is the **Old Capitol** (www.uiowa.edu/~oldcap), which sits on a wide, grassy mall in striking contrast to downtown's tight grid of streets. The modest gold-domed capitol was the seat of government in Iowa from 1846 to 1857, when Iowa City served as the capital of the Iowa Territory and then as the first state capital.

Inside is a museum with re-created chambers of the Iowa House, Senate

JAMES VAN ALLEN: PIONEER OF THE SPACE RACE

A crucial figure in America's quest to conquer space, Mount Pleasant, Iowa, native James Van Allen was for many years a professor of physics at the University of Iowa, where he helped develop Explorer I, America's first satellite launched into Earth's orbit. He went on to work on many more spacecraft. The Van Allen Belts, energy rings encircling the Earth discovered after the launch of Explorer I, were named after him.

and Supreme Court, and offices of the governor and other state officials. There are also rotating exhibits related to Iowa history in the basement. Guided tours are available. Behind the capitol is a nice portico looking out toward the river and the campus beyond.

Adjacent to the capitol is MacBride Hall, which houses the **Museum of Natural History** (www.uiowa.edu/~nathist), a first-rate (and free!) collection of exhibits spread out over several floors. The ground floor features some nice displays of plants, animals and geological phenomena. Even better are the exhibits upstairs, which include displays of Iowa's natural and cultural past, including Native American history and the development of agriculture. Learn about the ancient sea that once covered the area around Iowa City, and check out the many dioramas—don't miss the giant ground sloth.

There are even more dioramas in the third floor's room dedicated to mammals: the giant anteater and Atlantic walrus are particularly impressive. Look up

Iowa City's Old Capitol

to see the whale skeleton. Across the hall is the hall of birds, with more dioramas, a reconstruction of an extinct dodo and an amazing cyclorama, a 360-degree painting accessorized with mounted birds and audio effects that depicts a huge flock on a Pacific island.

Unfortunately, powerful floods that swept through the area in 2008 forced the closing of the **University of Iowa Museum of Art** (http://uima.uiowa.edu), which had to vacate its home on the west bank of the Iowa River. However, nearly its entire collection was saved and dispersed to several different locations, including other campus buildings and the art museums in Cedar Rapids and Davenport, until it can once again find a home. Contact the university to see if the museum has reopened. When it does, visitors can once again admire its extensive number of modernist works, including pieces by artists such as Matisse, Picasso and Miro, and many works of abstract expressionism.

About a mile and a half west of **Kinnick Stadium**, the **University of Iowa Athletics Hall of Fame** (www.hawkeyesports.com/hallfame/iowa-hallfame.html) brings to life a parade of Hawkeye greats in numerous sports, including 1939 Heisman Trophy winner Nile Kinnick and the many top wrestlers produced by the university. The university is also renowned for its medical facilities, and there's an on-campus **Medical Museum** (www.uihealthcare.com/depts/med museum/medmuseum.html) with frequently changing exhibits looking at a variety of topics in health and medicine.

Several Iowa City attractions are actually located in the adjacent city of Coralville. The **Iowa Children's Museum** (www.theicm.org), housed in the **Coral Ridge Mall**, is a large facility with many rooms full of interactive exhibits that will keep kids occupied, whether they want to build and race wooden cars to learn about the laws of motion or use carpenter's tools to put up a fort. A new aviation exhibit gives visitors the chance to use a flight simulator. There are numerous special programs, too.

A much more tranquil experience is found at the **Iowa Firefighters Memorial** (http://iowafirememorial.org), located north of I-80 in Coralville and next to Oak Hill Cemetery. There's a simple statue and memorial wall, and a small museum with firefighting artifacts and mementos. Coralville's **Antique Car Museum of Iowa** (www.acmoi.com) has plenty of "horseless carriages" dating back to the earliest years of the automobile, as well as an antique gas station and a model train display.

Near the firefighters memorial, the **Johnson County Historical Society Museum** (www.jchsiowa.org) in Coralville's Iowa River Landing Development has a huge number of artifacts on display illustrating local and area history, from pioneer settlers and Mormons who passed through Iowa on their epic trek to more contemporary residents.

The historical society operates a number of other local sites, including the

---

NILE KINNICK: A GRIDIRON GREAT

An All-American football player at the University of Iowa in the late 1930s and one of the all-time greats, Nile Kinnick won the Heisman Trophy in 1939. He is remembered for giving one of the strongest, most erudite acceptance speeches in the history of the award.

Kinnick died in a training flight while preparing to enter combat in World War II. The Hawkeyes' football stadium is named after him, and a large bronze statue of Kinnick stands in front of the stadium.

The Iowa Firefighters Memorial in Coralville

Iowa River Gazebo, located at the pedestrian bridge that links Coralville and Iowa City, and the **1876 Coralville Schoolhouse,** restored to its authentic appearance. The **Plum Grove Historic Home,** located in Iowa City, is a modest redbrick Greek Revival structure that was the home of Iowa's first territorial governor.

If you're into more offbeat sights, swing by Iowa City's Oakland Cemetery for a look at the **Black Angel**—it's easy to find on the winding paths. The 8½-foot-tall statue is the subject of many local legends, and is a popular gathering spot on Halloween.

Iowa City is a major cycling area— ask at the visitors center for a map of local bike trails. Other outdoor fun can be found north of the city at **Coralville Lake** (www.mvr.usace.army.mil/Coralville /default.htm), which offers fishing, camping, swimming, boat ramps and trails, as well as **Devonian Fossil Gorge** (www.mvr.usace.army.mil/coralville/devonian _fossil_gorge.htm), a prehistoric site marking the location of an ancient sea that covered the Iowa City area some 375 million years ago. A walkway leads past numerous notable geologic features left behind after the waters receded.

Once you've had your fill of Iowa City, head north on I-380 to **Cedar Rapids.** Spreading past the banks of the Cedar River, it is the second largest city in Iowa and a significant outpost of the great Midwestern breadbasket: area employers include Archer Daniels Midland, Cargill and

The Quaker Oats building on the Cedar River

Quaker Oats, whose riverfront facility infuses downtown with the pleasant smell of oatmeal.

City Hall is located on an island in the river, a distinction Cedar Rapids shares with Paris. NFL quarterback Kurt Warner honed his gridiron skills as a high school quarterback in Cedar Rapids, while Ashton Kutcher got his first taste of show biz while growing up here before heading for Hollywood.

The oldest standing mosque in North America sits in the middle of a residential neighborhood just north of downtown and west of the river. The modest structure has been serving local Muslims since 1934.

Cedar Rapids was one of the hardest-hit communities of Iowa's epic 2008 flood, with the Cedar River rising to more than 30 feet, destroying thousands of homes and causing untold damages to many other buildings—water went well over the second floor in some places.

One of the most visible reminders of the flood can be seen at the **National Czech & Slovak Museum & Library** (www.ncsml.org) a few miles south of downtown. The museum commemorates the huge number of immigrants who arrived beginning in the mid-1800s, drawn in part by the many industrial jobs available in the city. The very existence of the museum is impressive in the aftermath of the flood: after being inundated with 8 feet of water and mud, the entire building was moved. Specially built steel beams and hydraulic jacks picked up the 17,000-square-foot, 1,400-ton structure and carried it 500 feet to its new location, farther from the river and with the main floor elevated 3 feet higher than its previous level.

The museum, which has since expanded and plans to reopen to the public in the summer of 2012, has exhibits depicting the lives of Czech and Slovak immigrants both before and after their arrival in Iowa, as well as an exhibit looking at the historic 2008 flood and the community's response. The adjoining neighborhoods of **Czech Village** and **New Bohemia** were some of the original residential districts settled by the immigrants. Like the museum, they also suffered severe damage from the

Sykora Bakery, part of the Czech Village in Cedar Rapids

flood, but have begun to rebound, with several shops and restaurants along a couple blocks of 16th Avenue Southwest. Stop in at **Sykora Bakery** (www.sykora bakery.com) for some *kolace* or other delicious Czech pastries.

In addition to the large Czech and Slovak presence, Cedar Rapids has a significant African American community, as well as the **African American Museum of Iowa** (www.blackiowa.org) on the east bank of the river opposite the National Czech and Slovak Museum. Since recovering from the flood, the museum has continued its permanent and changing exhibits, which have examined such topics as the service of African Americans in the military, historic African American towns and African American coal miners in Iowa.

Plenty of other flood restoration efforts have taken place around Cedar Rapids, including **CSPS Hall** (http://legionarts.org), a former Czech social hall closer to downtown that has spiffed up its exterior. The hall houses a local art center that includes galleries, a studio theater and the main auditorium for music and other performing arts.

Downtown's numerous attractions include the **Carl & Mary Koehler History Center** (www.historycenter.org), with permanent exhibits on the history of the city and surrounding Cedar River Valley. Of special interest for younger visitors are the "time travelers" room, with numerous interactive displays, and the opportunity to dig for fossils. The museum also offers scavenger hunts for kids of all ages. Unfortunately, the Cedar Rapids **Science Station** (www.sciencestation .org) lost many exhibits when floodwaters hit its riverfront home, which it had to leave, setting up temporarily in the **Lindale Mall** with limited exhibits geared more toward younger children.

The Carl & Mary Koehler History Center

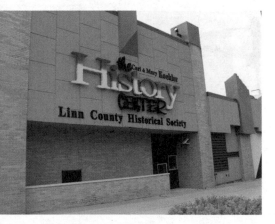

Farther from the river is the **Iowa Masonic Library and Museum** (http://grandlodgeofiowa.org/?page_id=888), a striking white marble building with some nice art deco touches, including stylized lion sculptures by the front door. Inside is a museum of Masonic art, regalia and equipment from all over the world as well as other historic artifacts, including collections of

Museum of Art, Cedar Rapids

Egyptian and pioneer American objects. The library holds a huge collection of titles, more than 5,000 of which focus on Iowa history.

Nearby is the **Cedar Rapids Museum of Art** (www.crma.org), with galleries covering more than 2,000 years and encompassing everything from Roman sculpture to more contemporary pieces, including the world's largest collection of works by Grant Wood. The museum's large glass atrium rises across the street from Greene Square Park, a pleasant spot for a short stroll.

Wood's studio is located a few blocks away in a modest redbrick building tucked behind a funeral home. It was here, in a well-lit loft space, that Wood worked from 1924 to 1934, painting *American Gothic* and many other works. The studio is open only on weekends.

Back in Cedar Rapids, take a look at the opposite extreme of Wood's simple Midwestern style at **Brucemore** (www.brucemore.org), a large estate with a Queen Anne-style mansion that has been occupied over the past 150 years by some of Cedar Rapids' leading families, including the relatives of meat-packing and cereal tycoons.

The most recent occupants went all out when remodeling the house, adding a Tahitian Room, which had a simulated rain shower on the roof of its "hut," as well as a northwoods-themed room with a bearskin rug. They also kept lions for pets as well as lots of German shepherds, and the animals are now buried in an on-site pet cemetery. The estate sprawls over more than 25 acres and includes some breathtaking outdoor gardens and numerous other features. Cultural events are frequently held at the site.

Looking for a break from the urban whirl of Cedar Rapids? Head over to **Ushers Ferry Historic Village** (www.ufhv.com), a re-created village from the turn of the 20th century where visitors can visit 20 historic buildings, including stores and workshops.

For an even more verdant experience, **Indian Creek Nature Center** (www.indiancreeknaturecenter.org) has several natural habitats, including prairie, woodland and wetland, as well as a maple sugar house, an indoor beehive and mounted animals like a red fox, coyote, hawks and waterfowl. More than 10 miles of trails wind through the site. Just north of Cedar Rapids near Toddville is **Wickiup Hill Outdoor Learning Area** (www.mycountyparks.com/County/Linn/Park /Wickiup-Hill-Outdoor-Learning-Center.aspx), another nature area with trails and wildlife displays, as well as exhibits focused on Native American life and the diversity if Iowa's ecosystems.

The **Cedar Valley Nature Trail** (www.cedarvalleytrail.com) is the showpiece of the Cedar River Valley's many trails: a paved path for cyclists, walkers, in-line skaters and cross-country skiers that runs from Cedar Rapids to Waterloo/Cedar Falls, passing through pleasant landscapes of forest, wetlands and farm fields. Check with the Cedar Rapids Area Convention & Visitors Bureau about a trail map.

If you've made the trip to Anamosa on the Grant Wood Scenic Byway, or if you're just interested in seeing an especially impressive collection of motorcycles, check out the **National Motorcycle Museum** (www.nationalmcmuseum.org). A bike lover's dream, this massive shed just off US 151 has a *ton* of Harleys and other makes stretching back more than 100 years, with most polished to a glistening sheen. Police, military and racing models are packed in among choppers and street bikes, while vintage advertisements and race posters cover the walls. There are displays dedicated to noted motorcycle enthusiasts Steve McQueen and Evel Knievel, as well as historic cycles like the one Peter Fonda rode in *Easy Rider*. The museum also has oddities like a Harley snowmobile (?!?!). It's well worth the price of admission.

One of the more unusual museums you may ever visit is the **Anamosa State Penitentiary Museum** (www.asp history.com). It might seem odd to have a museum dedicated to a prison— especially one that's still in operation— but the castlelike structure known as the "White Palace of the West" welcomes visitors to see its exhibits, including a replica cell. Open since 1872, the prison is Iowa's largest and has housed such notables as serial killer John Wayne Gacy and John Wesley

The exterior of Grant Wood's studio in Cedar Rapids

Elkins, sentenced to life in 1889 at the age of 11 for killing his parents. (He was paroled after 12 years at Anamosa and lived a long life with no further trouble with the law.)

After *that* pair of museums, you may want to take a nice quiet stroll along Main Street, stopping for a cold drink or snack and perhaps a visit to the **Grant Wood Art Gallery** to view some of Wood's pastoral Iowa scenes.

Another option is **Wapsipinicon State Park** (www.iowadnr.gov). This rugged park just outside Anamosa is one of Iowa's oldest. It sits on Dutch Creek and features moss-covered sandstone and limestone bluffs and caves, including the legendary Ice Cave, a perfect place to retreat on a hot summer day. Deer, wild turkeys and beavers can be seen around the banks of the creek, which is also a nice spot for fishing for catfish, bullhead and bass.

Circling back to Iowa City, perhaps with a stop in **Mount Vernon** for a meal at the renowned **Lincoln Café** (see *Dining*), you can hop onto I-80 for the short drive over to **West Branch**. Here, the **Herbert Hoover Presidential Library and Museum** (http://hoover.nara.gov) and the surrounding **Herbert Hoover National Historic Site** (www.npsgov/helo) make up a good chunk of the tiny town, which that was the boyhood home of the 31st president, the only one born in Iowa.

The museum has a number of galleries detailing the many historic events during Hoover's presidency, including, of course, the Great Depression. It also traces his early life in Iowa and on the West Coast, as well as his time spent traveling the world as a mining engineer and his efforts to alleviate hunger in Europe

FOLLOWING THE GRANT WOOD SCENIC BYWAY

Known for his iconic painting of a Midwestern couple in front of a gothic window, Grant Wood is Iowa's artist, spending most of his life in and around Cedar Rapids, including a decade of prolific work in his downtown studio.

Today, reminders of Wood's inspiration can be found in the fields and farmhouses that spread out in the small towns and wide open countryside of northeast Iowa, which can be seen along a collection of roads known as the Grant Wood Scenic Byway (http://byways.org/explore/byways/2183). Most of the Wood-related attractions are found on the section of the route that runs from Cedar Rapids to his hometown of Anamosa, 20 miles to the east.

Begin the driving tour by following either US 151 or country roads E34 and X28 from Cedar Rapids to Stone City, nestled among limestone cliffs along the Wapsipinicon River. Wood established an art colony here during his time at his studio in Cedar Rapids, and also produced a painting named after the town. Stop off for a bite or a drink at the General Store Pub (http://generalstore pub.com), a limestone-walled roadhouse with a deck looking out over the river's flowing waters.

From Stone City, it's a short distance to Anamosa, where Wood was born in 1932 and is buried in the city's Riverside Cemetery. Downtown's Grant Wood Art Gallery (www.grantwoodartgallery.org) pays tribute to Wood, as does an annual art festival (www.anamosachamber.org/grantwoodartfestival). Wood attended Antioch School while growing up on a farm outside Anamosa, and the one-room schoolhouse has been preserved to look as it did when he was a student there. The scenic byway then continues to the east, passing through the towns of Wyoming, Monmouth and Baldwin before reaching Maquoketa and then continuing on to Bellevue on the Mississippi.

The *American Gothic* house (www.wapellocounty.org/americangothic) is actually located in the town of Eldon, more than 100 miles south of Cedar Rapids. There's a small museum by the house, and you may have to get in line to take a picture of it on a beautiful summer day. It's worth a visit.

following both World Wars. There is a replica of Hoover's suite at the Waldorf-Astoria Hotel in New York, where he lived for many years after his presidency, and a large display dedicated to his love of fishing.

The surrounding grounds include the house in which Hoover was born, a school and Quaker meetinghouse he attended as a child, his father's blacksmith shop and a street of historic homes reconstructed to look as it did

Herbert Hoover's birthplace in West Branch

in Hoover's boyhood. Hoover and his wife, Lou, are buried on a quiet hillside, reached from the museum by following walking trails across a rustling prairie.

IN THE AREA

ACCOMMODATIONS

Cedar Rapids has many chain hotels, both downtown and in outlying areas along major highways. Accommodations in Iowa City often fill up well in advance for major campus events like football games and graduation.

Belmont Hill Victorian Bed & Breakfast, 1525 Cherokee Drive Northwest, Cedar Rapids. Call 319-366-1343. Tucked away in a carriage house behind a restored Victorian home are three charming guest rooms featuring high ceilings, exposed brick walls, oak and walnut beds and an overall shabby elegance. Breakfasts are delicious, especially with the view of the many trees and verdant gardens. Inexpensive to Moderate. Website: www.belmonthill.com.

Brown Street Inn, 430 Brown Street, Iowa City. Call 319-338-0435. On B&B-heavy Brown Street, this Dutch Colonial–style bed & breakfast has five guest rooms plus a large suite on the third floor. All are simply yet tastefully furnished and all have private baths. The entire house has a very open, airy feel, making for a relaxing stay. It's on the north side of town, a short distance from the campus and downtown. Inexpensive to Moderate. Website: www.brownstreet inn.com.

Country School Retreat, 483 Wapsi Banks Road, Anamosa. Call 319-350-8657. This rural getaway perched on acreage between the Wapsipinicon River and Buffalo Creek is perfect if you're exploring Grant Wood country and really want to experience the landscape that inspired his work. There's a kitchen, two bathrooms, a master bedroom and two additional bedrooms with twin beds. Very quiet and peaceful—ideal for a weekend where you just want to disappear into the country. Moderate. Website: www .countryschoolretreat.110mb.com.

Golden Haug Bed & Breakfast, 517 East Washington Street, Iowa City. Call 319-354-4284. This is a funky bed & breakfast with a real college-town vibe just a few blocks from downtown's cultural scene and restaurants. There are five comfortable rooms, each stocked with refreshment baskets containing chocolate and popcorn to satisfy snack cravings. The adjacent guest house has rooms designed for longer stays, with kitchen and laundry facilities available. Moderate. Website: www.goldenhaug.com.

Iowa House Hotel, 121 Memorial Union, 125 North Madison Street, Iowa City. Call 319-335-3513. Location is the prime draw of this hotel on the upper floors of the university's downtown student union, with standard rooms and numerous amenities, including a fitness center, laundry service, washing machines and a business center. Some rooms have nice views of the river. There's a complimentary breakfast and free parking across the street. Moderate,

although rates go up significantly on football weekends. Website: http:// imu.uiowa.edu/iowahouse.

Mission House Bed & Breakfast, 228 Brown Street, Iowa City. Call 319-358-2854. A Spanish-style home incongruously set down in the Midwest, its interior continues the Southwestern theme with Navajo rugs and semi-rustic decor in the rooms. All rooms have private baths. Very relaxing and comfortable, especially when you're sitting on the front porch on a pleasant afternoon. Moderate. Website: http://missionhousebedand breakfast.com.

Smiths' Bed & Breakfast, 314 Brown Street, Iowa City. Call 319-338-1316. Yet another B&B on Brown Street, this one has three simple yet pleasant rooms, including a larger room on the first floor with a sitting area that's perfect for curling up with a book. On-site massages are also available and are a great option on a long weekend. Inexpensive. Website: http://smithsbandb.home.mchsi.com /smith_bb/Welcome.html.

DINING

Al's Blue Toad, 86 16th Avenue Southwest, Cedar Rapids. Call 319-265-8623. This Czech Village bar and grill serves up everything from classic American pub grub like burgers, nachos and chicken wings to old country favorites including goulash and cabbage roll. Entrée salads and large plates such as steak and grilled pork loin are on the menu, too. A nice place to stop after you've taken in the nearby National Czech & Slovak Museum & Library. Inexpensive. Website: www.bluetoadcr.com.

Atlas World Grill, 127 Iowa Avenue, Iowa City. Call 319-341-7700. Tasty dishes encompassing a wide fusion of cuisines—many made with locally grown and raised ingredients—are the rule at this friendly restaurant popular with students, professors and locals alike. The menu has everything from Jamaican jerk chicken and Creole shrimp to the ubiquitous Iowa pork chop and a gourmet mac and cheese. Daily specials are worth checking out, as is the wide slate of sandwiches and burritos—including a Thai chicken and a Greek salad version—at lunchtime. Desserts are delicious. It's also a popular spot for cocktails on the patio or inside at the bar. Moderate. Website: www.atlas iowacity.com.

Bob's Your Uncle, 2208 North Dodge Street, Iowa City. Call 319-351-7400. Good all-American food is served at this bar and grill adjacent to the Travelodge Motel off I-80. Locals and visitors alike come in for meat loaf, fried shrimp and steak, as well as some nice seafood and pasta dishes and a wide selection of burgers and sandwiches. Bob's Your Uncle is especially known for its pizza, including several specialty pies. Moderate.

Website: www.bobsyourunclepizza cafe.com.

Daniel Arthur's, 821 Third Avenue Southeast, Cedar Rapids. Call 319-362-9340. Fine dining in a converted 19th-century mansion. Brick walls and a fireplace create an intimate atmosphere. Start with any one of the enticing appetizers. Fresh seafood is flown in daily, and the menu also has fresh-cut steaks as well as options for vegetarians. There's a nice wine list and live music five nights a week. Reservations recommended. Medium to Expensive. Website: www.daniel arthurs.net.

Devotay, 117 North Linn Street, Iowa City. Call 319-354-1001. Eclectic dishes are served up in a funky, laid-back atmosphere at this spot near the University of Iowa campus. Largely a tapas joint, with selections like grilled calamari and crudités of vegetables among the many offerings. There are also entrées, everything from paella to marinated tofu to pork roulade (this *is* Iowa, after all). Dishes are made with fresh ingredients and wonderfully prepared. Moderate. Website: www.devotay.net.

Hamburg Inn #2, 214 North Linn Street, Iowa City. Call 319-337-5512. A longtime landmark greasy spoon that packs in students for its burgers and fried fish, as well as breakfasts accompanied by chicken-fried steak or grilled pork tenderloin. *Not* the place for a healthy meal, although there are a few salads on the menu. Inexpensive. Website: www.hamburg inn.com.

Iowa River Power Restaurant, 501 First Avenue, Coralville. Call 319-351-1904. In a former flour mill on the Iowa River, this steak and seafood joint serves up some nice cuts of beef, including a good rib eye and New York strip, as well as the inevitable pork chop, smoked over applewood. There's also a juicy and flavorful prime rib. Shrimp, salmon and grilled tuna are among the seafood offerings. Medium. Website: www.powercompanyrestaurant.com.

Joensy's, 101 West Main Street, Solon. Call 319-624-2914. In a little country crossroads on the winding road between Iowa City and Mount Vernon sits a provider of a true Iowa classic: the pork tenderloin sandwich. Not to be confused with a pork chop, this is a slab of meat that is pounded into a thin and tender strip, breaded and deep-fried into a crispy patty, then served up on a hamburger bun, which it spills out of on all sides. (You won't finish it unless you are absolutely starving.) Many aficionados like theirs with mustard, onions and pickles. Don't expect a fine-dining atmosphere: this is a small-town tavern with a faithful yet friendly crowd of locals. Inexpensive.

Lighthouse Inn Supper Club, 6905 Mount Vernon Road Southeast, Cedar Rapids. Call 319-362-3467. This is an authentic roadside inn with roots along the route that ran from Cedar Rapids to Iowa City when the latter was the state capital. The menu features classic all-American cooking like steaks, seafood and broasted chicken. Hang out in "Josie's Dive," where bartenders pour strong, old-school cocktails, and listen to the house jazz band on Friday and Saturday nights. Moderate to Medium. Website: www.crlighthouseinn.com.

Lincoln Café, 117 First Street West, Mount Vernon. Call 319-895-4041. At the opposite end of the culinary spectrum from Joensy's, this little storefront on a steep, small-town main drag serves some of the most innovative and refined cooking in Iowa—or the Midwest, for that matter. The changing menu has a small selection of main dishes that feature incredibly fresh ingredients and skillful preparation with an eclectic array of flavors, including touches of cuisines from around the world. Different meats and fish are regularly highlighted at dinner, and there are also sandwiches, salads and a children's menu. Side dishes and desserts are just as memorable. Medium to Expensive. Website: www .foodisimportant.com.

Linn Street Café, 121 North Linn Street, Iowa City. Call 319-337-7370. Elegant yet relaxing dining with a menu that changes regularly and may include choices like pan-seared duck breast, risotto with saffron and New Zealand rack of lamb. Perfect for a romantic evening, especially if you opt for the decadent desserts. Medium. Website: www.linnstreetcafe .com.

The Mill, 120 East Burlington Street, Iowa City. Call 319-351-9529. This low-key downtown joint right off campus is a favorite hangout with students: you may see everything from graduate creative writing students discussing literature to undergrads celebrating after a Hawkeye win. The menu is nothing fancy, just tasty pizzas, pastas, burgers and sandwiches. There's a children's menu as well. The Mill has live music many nights. Inexpensive. Website: http://icmill.com.

The Motley Cow, 160 North Linn Street, Iowa City. Call 319-688-9177. Light and tasty dishes make this small, unpretentious café near campus a good place for a relaxing lunch or dinner. The menu changes with the seasons and features meats and fresh produce from local providers. There are also regular specials and a nice wine list. The outdoor patio is wonderful for a bottle of wine and an appetizer or two on warm days. Moderate to Medium. Website: www .motleycowcafe.com.

Red Avocado, 521 East Washington Street, Iowa City. Call 319-351-6088. An all-organic vegan restaurant with a frequently changing menu that may include dishes made with tofu, polenta and portobello mushrooms, as well as all sorts of fresh vegetables, often in tasty sauces. Yummy pastas as well. No meat, fish or dairy in anything. Moderate to Medium. Website: www.theredavocado.com.

Red's Alehouse, 405 North Dubuque Street, North Liberty. Call 319-626-2100. In a small town just north of Iowa City, this bar and grill serves substantial steaks and seafood and a full smorgasbord of sandwiches. But the real draw is the beer to wash down your meal: nearly 20 brews are on tap here, including obscure microbeers and some good Belgian ales. What's on tap changes frequently, and there are plenty of bottled beers as well. Rounding it out are wines and specialty cocktails. Moderate. Website: http://redsalehousenl.com.

Share Wine Lounge, 210 South Dubuque Street, Iowa City. Call 319-354-4640. A different type of drinking and dining is found at this chic bistro: more than 40 wines are available to try along with a wide array of small and large plates. Dishes tend toward the light and fresh, but there are still plenty of red meat selections as well as soups and salads that make just the right complement to an inviting glass. Medium. Website: www.share winelounge.com.

Vernon Inn, 2663 Mount Vernon Road Southeast, Cedar Rapids. Call 319-366-7817. Delicious Mediterranean options star at this neighborhood restaurant, known affectionately around town as "The Greek Place." Have some chicken or fish with Greek spices and just the right touch of garlic and lemon. Of course, there are gyros and several other lamb dishes, along with lighter choices like Greek salads. Finish up with some sweet baklava. Moderate.

Vino's Ristorante, 3611 First Avenue Southeast, Cedar Rapids. Call 319-363-7550. An intimate, dimly lit space with white tablecloths and art on the walls, perfect for a special dinner. There's a nice choice of both Italian specialties and more contemporary entrées, with an emphasis on seafood dishes. The adjoining lounge has the comfortable feel of an old study or library, with walls of books lining the

room and cushioned seating. It's a nice spot to sip a cocktail or after-dinner drink or share a bottle of wine. Moderate to Medium. Website: vinosristorante.com.

Vito's on 42nd, 4100 River Ridge Drive Northeast, Cedar Rapids. Call 319-393-8727. Cedar Rapids' tour of ethnic dining continues at this casual Italian café with redbrick walls. Vito's is known for its pizzas and pastas, as well as specialties like chicken piccata. There's a lengthy list of sandwiches and salads, too. Specials are featured throughout the week. Moderate. Website: www.vitoson42nd.com.

Zins Restaurant, 227 Second Avenue Southeast, Cedar Rapids. Call 319-363-9467. This swanky downtown eatery in a historic building features lots of tasty small plates perfect for

Prairie Lights Bookshop, Iowa City

sampling a variety of flavors. There are also full-size entrées, including steaks and chops. An extensive menu of drinks complements the varied food offerings. Moderate. Website: www.zinsrestaurant.com.

SHOPPING

Czech Cottage, 100 16th Avenue Southwest, Cedar Rapids. Call 319-366-4937. A store full of Czech and Slovak gifts and specialty items, including intricate glassware, China and jewelry. Check out the extensive selection of Christmas tree ornaments and other holiday items. Website: http://czechcottage.com.

Gameday Iowa, 821 Melrose Avenue, Iowa City; also 805 Second Street, Coralville. Call 319-338-3133. *The* place to pick up official Iowa Hawkeyes merchandise, with a huge selection inside a cavernous store. Jerseys, sweatshirts, hats and all sorts of accessories. Website: www.game dayiowa.com.

Iowa Artisans Gallery, 207 East Washington Street, Iowa City. Call 319-351-8686. More than 200 artists display their wares at this downtown shop, which specializes in handmade American craft items. You can spend hours perusing the offerings, many of which make excellent and unique gifts. Website: www.iowa-artisans -gallery.com.

Prairie Lights, 15 South Dubuque Street, Iowa City. Call 319-337-2681.

A classic college town bookstore with an endless number of titles in subjects ranging from all-encompassing to the most minute and esoteric. Sprawls over three floors and includes a large children's section and an upstairs coffeehouse that hosts frequent readings. A must-visit for book aficionados. Website: www .prairielights.com.

RECREATION AND ENTERTAINMENT

Cedar Rapids Kernels Baseball Club, 950 Rockford Road, Cedar Rapids. Call 319-363-3887. The Kernels play at Veterans Memorial Stadium, which holds more than 5,000 fans and sits on the west side of town. An affiliate of the Los Angeles Angels of Anaheim, the team offers numerous ticket deals and promotions throughout the season. Website: http://web.minorleaguebaseball.com /index.jsp?sid=t492

Englert Theatre, 221 East Washington Street, Iowa City. Call 319-688-2653. A grand old-style marquee

heralds this downtown venue which has hosted all kinds of live music acts, from folk to country, jazz to rock, as well as other live entertainment. Plenty of shows sell out, so it's worth getting tickets early if you plan to be in town. Website: www.englert.org.

Iowa River Water Trail/Johnson County Conservation, F. W. Kent Park, 2048 IA 6 North, Oxford. Call 319-645-2315. The Iowa River flows unhindered by dams for more than 70 miles from Iowa City to the Mississippi, making it an ideal stretch for paddlers. Put-in and take-out points near Iowa City include Sturgis Ferry Park, Hills Access or River Junction Access. Camping is available in some areas. Website: http://iowariverwater trail.com.

Paramount Theatre, 123 Third Avenue, Cedar Rapids. Call 319-398-5211. In the process of being rebuilt after suffering severe flood damage, this ornate theater has a long history of showcasing live entertainment, including music and drama productions. Website: www.uscellularcenter .com/PT/pt.html.

Riverside Theatre, 213 North Gilbert Street, Iowa City. Call 319-338-7672. Iowa City's lone professional theater company stages numerous plays every season, including both classic shows and new works. It also produces the annual Riverside Theatre Shakespeare Festival. Website: www.riversidetheatre.org.

Theatre Cedar Rapids, 102 Third Street Southeast, Cedar Rapids. Call 319-366-8592. A longtime community theater company that puts on musicals, comedies, dramas and classic productions. Many performances are held in an ornate yet intimate 500-seat auditorium, while others are performed in a smaller studio theater. Website: www.theatrecr.org.

OTHER CONTACTS

Jones County Tourism Association, 120 East Main Street, Anamosa, 52205. Call 1-800-383-0831. Website: www.jonescountytourism.com.

Cedar Rapids Area Convention & Visitors Bureau, 119 First Avenue Southeast, Cedar Rapids, 52401. Call 319-398-5009. Website: www.cedar-rapids.com.

Iowa City/Coralville Area Convention and Visitors Bureau, 900 First Avenue/Hayden Fry Way, Coralville, 52241. Call 319-337-6592. Website: www.iowacitycoralvillearea.org.

Mount Vernon-Lisbon Community Development Group, P.O. Box 31, Mount Vernon, 52314. Call 319-210-9935. Website: www.visitmvl.com.

Main Street West Branch, 109 North Downey Street, West Branch, 52358. Call 319-643-7100. Website: www.mainstreetwestbranch.org.

7 The Amana Colonies and Kalona:
STEP BACK IN TIME

Estimated length: It's about 30 miles between the two communities.

Estimated time: You could spend a day or two in each place or do them both in a weekend. Although both are just a short distance from Cedar Rapids and Iowa City, they deserve their own chapter due to the many options they offer visitors.

Getting there: The Amana Colonies are about 5 miles north of I-80 off US 151; alternatively, you can take US 151 South from Cedar Rapids or US 6 West from Iowa City for a more scenic route. Kalona is about 20 miles south of Iowa City on IA 1.

Highlights: These are two of the most popular tourist destinations in Iowa, with a plethora of shopping opportunities and a chance to experience major communities of two prominent groups in American history: in Kalona, the largest Amish settlement west of the Mississippi; and in the Amana Colonies, a communal society established by descendants of 19th-century pioneers known as Pietists. Both Kalona's Historical Village and numerous restored historical buildings in the Amana Colonies provide examples of living history, showing how the ancestors of present-day residents lived and worked.

D on't get the two groups mixed up. Despite the somewhat similar sound of "Amana" and "Amish," they're not at all related to each other, even though both have roots in Germany and came to America seeking religious freedom.

Start off in the Amana Colonies, which consists of seven villages clustered in the rolling countryside, with the first stop being the main village of Amana. The Amana Colonies Visitors Center (http://amanacolonies.com/pages/directory /amana-colonies-visitors-center.php) has a ton of information for visitors, including a map that will help you find your way around the individual villages.

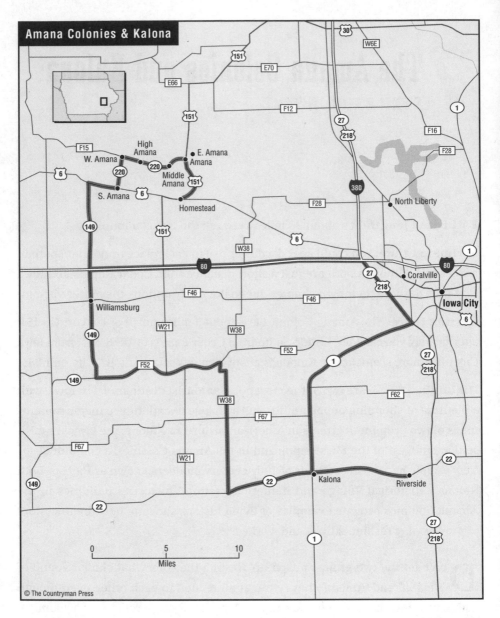

Amana Colonies & Kalona

Down the street from the visitors center is the **Amana Heritage Museum** (www.amanaheritage.org/museums.html), which has many rooms detailing the fascinating history of the colonies, from the original settlers who arrived in Iowa in the mid-1800s, through the communal society's end in the 1930s, and eventually to the community's new identity as a major manufacturer of home appliances and the biggest tourist attraction in Iowa. There's an admission charge for the museum, which can include admission to the other half-dozen Amana heritage sites scattered throughout the villages. Many of the sites have limited hours; check with the museum or visitors center for specific times.

The heritage sites also include the **Communal Kitchen and Copper Shop** in Middle Amana, the only surviving example of one of the most unique features of life in the old communal society: there were no kitchens in individual homes; instead, food was prepared by teams of women in kitchen buildings like this one throughout the colonies. (Meals were eaten communally as well, with large groups sitting down together at mealtimes.) Guides give a detailed talk on the structure and running of the communal kitchen and the food served in the colonies. Down the street, the cooper shop demonstrates the art of making barrels.

The **Communal Agriculture Museum** in South Amana, which is usually open only by appointment, contains a large collection of farm implements as well as photographs that show the colonists' farming techniques. It is located in a historic 19th-century barn that was used to house oxen and is still quite sturdy, with large beams holding up the roof.

Three historic sites are clustered in the village of **Homestead.** The **Homestead Store Museum** features displays on the variety of crafts and trades that sustained the colonists, along with models of some of the colonies' original buildings. The **Amana Community Church Museum** is dedicated to the importance of religion in the colonists' lives, with guides explaining the different aspects and practices of their faith. It's a very simple building without any sort of decoration or religious icons, reflecting the simple way colonists worshiped. Visitors may also attend Sunday services at the **Amana Church** in Middle Amana, where the service is conducted in a combination of German and English that dates back to the colonies' early years.

Finally, the **Homestead Blacksmith Shop** has demonstrations not just of blacksmithing, but also of printmaking and bookbinding, as well as

The Amana Colonies Visitors Center, a good starting point for tourists

displays of tools used in those and other trades. The shop is usually open only on Saturday. Interestingly, Homestead was not part of the original settlement of the Amana Colonies, but was founded later as a train terminal for the railroad that came through the Iowa River Valley.

In **South Amana**, the **Barn Museum** holds one of the more unusual collections in the colonies: a spread of miniature buildings forming whole communities, including Amana buildings, Abraham Lincoln's boyhood village of New Salem, a Northern California logging camp and a Great Plains settlement of Native Americans. Created by a retired farmer who began the craft of miniatures well into his 50s with a barn scaled 1 inch to the foot, the buildings are remarkably intricate in their detail, right down to the curtains and windowpanes.

In addition to the individual sites, walking tours of the villages are available, beginning at the Amana Heritage Museum. There are also special tours dedicated to industry in the colonies—including a visit to Amana's famous woolen mill and other industrial sites—and colonial winemaking, which of course includes wine tasting. Self-guided audio and GPS tours are also available; check at the visitors center for details.

Shopping is the big attraction for many visitors to the Amana Colonies, with a variety of shops clustered along the narrow village streets, especially in the main village of Amana (see *Shopping*).

Kalona is home to more than 1,000 Amish, who first arrived in the area in

---

ORIGINS OF KALONA'S NAME

Founded as a stop on the railroad, Kalona grew to prosperity, as did many towns in Iowa, as goods and people moved west along the rails. How Kalona got its name, however, is a unique story: when the railroad first arrived, a farmer whose land it crossed proposed the name Myersville. This was rejected, and so the farmer proposed the name Kalona, which was accepted, most importantly by railroad officials. But while it may have sounded agreeable to them, it was actually the name of the farmer's prize bull!

Kalona thus gained the nickname "Bulltown," which stuck for many years until it became "Quilt Capital of Iowa."

THE DIFFERENT ORDERS OF AMISH

The Amish are divided into different groups: the Old Order Amish, who are probably the most well known, shun electricity, telephones, cars and many other modern technologies, while the Beachy Amish use electricity, phones and automobiles and own modern appliances and farm equipment. The New Order Amish are a hybrid of the two groups.

All Amish, however, dress similarly in simple clothes and live in close communities in which families assist each other, with barn raising perhaps the best-known example of members coming together for the good of the community. The Amish believe in a literal interpretation of the Bible and worship in their homes rather than in a church building, a legacy of the time when they were persecuted for their faith in 16th-century Germany and Switzerland before coming to America.

Meanwhile, the Mennonites, who also have a presence in the Kalona area, share roots with the Amish and share some of the same religious beliefs, but in general use modern technology, including automobiles and electricity.

1846. The town and surrounding Amish farms are a true throwback to an earlier time, with Amish buggies making their way down country lanes and life moving at a slower pace in the shops and cafés. Shops line downtown streets and narrow roads that stretch past farms in the rolling countryside.

Kalona can be reached from the Amana Colonies either by following country roads south of I-80, or by driving east to Iowa City and then following IA 1 South about 20 miles.

In addition to the Amish, whose fine furniture and other handiwork can be seen in local shops, Kalona's history can be discovered at the **Kalona Historical Village** (www.kalonaiowa.org/KHV.htm), which traces the town's history back to its earliest days. The historical village was established in 1969, when the depot was picked up and moved soon after trains stopped coming to town.

Today, the village comprises some 15 buildings, including the **Snyder Log House,** built in 1842 and thought to be one of the oldest houses in the area. It displays a rope bed, spinning wheel and cast-iron stove. The **Wahl House** has a large selection of antiques, while the **Grandpa House** is a fine example of an

Amish "retirement home," in which the older generation would live after handing over management of a family farm to the next generation.

The **Kempftown Store** was an Amish general store that carried everything under the sun for local farmers. The **Loom House** was dedicated to weaving and displays two looms, one from the 19th century, and a coverlet and rugs. **Straw College** was actually a one-room schoolhouse named Summit School, built in the mid-1800s, which gained its nickname due to the straw stuffed behind the walls for insulation and warmth during harsh Iowa winters.

Other buildings in the village include a historic church and a mill still used for grinding corn and wheat during Kalona's annual Fall Festival, which features demonstrations of all sorts of crafts and pioneer skills and plenty of delicious homemade goodies.

There are also several small museums in the village, including the **Quilt and Textile Museum** (www.kalonaiowa.org/KQTM.htm), with changing displays of nearly 400 historical quilts and the largest display of antique spool cabinets in the United States. Kalona is known as the quilt capital of Iowa, and the annual **Kalona Quilt Show and Sale,** held in April, displays hundreds of quilts at the town's community center.

The **Wahl Museum** is a tribute to the craftsmanship of Kalona's early days, and displays an old telephone switchboard, newspaper office equipment and other historic items. The **Agriculture Museum** has antique farm equipment and automobiles, while the **Reif Family Rock and Mineral Display** contains a collection of fascinating gems and crystals. The **Iowa Mennonite Museum** has numerous artifacts pertaining to both the Mennonites and Amish, including a shuttle loom still used by Mennonite artisans.

The Kalona Area Chamber of Commerce has information on numerous tours of local history available to visitors. Some tours conclude with a big family-style meal in a local home.

Kalona's quilt heritage continues with the numerous barn quilts found on many of the two-lane roads that wind through the countryside. There are around 100 barn quilts in the Kalona area and at least three driving tours that take visitors past numerous examples of the folk art; check with the chamber of commerce or online at www.barnquiltsonline for details. You can also see examples of quilt work on Kalona's **Quilt Block Walking Tour:** with more than 40 quilt designs are installed in the bricks of downtown's sidewalks.

Finally, for a different sort of historical pilgrimage, Trekkies may want to scoot over to **Riverside,** future birthplace of *Star Trek* lead character Captain James T. Kirk. According to *Star Trek* trivia, the leader of the USS *Enterprise* will be born in this Iowa town in 2233.

It may seem strange, going to a place that won't actually be known for anything for a loooong time, but devoted fans still make the pilgrimage, taking in a model of the USS *Riverside* (which looks just like the *Enterprise*) in Legion Park, as well as visiting the **Voyage Home Museum,** which has memorabilia from the television show as well as exhibits on local history. The optimistic town even hosts Trekfest (www.trekfest.org) every June, which draws Trekkies and other visitors to town for a variety of events.

IN THE AREA

ACCOMMODATIONS

Amana Colonies Guest House Motel, 4712 220th Trail, Amana. Call 319-622-3599 or 1-877-331-0828. This lodging in the heart of the main village's shopping and dining has nearly 40 rooms in two buildings, including a 125-year-old sandstone structure, which was previously a communal kitchen, and a more contemporary motel building. A good value and an excellent location. Inexpensive. Website: www.theguesthousemotel.com.

Annie's Garden Guest House, 716 46th Avenue, Amana. Call 319-622-6854 or 1-866-622-6854. A bed & breakfast with three guest rooms, well situated to shopping and strolling in the main Amana village. Beds are comfortable and the rooms feature antique furnishings and private baths. Breakfast is a country spread with delicious baked goods and fresh fruit. A pleasant garden adds to the relaxing atmosphere. Moderate. Website: www.timeandtides.com.

The Carriage House Bed & Breakfast, 1140 Larch Avenue, Kalona. Call 319-656-3824. A mile outside of Kalona, The Carriage House offers two rooms in an adjunct to a rural spread that sits among Amish farms, with buggies passing by on the road and horse-drawn plows moving through the fields. It's perfectly quiet, a fine spot for a weekend getaway. One room features a Murphy bed and private bath, while the second room's bath has a clawfoot tub. A big country breakfast includes entrées like stuffed French toast, omelets and biscuits and gravy. There's a unique payment policy—a rate range is listed, and guests pay what they feel their stay is worth. Moderate. Website: www.thecarriagehousebb.net.

Die Heimat Country Inn, 4434 V Street, Homestead. Call 319-622-3937 or 1-888-613-5463. This Amana Colonies B&B is housed in a former communal kitchen building. There are nearly 20 comfortable guest rooms with a choice of full-, queen- and king-sized breads. A substantial buffet breakfast will get you fueled up for a day of shopping or sight-seeing in Homestead and the other villages. Moderate. Website: www.die heimat.com.

Ethel's Gourmet Kitchen Bed & Breakfast, 1070 IA 1, Kalona. Call 319-656-2481 or 319-936-6131. Ethel's consists of a pair of rooms in a residence outside of Kalona among the rolling fields and large Amish community. Rooms have queen beds, and one has a private bath. Breakfast is big and hearty, with yummy baked goods. Amenities include evening drinks and dessert. Moderate. Web-site: www.ia-bednbreakfast-inns.com /ethelsbandb.htm.

Rose's Place Bed & Breakfast, 1007 26th Avenue, Middle Amana. Call 319-622-6097 or 1-877-767-3323. This handsome redbrick structure in one of the smaller Amana villages has three good-sized guest rooms with private baths. There's also a spacious common area with a piano that's nice for reading or relaxing. Breakfast is a tasty selection of eggs, meats and baked goods. Inexpensive. Website: www.iowacity.com/amanas /rosesbb.

Village Guest Suite, 4312 F Street, Amana. Call 319-622-6690 or 1-866-624-6690. An elegant yet affordable bed & breakfast right in the middle of Amana's sights and shops. Two large suites take up much of the first and second floors, with the first-floor suite including a Jacuzzi tub and the second-floor suite featuring a private balcony that looks out over the vil-lage. An adjoining second-floor suite is smaller, but has a queen-sized bed and full bath. Inexpensive to Moder-ate. Website: http://villageguestsuite .com/suites.html.

Zuber's Homestead Hotel, 2206 44th Avenue, Homestead. Call 319-622-3911 or 1-888-623-3911. A true old-fashioned hotel updated with modern conveniences, this lodging just a short drive from the main vil-lage of Amana is a collection of theme rooms, including several cele-brating Iowa as the heart of Ameri-can farm country and two honoring University of Iowa sports teams. Other rooms have artifacts commem-

orating the original Amana Colonies settlers, and all rooms are furnished with antique and period items, comfortable beds and nice baths. A full breakfast comes with your stay. Moderate. Website: www.zubershome steadhotel.com.

DINING

The Colony Inn, 741 47th Avenue, Amana. Call 319-622-2300. Since 1935, this restaurant has set the standard for the Amana Colonies famous family dinners, with big platters of meat and large bowls of hearty side dishes like mashed potatoes and vegetables. Main dishes include both American and German choices such as fried chicken and ham or Swiss steak and Wiener schnitzel, with different sausages on the menu as well. Breakfast is good, too, with big plates of eggs, pancakes, bacon and sausage. Moderate.

Ox Yoke Inn, 4420 220th Trail, Amana. Call 319-622-3441 or 1-800-233-3441. A charming country inn on the outside with heaping portions of American and German favorites inside. As with several other restaurants in the Amana Colonies, many dishes are served family-style, with mashed potatoes and other sides coming to the table in big bowls. You can also find delicious steaks and several seafood options, as well as German dishes like Wiener schnitzel and sauerbraten. Leave room for the tempting cakes and pies served for

dessert. There's a second location just off I-80. Moderate. Website: www .oxyokeinn.com.

Ronneburg Restaurant, 4408 220th Trail, Amana. Call 319-622-3641 or 1-888-348-4686. Housed in one of the old communal kitchens, this restaurant has a classic meat-and-potatoes menu, but with a German twist: Bavarian chicken and dumplings are on the menu, as are schnitzel and sauerbraten. You can also get steaks and seafood and some tasty sandwiches. Black forest brownie is a wonderful dessert. Moderate. Website: www.ronneburgrestaurant.com.

Tuscan Moon Grill on Fifth, 203 Fifth Street, Kalona. Call 319-656-3315. An authentic bistro dining experience in down-home Kalona, this restaurant features a fusion of several cuisines: Italian dishes prevail, of course, including some nicely prepared pasta choices, but there are also all-American favorites like expertly grilled steaks and seafood. Extensive wine list and full bar. Medium to Expensive. Website: http://tuscan -moon.com.

SHOPPING

You could easily spend all day shopping in the Amana Colonies: a large number of arts and crafts shops, art galleries and food shops line the streets of Amana and other villages, and this is in no way a comprehensive listing. Take time to simply stroll through Amana and be surprised by what you find around the next corner.

Amana Arts Guild Center, 1210 G Street, High Amana. Call 319-622-3678. A gallery and museum of Amana folk art with a shop that sells items like brooms, baskets, quilts, rugs and other decorative and household items produced by local artisans. Also displays artwork and runs an annual art show. Website: www .amanaartsguild.com.

Amana Furniture & Clock Shop, 724 48th Avenue, Amana. Call 1-800-247-5088. Beautiful, handcrafted designs in walnut, cherry, maple and oak, with a huge selection of clocks ranging from small bedside models to large grandfather clocks, as well as

items for the bedroom, dining room, living room and office. Worth a visit just to watch the craftsmen at work and learn about the long history of furniture and clock making in the Amana Colonies. Website: http:// amanafurniture.com.

Amana Meat Shop & Smokehouse, 4513 F Street, Amana. Call 319-622-7586 or 1-800-373-6328. This smokehouse, which dates to 1855, offers big smoked hams as well as bacon, sausage, steaks and other meats, with plenty of free samples. Locally made cheeses, jams and jellies are for sale as well. Website: www.amanameat shop.com.

Amana Woolen Mill, 800 48th Avenue, Amana. Call 319-622-3432 or 1-800-222-6430. You can spot this landmark mill looming at one end of the main Amana village. Go inside for a look at working looms; the mill has been spinning out blankets and other wool items since 1857, and there are some very nice items for sale in the on-site shop, including sweaters and other apparel. Website: www.amanawoolenmill.com.

Collectively Iowa, 4709 220th Trail, Amana. Call 319-622-3698. A neat little wine shop with dry, semi-sweet and dessert wines made from Iowa grapes. There's a tasting room and a knowledgeable staff that can recommend vintages. Try a few wines and perhaps sample items from the food menu, including personal pan pizzas. Website: http://ciwines.com.

Custom Cutlery & Ironworks, 822 48th Avenue, Amana. Call 319-622-3482. Handcrafted steel kitchen knives come off the forge at this shop behind Amana Woolen Mill. It also turns out hunting knives and other iron items like fireplace tools and home accessories. There's an industrial machine shop museum, too. Website: www.customcutlery.com.

High Amana General Store, 1308 G Street, High Amana. Call 319-622-3232. A step back in time to an era of small-town shops, with its wooden floors, old-fashioned display cases, barrels holding wares and a tin ceiling overhead. Everything from vintage candies and specialty foods to toys, gifts and domestic items like handmade soaps can be found on its well-stocked shelves. Website: www.amanaheritage.org/highstore.html.

Kalona Antique Company, 211 Fourth Street, Kalona. Call 319-656-4489. An impressive collection of items can be found in this antique mall housed in a 19th-century church building. Peruse the offerings of 20 vendors, including those who sell furniture, glassware and the quilts for which Kalona is famous. Keep your eyes peeled for monthly specials, which can include some real treasures. Website: http://kac.kctc.net.

Kalona Bakery, 209 Fifth Street, Kalona. Call 319-656-2013. Known for its pies, cakes and breads as well as pastas, which you can watch workers create in an on-site viewing room. Pick up some homemade potato salad for a picnic in the countryside. Website: http://kalonabakery.com.

Kalona Cheese Factory/Twin Country Dairy, 2206 540th Street Southwest, Kalona (4 miles north of town on IA 1). Call 319-656-2776. This rambling brick building, established by Amish and Mennonite farmers in the 1940s and still one of only a few cheese factories in Iowa, stocks more than 200 varieties of cheese, plus sausages, condiments and other gour-

---

THE KALONA BAR

Not a local tavern—this is Amish country, after all— the Kalona Bar is a confection of vanilla ice cream covered in chocolate and rolled in graham cracker crumbs. This delicious treat is available at some shops in town.

met items. Watch fresh cheese curds being made through an observation window. Website: http://twincountry dairyinc.com.

Kalona Furniture Company, 210 Fifth Street, Kalona. Call 319-656-2700. Fine, handcrafted Amish furniture, including sturdy bedroom sets, living and dining room items and children's pieces, with designs in oak and cherry woods. Even if you don't buy anything, it's still worth taking a look at the impressive craftsmanship. Website: www.kalonafurniture.com.

Kalona General Store, 121 Fifth Street, Kalona. Call 319-656-2700. All kinds of merchandise line the shelves at this old-fashioned emporium, including games, toys and puzzles, as well as a plethora of food items like fresh fudge and tempting Amish cashew crunch candy. On the flip side, there are a lot of health and wellness items, too. Website: www .kalonageneralstore.com.

Lehm Books & Gifts, 4536 220th Trail, Amana. Call 319-622-6447 or 1-800-840-2387. A well-stocked emporium with all sorts of titles, including novels, sports and history books and cookbooks, as well as selections for children. There's a nice selection of volumes related to the Amana Colonies as well. This shop also sells gifts and collectibles, with an emphasis on dolls and figurines and holiday items. Website: www.lehmbooksand gifts.com.

Millstream Brewing Company, 835 48th Avenue, Amana. Call 319-622-3672. This microbrewery pumps out Iowa-themed brews in a small building across from the large Amana Woolen Mill. The tasting room offers free samples of the ales, stouts and many other varieties, and there's a pleasant beer garden right outside the front door, a nice place to take a break from shopping the many stores in Amana. Thick and creamy root beer and cream soda will keep kids happy. Website: www.millstream brewery.com.

Village Winery, 752 48th Avenue, Amana. Call 319-622-3448 or 1-800-731-7142. A combination winery and gift shop, with a large selection of Hummel figurines alongside the fruit and berry wines, which may be sampled in the tasting room. There are several other types of figurines for sale, as well as beer steins and numerous Christmas items. Website: www.thevillagewinery.com.

RECREATION AND ENTERTAINMENT

Amana Kolonieweg Recreational Trail. For cyclists, there's nothing more pleasant than rolling down this trail that winds for 4 miles between the villages of Amana and Middle Amana, including sections passing a lake and a canal levee. Walkers, meanwhile, will enjoy the **Amana Nature Trail**, a 3-mile loop through thick forest with a view from the bluffs overlooking the Iowa River. This area is rich in Native American history, too, with some burial mounds nearby in the woods and a fish weir on the river. Check with the visitors center to see about maps of the trails. Website: www.amanacoloniestrails .org.

Iowa Theatre Artists Company, 4709 220th Trail, Amana. Call 319-622-3225. This professional company presents musicals and other entertaining performances in an intimate theater space on the second floor of a historic building adjacent to the Amana Colonies' visitors center. There's a lounge on the first floor that serves beer and wine. Website: www.iowatheatreartists.org.

Old Creamery Theatre, 39 38th Avenue, Amana. Call 319-622-6194 or 319-622-6034. This long-standing professional company puts on a wide variety of shows in two spaces, everything from classic theater to comedies, dramas to musicals and children's productions. The 300-seat theater has good views of the stage and comfortable seats. Website: www .oldcreamery.com.

OTHER CONTACTS

Amana Colonies Convention & Visitors Bureau, 622 46th Avenue, Amana, 52203. Call 1-800-579-2294. Website: www.amanacolonies.com.

Kalona Area Chamber of Commerce, 514 B Avenue, Kalona, 52247. Call 319-656-2660. Website: www .kalonachamber.com.

8 Waterloo/Cedar Falls:
ATTRACTIONS ALONG THE RIVER

Estimated length: Fairly short and compact, with most attractions sprinkled throughout both cities, and a few side trips totaling 10 to 20 miles.

Estimated time: You could easily get a taste of at least one city in a day, and do both of them in a weekend. Side trips would add another day or two.

Getting there: It's a 45-minute drive from Cedar Rapids on I-380, and this area can also be reached on US 20, which runs from Dubuque on the Mississippi River all the way across the state.

Highlights: A stroll through Cedar Falls' historic downtown and over to the riverfront ice house museum. Grout Museum District. Exploring nature trails.

Home to a massive John Deere tractor works and several other plants displaying the green and yellow icon of the internationally known farm equipment maker, these twin cities on the Cedar River are manufacturing towns that maintain a healthy amount of culture and recreation. Cedar Falls is home to the University of Northern Iowa, one of three large public institutions of higher learning in the state.

Begin your visit in **Cedar Falls,** which has a visitors center just off the riverfront in a converted historic gas station, including restored pumps out front and a vintage vending machine inside. There are numerous historical attractions (www.cfhistory.org), beginning with the nearby **Ice House Museum,** which is easy to spot, with a 100-foot diameter roof on the circular building. Once inside, marvel at the single post that holds up the roof.

The museum is a showcase of the ice industry in Cedar Falls' earlier years, when huge blocks of ice were wrenched from the frozen river and stored in the

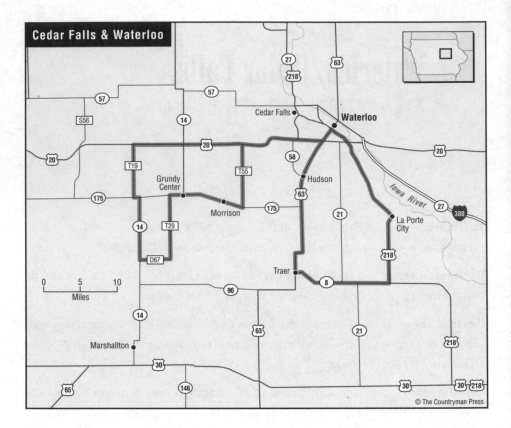

Cedar Falls & Waterloo

© The Countryman Press

ice house, which could hold thousands of tons of ice. There are numerous artifacts on display, including a life-sized ice wagon. The museum also has exhibits detailing Cedar Falls' old Main Street, including the facades of many downtown shops.

Numerous historic structures stand throughout town, a reminder of Cedar Falls' bustling days as an important river and railroad center. A **self-guided walking tour** of the city is available—check with the Cedar Falls Visitors Center (6510 Hudson Road; 319-268-4266 or 1-800-845-1955) for a copy. The tour leads several blocks from the riverfront, down Main Street and the surrounding area, passing several examples of **public art** that have been erected on the streets of the city. It highlights many historic commercial buildings and Victorian homes, including the **Victorian Home & Carriage House Museum**, a cupola-topped Italianate manse with period furnishings and permanent exhibits like the **William J. Lenoir Model Train Collection**, which features detailed locomotives built from scratch. **Overman Park** is the oldest public park in the city, while the **Oster Regent Theatre** is a grand old edifice that began as a live theater and served for many years as a movie house before once again becoming a showplace for live performances when it was given to a local theater company.

Also on the tour and adjacent to the visitors center is the **Little Red Schoolhouse Museum,** which dates to the earliest years of the 20th century and was moved to its current site. It has been refinished to look as it did in its days as an active school, including a potbelly stove and vintage textbooks and lunch pails. The **George Wyth House** is a few blocks away and is open by appointment. It has features of both art deco and arts and crafts home construction, with period artifacts found in many rooms. It was previously home to the **Viking Pump Museum,** which is now located at the company's main office and commemorates the long history of the local pump manufacturer, including a display that shows the making of a pump from beginning to end (Wyth was president of Viking for 40 years).

A unique piece of local history is found at a Main Street storefront that houses the **Iowa Band Museum** (www.cedarnet.org/cfband/museum.html). Also

open by appointment, the museum traces the history of the Cedar Falls Municipal Band, which has been playing tunes for more than 100 years. It is located in the tin-ceilinged band hall and includes a rehearsal room with mahogany conductor's podium. Vintage instruments and historic photographs are also on display, as are old band uniforms. To this day, the band plays concerts on Tuesday evenings at the band shell in Overman Park downtown—ask at the visitors center for details.

On the campus of the University of Northern Iowa, the **University Museum** (www.uni.edu/museum) has exhibits devoted to a hodgepodge of history, science and the natural world, including plenty of mounted animals. Check out the 16-foot-long python skin and the impressive collection of fossils, including a mastodon trunk found in Iowa. There's also a fine collection of ceremonial masks from around the world and lots of photographs of local history, as well as frequently changing temporary exhibits.

The university also has the **Marshall Center One-Room School,** a white clapboard building that was moved across the state to its home on campus. Unique among older schoolhouses, the restored structure has double doors and a telephone that was installed in the 1920s. There is also the **Bennington Number Four School** in Waterloo.

Finally, the **Hearst Center for the Arts** (www.cedarfalls.com/index.aspx?NID =160) has a collection of works by local and regional artists as well as temporary exhibits by national and international masters. There's also an outdoor sculpture garden that is open May through October, with art set among a pleasant spread of plants and trees.

Neighboring **Waterloo** is no slouch in the museum department: its **Grout Museum District** (www.groutmuseumdistrict.org) encompasses five separate attractions clustered around a few blocks of downtown. Start off at the **Grout Museum of History & Science**, which focuses on local history with a collection of neat bric-a-brac that includes a Maytag Car, a luxury automobile of its time that was built in Waterloo, an early tractor and a large whistle used by a longtime local meatpacking company. The **Bluedorn Science Imaginarium** is perfect for kids: it has lots of interactive exhibits that let visitors build a robot, operate a hot air balloon and learn about all kinds of weather phenomena.

Also part of the Grout District is the **Rensselaer Russell House Museum.** One of the oldest homes in the area, the brick Victorian has period details and fur-

THE SULLIVAN BROTHERS: TOGETHER FOR COUNTRY

An inspiration for the movie *Saving Private Ryan,* the story of the Sullivan brothers has become legendary: the five Waterloo siblings, ranging in age from 27 to 19, enlisted in the U.S. Navy less than a month after the Japanese attack on Pearl Harbor. They asked that they all serve together, a request the Navy granted.

The brothers were assigned to the USS *Juneau* and saw action during the lengthy series of battles around the island of Guadalcanal. In August 1942, the ship was hit by Japanese torpedoes and sank. All five Sullivan brothers died as a result. Later, their sister served with the WAVES, a woman's unit of the Navy. Contrary to popular belief, no law was passed after the Sullivan's death preventing siblings from serving on the same ship.

In addition to displays commemorating the Sullivan Brothers at the veterans museum, the convention center in Waterloo is named for them and a public park stands on the site of their former home. Their graves are in Waterloo's Calvary Cemetery.

nishings and lovely gardens. The **Snowden House** is another Victorian residence, used primarily for special events.

But perhaps the most interesting is the **Sullivan Brothers Iowa Veterans Museum.** Named for the five local brothers who famously served and died together in World War II, the large museum honors veterans from the Civil War through the present. The museum provides visitors with dog tags to guide them through the exhibits, which include video histories of veterans, large-scale dioramas depicting scenes from different wars and a replica of the ship the five Sullivan brothers were stationed on when it sank in the Pacific. A few blocks away on the banks of the Cedar River sits **Soldiers and Sailors Park.**

Art lovers will want to see the **Waterloo Center for the Arts** (www.waterloo centerforthearts.org), which houses an excellent collection of works by artists from both the Midwest and farther points on the globe, including the largest public Haitian art collection in the United States. The museum's **Phelps Youth Pavilion** is a children's wing with more than 40 interactive exhibits. Young visitors can milk a model cow, drive a virtual tractor through a Grant Wood painting and try digital finger painting. There's a beautiful sculpture garden outside.

Of course, ask any local and they'll tell you Waterloo means tractors: farm equipment giant John Deere may have its headquarters in its founding city of Moline, Illinois, but Waterloo makes a case for the industrial heart of the company, with more than 5,000 employees spread out over half a dozen area plants, including the main tractor works and a large diesel engine works.

Tours of both the tractor plant and engine plant are available; visitors must be at least 13 years old and reservations must be made in advance. A new Deere museum to complement the one in the Quad Cities is also scheduled to open in Waterloo.

Still in Waterloo, the Dan Gable International Wrestling Institute & Museum (www.wrestlingmuseum.org), named after one of Iowa's many home-grown legendary grapplers, has an exhaustive array of exhibits related to the sport most identified with Iowa. Kids will love getting in the replica ring dedicated to pro wrestling, while other exhibits and artifacts stretch all the way back to ancient times: see artwork of wrestling at the first Olympics and of a young Abe Lincoln wrestling. Other displays highlight modern Olympic and other champion wrestlers and wrestling clips from movies. There's a research library as well.

The Cedar Valley around Cedar Falls and Waterloo is an ideal spot for outdoor activities, with numerous parks and more than 80 miles of hiking and bicycling trails running through the two main cities and into neighboring communities. The Cedar Trails Partnership (www.cedartrailspartnership.org) is a clearinghouse of information on local trails, including trail maps. Trails include the Cedar Valley Nature Trail (www.cedarvalleytrail.com), which runs more than 50 miles from Cedar Falls and Waterloo, following the route of the Cedar River through rolling countryside while passing parks and wildlife areas. The nearby Waverly Rail Trail is another popular choice for bicycling through bucolic country, crossing several bridges over its 7½ miles.

The native prairie landscape has been restored in some places, such as Prairie Lakes Park (www.cedarfalls.com/index.aspx?NID=160) adjacent to the Cedar Falls Visitors Center, a nice spot for bird-watching. Other examples of prairie can be found at Big Woods Lake as well as the University of Northern Iowa's Campus Prairie and Tallgrass Prairie Center.

For a nature experience in the heart of the city, head to Hartman Reserve

Nature Center (www.co.black-hawk.ia.us/hartman) in Cedar Falls, a wooded isle with a variety of landscapes including woods, prairie and ponds spread out on a bluff that descends to the Cedar River. There's an interpretive center where visitors can learn about the many birds that call the center's lands home, as well as several trails with scenic views.

Nearby, **George Wyth State Park** also has diverse habitats traversed by trails which make for excellent exploration and provide opportunities to spot wildlife like white-tailed deer and many different varieties of birds. The park also has numerous lakes for swimming, boating and fishing. The **Cedar Valley Paddlers Trail** follows a loop along the Cedar River and through lakes in George Wyth State Park and the Hartman Reserve Nature Center, passing by riverbanks clustered with native plants.

The **Cedar Valley Arboretum and Botanic Gardens** (www.cedarvalley arboretum.org) in Waterloo is a beautifully landscaped collection of gardens, including a rose garden with varieties popular in northeast Iowa, as well as a labyrinth of looping hedges and a children's garden with a "dinosaur dig" and a railway garden. A walking trail leads through an expansive prairie studded with native plants.

There are some nice road trips out of Cedar Falls and Waterloo. Heading south soon brings you to **Hudson,** home of **Hansen's Farm Fresh Dairy** (www .hansendairy.com), a working dairy farm with daily milking demonstrations, part of a tour that shows the entire process of bringing milk from cow to market. (Call ahead to schedule a tour) There are also some wallabies hopping around.

Moving on, continue south to **Traer,** whose typical small-town downtown has a most unique architectural feature: the **Winding Stairs** (www.traer.com), an outdoor spiral staircase heading up to the second floor of a building on Second Street. The staircase dates back more than a century, when the town's newspaper publisher was seeking more space in his cramped office and found it by building the iron staircase outside. When the town widened the sidewalks several years later, the publisher simply moved the stairs farther out and added a catwalk to reach the office. The staircase has become so celebrated that Traer throws an annual Winding Stairs Festival.

The staircase's building is owned by the local historical society, which also operates the **Traer Historical Museum** (www.traermuseum.com). Exhibits include a Civil War cannon and an exhibit dedicated to "Tama Jim" Wilson, a local resident and the longest serving U.S. Secretary of Agriculture, holding the position beginning in the late 1800s.

Traer's other sights include the **Traer Salt & Pepper Shaker Gallery**, one of the largest collections of the indispensable kitchen items. Find out about the many different types of shakers you never knew existed, fashioned in porcelain, glass, metal and other materials. Then head over to the **Wilson Nature Preserve** (http://traermuseum.art.officelive.com/wilsonnaturepreserve.aspx), a restored prairie landscape studded with wildflowers that also includes a butterfly garden and an Iowa native tree area.

Loop back toward Cedar Falls and Waterloo, stopping along the way in **La Porte City**. The large **FFA Historical & Ag Museum** (www.lpcmuseum.com) covers local history with both permanent and temporary exhibits that include many historical artifacts.

The other recommended road trip is to Grundy County to the west of Cedar Falls and Waterloo. The county is known for its **Barn Quilts** (www.grundycounty ia.com/Quilt_Website/indexbq.htm), and there's a 64-mile driving loop that runs past more than 50 fine examples of this folk art. Both a map and audio tour of the route are available, which also meanders past the **Grundy County Welcome Center** and through the county seat of **Grundy Center**, passing many small shops along the way.

Grundy Center is also the site of the **Herbert Quick Schoolhouse**, named for a journalist and author who penned nearly 20 books, including a trilogy of "Iowa novels" in the 1920s that depicted Midwestern life. It's restored to the way it was when Quick was a student there. In the nearby town of **Morrison**, the **Grundy County Heritage Museum** has more than 100 mounted birds, mammals and amphibians, as well as exhibits dedicated to Native American and pioneer life. There's also the log cabin of the county's first white settler, a one-room schoolhouse and a vintage railroad caboose.

IN THE AREA

ACCOMMODATIONS

There is an extensive selection of chain hotels and motels in Cedar Falls and Waterloo, with many clustered at the Butterfield Road/IA 27/ 58 and US 218 exits off I-380, as well as along University Avenue.

Black Hawk Hotel, 115 Main Street, Cedar Falls. Call 319-277-1161 or 1-800-488-4295. A beautifully restored historic hotel in the heart of Cedar

Falls' charming downtown. Rooms are tasteful and charming, with comfortable beds, luxurious baths and all the modern amenities. Larger suites are available, as are rooms in buildings adjacent to the main hotel. There's a hip martini bar just off the lobby. Moderate. Website: www.black hawk-hotel.com.

Carriage House Inn Bed and Breakfast, 3030 Grand Boulevard, Cedar Falls. Call 319-277-6724. Overlooking Castle Hill Park and just a short distance from the Hartman Reserve Nature Center and Riverside Trail, this quiet retreat has two large suites, each decked out with double whirlpool, fireplace and skylight. The queen-sized beds, including one in antique oak and another in Rococo Revival walnut, are comfortable, and the refrigerator with complimentary beverages is a nice touch. Moderate.

University Inn, 1711 University Avenue, Cedar Falls. Call 319-277-1412. Basic, comfortable lodging with good-sized rooms, convenient for university visitors and close to many attractions. Amenities include continental breakfast and a fitness center. Inexpensive to Moderate. Website: www.universityinncf.com.

Wellington Bed & Breakfast, 800 West Fourth Street, Waterloo. Call 319-433-1205. This rambling historic Colonial Revival home features carved woodwork, stained and beveled glass and parquet floors.

There are three guest suites, and breakfast is served in the rooms. Moderate.

DINING

The Cedar Falls Brown Bottle, 1111 Center Street, Cedar Falls. Call 319-266-2616. Website: www.thebrownbottle.com. And the **Waterloo Brown Bottle,** 209 West Fifth Street, Waterloo. Call 319-232-3014. Website: www.brownbottlewaterloo.com. These two family-owned Italian restaurants do a fine job of serving up favorite comfort foods like lasagna, manicotti and spaghetti, as well as some more innovative pasta choices and a full list of steaks, seafood and pizza. The Waterloo restaurant sits in the high-ceilinged, light-filled lobby of the historic Russell Lamson Building, while the Cedar Falls restaurant has a popular outdoor patio on the banks of the river with a view of the Ice House Museum. Moderate.

Cu Restaurant, 320 East Fourth Street, Waterloo. Call 319-274-8888. This intimate downtown dining room offers an enticing blend of flavors. Touches of cuisines from all over the world turn up in dishes like maple leaf duck, Cantonese noodles and Gorgonzola lamb. Steaks are broiled to perfection and there's a tasty selection of seafood offerings. The restaurant also has an extensive wine list, and the downstairs Cellar Bar is a relaxing spot to unwind over a glass of wine. Moderate to Medium. Website: www.curestaurant.com.

D+K Hickory House, 315 Park Road, Waterloo. Call 319-233-9111. A barbecue lover's nirvana, this simple wood-paneled room dishes out thick and tasty slabs of ribs with tender meat and delectable flavor. D+K also serves steaks, seafood and sandwiches, but this is first and foremost a temple to carnivores. A children's menu is available. Inexpensive to Moderate.

Doughy Joey's Peetza Joynt, 126 Brandilynn Boulevard. Call 319-277-2800. And 300 West Fourth Street, Waterloo. Call 319-274-0996. Big-city style pizza is served at these fun spots, which also offer calzones, pastas, sandwiches and salads. The Cedar Falls location has the look and feel of a sports bar, while the Waterloo site is a larger, more kid-friendly restaurant. Inexpensive to Moderate. Website: www.doughyjoeys.com.

The Fainting Goat, 118 10th Street Southwest, Waverly. Call 319-352-2335. This no-frills bar and grill with lots of favorite pub grub is just a short drive from Cedar Falls. Probably more varieties of fried appetizers and flavors of chicken wings than you'll find anywhere else. All sorts of burgers, sandwiches, a few dinner entrées and plenty of chicken choices. Have a beer and ask the bartender how the place got its name. Stays open until the wee hours and gets a little wild with music pumping out of the sound system. Inexpensive to Moderate. Website: www.thefainting goat.com.

Galleria De Paco, 622 Commercial Street, Waterloo. Call 319-833-7226. One of the most stunning and unique restaurant interiors you'll ever see: Michelangelo's Sistine Chapel paintings have been reproduced—in spray paint—on the ceiling of this fine dining spot, the work of a young artist who fled war-torn Bosnia and landed in the Cedar River Valley. The restaurant serves well-prepared steaks and other refined fare. Downstairs is a swanky cocktail lounge with innovative drinks. Moderate to Medium. Website: www.paco-rosic.com.

Mama Nick's Circle Pizzeria, 1934 Washington Street, Waterloo. Call 319-233-3323. A classic, old-school pizza parlor going on 50 years of family ownership. Nothing fancy, just pizzas with a variety of toppings and a few specialty pies, with a handful of sandwiches, pastas and fried entrées thrown in as well. Stick with the pizza—the cheese is hot and bubbly, while the rich tomato sauce has just the right spiciness. Inexpensive. Website: www.mamanicks.com.

Montage, 222 Main Street, Cedar Falls. Call 319-268-7222. Upscale casual place with exposed brick walls and brushed steel tables. The menu has a fusion of dishes like Asian pork, Southwestern chicken and jambalaya pasta, as well as old standbys like New York strip steak. There's also a full slate of specialty pizzas, including Thai, Mexican and goat cheese options. A lengthy list of beers, wines and specialty cocktails gives you something to sip while taking in the cool, subtle decor. A children's menu is available. Moderate to Medium. Website: www.montage-cf.com.

Newton's Paradise Café, 128 East Fourth Street, Waterloo. Call 319-234-0280. A former jewelry store is home to this retro diner with a modern menu: lunch includes choices like wraps with pesto chicken, turkey and raspberry aioli, and several salads alongside the burger, Reuben, and other standard diner fare. Breakfast is more straight up, with eggs, French toast and pancakes among the offerings. Although it closes midafternoon, there are dinner items available, including steaks, fish and chips, rack of pork and chicken dishes. Moderate. Website: www.newtonscafe.com.

The Pump Haus, 311 Main Street, Cedar Falls. Call 319-277-8111. A storefront bar and grill downtown, popular with the after-work and *Monday Night Football* crowd. Yummy burgers and sandwiches as well as wraps and salads are the stars of the menu. For spicy food lovers there are chili cheese fries and buffalo chicken. Televisions are installed in all the booths, so you won't miss a minute of the game. Inexpensive. Website: www.thepumphaus.com.

Rudy's Tacos, 2401 Falls Avenue, Waterloo. Call 319-234-5686. A stripped-down Mexican American café, the local outpost of a Quad Cities–based chain, with vinyl chairs facing Formica tables and pop culture artifacts on the walls. Don't let the kitschy atmosphere distract you from the food: the tacos, tostadas and enchiladas are cheap, tasty and made with exceptionally fresh ingredients. They taste even better with the excellent salsa and guacamole. Inexpensive. Website: http://rudystacos.com.

SHOPPING

Barn Happy, 11310 University Avenue, Cedar Falls. Call 319-266-0888. This country store in an old dairy barn features gift baskets filled with good, wholesome Iowa foods like honey, jam, candy and other goodies. They also sell plenty of other foods and home products. This is also a nice spot to grab a light lunch or snack, with soups, quiche, salads and pastries all served fresh and tasty. Website: http://barnhappy.net.

Basket of Daisies, 208 Main Street, Cedar Falls. Call 319-277-3286. All kinds of home decor items and accessories are for sale at this downtown space. Browse among the elegant home setups and floral arrangements along the shop's exposed brick walls.

The staff can answer your decorating questions and make recommendations if you're planning a big or small project. Website: www.basketofdaisies.com.

Mohair Pear, 2209 College Street, Cedar Falls. Call 319-266-6077. Retro heaven, with lots of vintage clothing, jewelry and accessories at this unique shop just off the UNI campus. The helpful and knowledgeable staff can assist you in locating hard-to-find items—or come up with something else that's just as good. Website: www.mohairpear.com.

World's Window, 214 Main Street, Cedar Falls. Call 319-268-1584. A funky, internationally themed shop, with gifts, housewares and accessories from all over the world. The store promotes fair trade practices that pay the makers of its products a fair wage and provide safe and healthy working conditions. Website: www.worldswindowcf.org.

RECREATION AND ENTERTAINMENT

Cedar Falls Raceway, 6200 West Bennington Road, Cedar Falls. Call 319-987-2537. A quarter-mile drag racing track with races every Friday and Saturday night from May through October, with Friday nights offering open racing for everyone. The raceway also hosts special events. Website: www.cedarfallsraceway.com.

CrawDaddy Outdoors, 107 East Bremer Avenue, Waverly. Call 319-352-9129. This well-stocked outdoors store rents kayaks and canoes for float trips on local rivers, as well as camping gear for guided backpacking getaways in area forests. Also has snowshoes and cross-country skis for winter fun. Website: www.crawdaddyoutdoors.com.

Isle Casino Hotel Waterloo, 777 Isle of Capri Boulevard, Waterloo. Call 319-833-4753. The local gambling option, with 1,000 slot machines and table games including blackjack, craps, roulette and poker. There are three restaurants on the premises and live entertainment. Website: http://black-hawk.isleofcapricasinos.com.

Lost Island Water Park, 2225 East Shaulis Road, Waterloo. Call 319-233-8414. An endless number of thrilling slides are found at this park, as well as a few pools and an area for smaller children. Just outside is the Lost Island Adventure Park, which features one of the largest go-cart tracks in the Midwest. This family fun center also has two 18-hole miniature golf courses. Website: www.thelostisland.com.

Oster Regent Theatre, 103 Main Street, Cedar Falls. Call 319-277-5283. A local community theater in a historic downtown building. Productions include comedies, musicals and dramas. The theater space also hosts other performances. Website: www .osterregent.org.

OTHER CONTACTS

Cedar Falls Tourism & Visitors Bureau, 6510 Hudson Road, Cedar Falls, 50613. Call 1-800-845-1955. Website: www.cedarfallstourism.org.

Waterloo Convention & Visitors Bureau, 500 Jefferson Street, Waterloo, 50701. Call 1-800-728-8431. Website: www.travelwaterloo.com.

Grundy County Development Alliance, 705 F Avenue, Grundy Center, 50638. Call 319-825-3606. Website: www.grundycountyia.com.

Waverly Chamber of Commerce, 118 East Bemer Avenue, Waverly, 50677. Call 319-352-4526. Website: www.waverlyia.com.

9 Southeast Iowa:
SIMPLICITY IN SMALL TOWNS

Estimated length: About a 250-mile loop, beginning at the historic Villages of Van Buren County and then circling west, north, east and south, passing through the small cities of Ottumwa, Oskaloosa, Fairfield and Mount Pleasant.

Estimated time: Even though it's a fairly lengthy distance, you can hit several places in a day, and you can probably do the entire trip in a weekend. Plus, this trip can be broken up into shorter, more manageable trips.

Getting there: Reach the starting point by taking IA 2 West from US 61/218 (Great River Road) and driving about 30 miles to Bonaparte.

Highlights: Historical buildings galore in Bonaparte, Bentonsport and Keosauqua. The *American Gothic* house in Eldon. One of the most unusual collections of stuff *anywhere* at the Dumont Museum in Sigourney.

This shorter trip is a series of visits to historical villages interspersed with individual sights, with the route corkscrewing through several rural counties. The area is one of the less populated parts of eastern Iowa. Towns along the narrow country roads are a throwback, with few modern commercial strips and virtually no stoplights.

The first smaller tour-within-a-tour is a drive through the **Villages of Van Buren** (http://villagesofvanburen.com), a collection of rustic, off-the-beaten-path hamlets that make for a pleasant excursion. Begin in **Bonaparte,** the first of several towns on this trip that grew to prominence as steamboats plied the Des Moines River on their way to and from the Mississippi. **Bonaparte Mills** sits on the banks of the river and consists of a trio of redbrick buildings for which the river was the lifeblood of their operations, including a gristmill, woolen mill

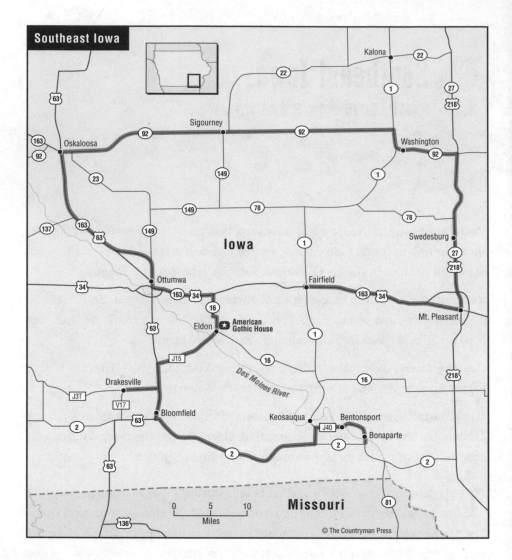

and pants factory. They are now home to a restaurant, shops and a hotel, respectively.

With the end of the steamboat era, Bonaparte and the other villages eased down into the sleepy country towns they have remained to this day. The **Bonaparte National Historic Riverfront District** (www.bonaparte-iowa.com) has several charming shops in historic downtown buildings. The **Aunty Green Hotel Museum** was the first brick home in Bonaparte and also served as a stagecoach stop for travelers heading west. Today, it houses the town's public library and historical museum.

Historic Bonaparte Pottery (http://bonaparte-pottery.com) is a pottery shop that was originally a 19th-century stoneware workshop. Archaeological digs at the site have uncovered numerous pieces of original pottery. Tours are available, and visitors also have the opportunity to make their own pottery.

Moving on to **Bentonsport,** another shopping opportunity awaits at **Bentonsport National Historic District** (www.bentonsport.com), with antiques and craft shops and artisans' workshops, including a blacksmith and potter in historic buildings. Nearby, a picturesque one-lane iron bridge spans the Des Moines River. Take a stroll across and back—it's a pedestrian-only bridge.

Bentonsport's **Indian Artifact Museum** (www.bentonsport.com/indianmuseum.html), located in the historic district, has one of the more interesting backstories of any museum in the state: it displays the vast collection of arrowheads of a local collector who has been gathering them for many years, and who designed and built the intricate inlaid panels holding the arrowheads from wood he scoured from the countryside around Bentonsport. (He's an avid outdoorsman who only eats meat he hunts himself, grinds his own wheat and corn, and grows his own fruits and vegetables.) Antlers, ax heads and other artifacts are also on display.

For another look at modern-day preservation of pioneer arts, come to the annual **Buckskinners Festival,** which includes demonstrations of blacksmithing, basket making and pottery, as well as knife and tomahawk throwing and blackpowder shooting. The dates vary; check with the Villages of Van Buren visitors center for details.

The next stop is **Keosauqua,** the largest town in the area, which has several historic buildings of its own, including the **Twombly Building**, a stone structure that once served as a dry goods store and newspaper office. It currently houses the town's historical museum. The **Pearson House,** a brick and stone home built in the mid-1800s, was a stop on the Underground Railroad, assisting fugitive slaves in their escape to freedom. The **Van Buren County Courthouse** is of note because it is the oldest continuously operating courthouse in Iowa and the second oldest in the United States. The Federal-style building has been restored since it was first built in 1846.

Nearby **Lake Sugema** is an angler's paradise, with fishing enthusiasts dropping lines for bass, bluegill, crappie, catfish and walleye in the 574-acre lake. The surrounding area is open for hunting, hiking and bird-watching, and includes

The *American Gothic* House in Eldon

Lacey-Keosauqua State Park, one of Iowa's largest state parks and home to many hiking trails.

Next, swing west over to **Bloomfield,** which has a historic tour of its own, mainly focusing on restored homes in a variety of styles, including Gothic, English Tudor, Colonial Revival and Queen Anne. Even the town's welcome center is in a restored 1910 Sears, Roebuck & Company mail order home. There is also an impressive French Renaissance courthouse with a picturesque bell tower.

From Bloomfield, follow the highway north and then take a short side trip west to **Drakesville,** home to an Amish community where the works of local craftsmen are displayed in the shops that pop up along gravel roads. Stop in one of the shops to pick up a map of the area.

Head north again on US 63 for a few miles, then jog east on a country road to **Eldon** and one of the more iconic images associated with Iowa. The *American*

Gothic **House** (www.wapellocounty.org/americangothic) sits on the far edge of town, its famous window sitting back from the street, in a neighborhood where houses begin to give way to rolling countryside.

The house has a rather interesting backstory: artist Grant Wood only glimpsed the house in passing and decided to use it as the backdrop for his famous work—the models posed separately in Wood's studio in Cedar Rapids and were not pleased with the finished painting! Furthermore, Wood received only $300 for the painting from the Art Institute of Chicago, which awarded him the money as part of a competition.

A small visitors center has exhibits about Grant Wood, the story of the painting and a sampling of different depictions of *American Gothic,* one of the most copied and parodied images in history.

After a quick look at Eldon's tiny downtown, you're off again: head north to US 34 toward **Ottumwa,** which has some nice lodging and dining options, then veer northwest to **Oskaloosa.** Although it's one of the larger cities in this part of Iowa, it is actually well known for **Nelson Pioneer Farm** (www.nelsonpioneer.org), which re-creates mid-19th-century farm life and includes 18 separate buildings, including a barn, smokehouse and the original farmhouse, as well as a "downtown" with general store, barbershop and other pioneer structures. It's also home to the only mule cemetery in Iowa, which honors two of the beasts who served in the Civil War. An adjoining museum has tons of historic artifacts, including Native American and military items and a miniature circus.

Yet another unique museum is waiting just down the road in the town of **Sigourney.** The **Dumont Museum** (www.dumontmuseum.com) is an overwhelming (and it truly is *overwhelming*) collection of bric-a-brac and pop culture detritus that includes…well, what *doesn't* it include? In addition to antique tractors, engines and farm toys, there are dolls, household items, buggies, pedal tractors, covered wagons, and…oh, just go and see it!

The museum also has perhaps the most complete collection of Roy Rogers and Dale Evans memorabilia, including a life-sized Roy above a bucking Trigger. The couple who undertook this vast collection had to move it years ago into a nearly 25,000-square-foot shed, but at this rate they eventually may have to find an even bigger home for all their stuff.

Shooting due east about 30 miles brings you to **Washington,** home to several historic sites, including the **Conger House Museum,** which has numerous displays and rooms with period furniture; the **D.A.R. Log Cabin,** which also has period furniture and antiques donated to the D.A.R., sponsor of the site; and the **F-Troop Military Museum,** a collection of military memorabilia stretching back to the Civil War and reaching all the way to the wars of the 21st century. Numerous barn quilts also can be found on country roads outside of town.

Drive a few miles east and then south until you come to the small community of **Swedesburg.** As you might guess, it was settled by Swedish immigrants, who first arrived in the mid-19th century. The town's **Swedish American Museum** commemorates this heritage, with a restored country store and artifacts and exhibits detailing farming techniques of the early settlers, including displays of how they drained the marshy soil and made it into productive farmland. The community also sponsors Swedish-themed festivals, including the annual **Midsommar Fest.**

Just south of Swedesburg is the larger city of **Mount Pleasant,** another Iowa community whose claim to fame is tractors, and lots of them: the **Midwest Old Threshers Heritage Museum** (www.oldthreshers.com) has dozens of old steam models and other antique tractors spread out on its grounds and inside several buildings. The collection goes beyond tractors to encompass every aspect of farm life in the early 20th century, with displays of vintage farm implements, windmills, a reconstructed 1915 farmhouse and a farm implement dealership. In another room is a large collection of antique dolls. Also on-site is the **Museum of Repertoire Americana,** which has a large collection of early theater memorabilia.

During the annual Old Threshers Reunion leading up to Labor Day, the area around the museum comes to life with the hiss and rumble of steam tractors moving across the sprawling grounds, puttering along next to antique cars, electric trolleys and other vintage vehicles. There are also demonstrations of farming techniques and live entertainment.

Finally, finish the roundabout trip with a visit to **Fairfield,** which has one of the more unusual features of rural Iowa: **Vedic City** (www.maharishivediccity .com), a community organized by the followers of Transcendental Meditation, whose founder, the Maharishi Mahesh Yogi, a guru from India, bought Fairfield's Parsons College after it closed in the early 1970s.

The college, renamed **Maharishi University of Management,** along with those who have settled in Vedic City, have helped pump up the local economy, and Fairfield today is a prosperous community with many shopping and dining options, including a few Indian restaurants and others serving exclusively organic and vegetarian dishes. All the buildings in Vedic City are designed according to principles laid down by the Maharishi, making for some interesting architectural features.

In addition, Fairfield is home to more than 200 visual and performing artists who have opened studios and galleries throughout town. An **art walk** is held the first Friday of every month. The town also has a **Carnegie Historical Museum**, part of a **heritage trail** that includes many historic homes and other buildings, including a 1910 armory.

IN THE AREA

ACCOMMODATIONS

Bonaparte Inn, 802 First Street, Bonaparte. Call 319-592-3823 or 1-800-319-3234. This former pants factory overlooking the Des Moines River has been transformed into a cozy lodging with exposed brick walls and hardwood floors. Rooms are large and airy, and the location is ideal for exploring the historic villages. Moderate. Website: http://bona parteinn.com.

Hattie Corn's Cottage, 21930 Wall Street, Bentonsport. Call 319-592-3152. A cozy, country-style, two-bedroom cottage just a few blocks from Bentonsport's downtown and riverfront, with modern amenities including a DVD player and central air-conditioning. A fully modern kitchen is on the first floor. Relax on the deck or screened front porch. Moderate. Website: http://showcase .netins.net/web/alexander.

Hotel Manning, 100 Van Buren Street, Keosauqua. Call 1-800-728-2718. Resembling the prow of a steamboat cutting through the nearby river, this historic hotel lined with balconies and distinctive window dormers has 16 bed & breakfast rooms with antique fixtures and comfortable beds. There are also 19 modern rooms in the **Riverview Inn,** a newer structure on the riverfront, and in a smaller motel building. Even if you're staying in the newer rooms, duck into the hotel and let the lobby's original pine woodwork and rosewood grand piano remind you of the steamboat era. Inexpensive (inn and motel) to Moderate (hotel). Website: www.thehotelmanning.com.

Hotel Ottumwa, 107 East Second Street, Ottumwa. Call 641-682-8051. A historic downtown hotel, built in 1917 and since updated, with modern rooms that include refrigerator and microwave. Complimentary breakfast is included with all rooms, and there's a restaurant as well as a hip watering hole, the Tom Tom Tap, with a large mural that celebrates the area's Native American heritage. Inexpensive to Moderate. Website: www .hotelottumwa.com.

Kountry Kottage, 31965 235th Road, Bonaparte. Call 319-592-3431. A rural retreat just a few miles from the historic attractions of both Bonaparte and Bentonsport, as well as hiking and fishing options. There's a single guest room with access to the living room, kitchen and dining area. Moderate. Website: http://showcase.netins .net/web/kountrykottage.

Mainstay Inn, 300 North Main Street, Fairfield. Call 641-209-3300. Conveniently located in downtown Fairfield just a short walk from many shops and galleries, this bed & breakfast has two guest rooms in the main building and three in an adjoining cottage. Both buildings have extensively remodeled interiors, with airy, well-appointed bedrooms and details like Persian rugs and fine oak furniture. Moderate. Website: www.main stayfairfield.com.

Mason House Inn Bed & Breakfast, 21982 Hawk Drive, Bentonsport. Call 319-592-3133. This historic inn, originally built for steamboat passengers on the Des Moines River, nicely complements the surrounding historic villages of Van Buren County. The inn's former pub, laundry room and general store have been converted into pleasant first-floor guest rooms, and there are several more rooms upstairs overlooking the river and stocked with antique furnishings, comfortable beds and a full cookie jar! You can even stay in a renovated caboose on the grounds. Moderate. Website: www.masonhouseinn.com.

McNeill Stone Mansion, 1282 C Avenue East, Oskaloosa. Call 641-673-4348 or 641-990-3521. From the imposing stone facade to the mahogany-accented interior, this is one of the more opulent lodgings you'll find in Iowa. Rooms are regal, with features like fireplaces and canopied four-poster oak beds. The penthouse suite, reached by a private staircase, measures some 1,500 square feet and occupies the former ballroom and billiard room. Breakfasts are extravagant as well, served at a long table beneath a crystal chandelier. In the afternoon, you might relax in the solarium or take a stroll around the grounds and check out the large fountain. Moderate to Medium. Website: www.thestone mansion.com.

Oak Meadow Delight Bed and Breakfast, 2814 Oak Meadow Drive, Ottumwa. Call 641-682-0580. A contemporary home with four guest suites that include king-sized beds and private baths. Relax on the large patio and admire the adjacent garden. Moderate. Website: http://oak meadowdelightbnb.com.

Seven Roses Inn, 1208 East Burlington Avenue, Fairfield. Call 641-209-7077. This countrylike estate across the street from Chautauqua Park serves wonderful meals in a bucolic, verdant setting just a short distance from downtown Fairfield. There are five guest rooms, each with a different color scheme and all with private bath. Common areas are elegant and classy. Moderate. Website: www.seven rosesinn.com.

DINING

Appanoose Rapids Brewing Company, 322 East Main Street, Ottumwa. Call 641-684-4008. This downtown microbrewery serves up all-American favorites with a twist, like mac and cheese with bacon and tomatoes, as well as a full slate of steaks and other entrées, plus, of course, a nice selection of beers brewed on-site. Moderate to Medium. Website: www .appanooserapidsbrewingcompany .com.

Bonaparte Retreat, 713 First Street, Bonaparte. Call 319-592-3339 or 1-800-359-2590. Behind the redbrick exterior of an old gristmill on the Des Moines River, this casual eatery serves big portions of all-American favorites like steak, fried chicken and ham. There are also several seafood options like Alaskan king crab claws, shrimp and scallops, and salads for those looking for a lighter meal. Mod-

erate. Website: http://bonaparte retreat.com.

First Street Grille, 719 First Street, Keosauqua. Call 319-293-6462. Down-home country cooking is the rule at this no-frills bar and grill along the trail of Van Buren's historic villages. Try some chicken or baby back ribs, and wash it down with one of the cold beers on tap. Inexpensive.

Top of the Rock Grille, 113 West Broadway, Fairfield. Call 641-470-1515. This clubby, spacious room serves great steaks, broiled to perfection and seasoned just right. There are also chicken and seafood dishes and some pasta options as well. Salads are served crisp with fresh ingredients, and sweet and decadent desserts include fried brownies and make-your-own s'mores. A nice selection of wines and specialty drinks complements the menu items. Medium. Website: www.topoftherock grille.com.

Vivo Restaurant, 607 West Broadway, Fairfield. Call 641-472-2766. Innovative cooking in a sleek yet casual atmosphere. Appetizers like beef carpaccio and tuna sashimi are tempting, but save room for your choice from the extensive list of entrées, which includes numerous steak, seafood and chicken options. Dishes are prepared with fresh ingredients, and there are numerous vegetarian choices. Moderate. Website: www.vivofairfield.com.

The White Buffalo, 100 IA 34 East, Albia. Call 641-932-7181. Part of the Indian Hills Inn, The White Buffalo offers a menu of all-American comfort food like grilled ham, chicken-fried steak, fried chicken and even liver and onions. Big burgers come with tasty fries. There are also steak and seafood choices and pizzas with a wide selection of toppings. You may prefer to dine in the adjoining lounge and catch the game on the big-screen TV. The western-themed decor is a nice contrast to the rolling Iowa prairie outside. Inexpensive to Moderate. Website: www.indianhillsinn .com.

SHOPPING

Greef General Store, 21964 Hawk Drive, Bentonsport. Call 319-592-3579. An old-fashioned general store filled with a colorful assortment of antiques and arts and crafts, with numerous toys and household items. The storekeepers also sell some divine fudge, and they are a good source of information on what to see in Bentonsport and the surrounding historic villages. Website: www.greef store.com.

Hel-Mart, 301 State Street, Farmington. Call 319-878-3576 or 319-371-6783. It's worth taking a short side trip from Bentonsport to see this rambling former woolen mill that houses not only a store, but also displays of dollhouses, rocking horses and a miniature train set. Try some of the store's yummy pies and ice cream for a pick-me-up.

Iron & Lace, Walnut Street and Hawk Drive, Bentonsport. Call 319-592-3222. Located in a rustic old blacksmith shop in the Bentonsport Historic District, this store features Queen Anne's lace pottery and iron and woven items, some created by the husband and wife who own the place. This means you can actually watch them create household and artistic items at their forge, loom and potter's wheel. It's a nice change of pace from other shops.

RECREATION AND ENTERTAINMENT

Hawkeye Canoe Rental, 20717 IA 1, Keosauqua. Call 319-293-3897 or 641-919-8276. Spend a day paddling the Des Moines River or Lake Sugema with a rental from this outfitter. Rentals include life jackets, paddles and shuttle service to and from the paddling spot. They are able to accommodate large groups as well.

The Raj, 1734 Jasmine Avenue, Vedic City (Fairfield). Call 641-472-9580 or 1-800-248-9050. A health spa focused on ayurvedic treatments in Iowa's community of Transcendental Meditation followers. Many treatments are available, including those that include overnight stays in the on-site hotel. Website: http://theraj.com.

Southern Iowa Speedway, 701 North I Street, Oskaloosa. Call 641-

673-7004. Stock cars rev their engines at this half-mile dirt track at the Southern Iowa Fairgrounds. Fans turn out in large numbers on Wednesday evenings throughout summer and into fall to watch races, including the IMCA stock car shootout every July. Website: www.rl promotions.com.

OTHER CONTACTS

Keosauqua Chamber of Commerce, P.O. Box 511, Keosauqua, 52565. Call 319-293-7737. Website: www.keo sauqua.com.

Villages of Van Buren, 902 Fourth Street, Keosauqua, 52565. Call 1-800-868-7822. Website: www.villagesofvan buren.com.

Davis County Welcome Center, 301 North Washington Street, Bloomfield, 52537. Call 641-664-1104. Website: www.visitdaviscounty.com.

Albia Area Chamber of Commerce, 18 South Main Street, Albia, 52531. Call 641-932-5108. Website: www .albiachamber.org.

Oskaloosa Area Chamber & Development Group, 124 North Market Street, Oskaloosa, 52577. Call 641-672-2591. Website: www.oskaloosa chamber.org.

Washington Chamber of Commerce, 205 West Main Street, Washington, 52353. Call 319-653-3272. Website: www.washingtoniowa chamber.com.

Henry County Tourism, 124 South Main Street, Mount Pleasant, 52641. Call 319-385-3101. Website: www .henrycountytourism.com.

Fairfield Iowa Convention & Visitors Bureau, 200 North Main Street, Fairfield, 52556. Call 641-472-2828. Website: www.travelfairfieldiowa .com.

10 Northern Iowa:
FROM *THE MUSIC MAN* TO THE DAY THE MUSIC DIED

Estimated length: Roughly 200 miles round-trip, from Mason City and Clear Lake west to Algona, then south to Fort Dodge, east to Iowa Falls and then back to Mason City.

Estimated time: Two to three days.

Getting there: Mason City and Clear Lake, either of which can serve as the starting point for this trip, are both easily accessible off I-35 running north-south or US 18 running east-west.

Highlights: A smorgasbord of *Music Man* memorabilia as well as the marionettes from *The Sound of Music* in Mason City. A historic, if tragic, spot in American popular music in Clear Lake, along with a scenic lakefront. A museum dedicated to hoboes in a small Iowa crossroads town. One of the greatest hoaxes in American history, in Fort Dodge, housed inside a replica frontier fort.

D istances begin to open up as this trip moves out of the more populated areas along eastern Iowa's rivers and into the wider spaces of the Great Plains. The cornfields get broader and spaces between towns more empty as you move west from Mason City and Clear Lake, passing underneath the big blue sky.

Mason City welcomes visitors with a sign featuring a trombonist in homage to native son Meredith Willson, who based much of *The Music Man* on his hometown, including several key characters drawn from his childhood acquaintances.

A nostalgic trip down the streets of River City is found at the **Music Man Square** (www.themusicmansquare.org), which is based entirely on the sets from the 1962 movie of Willson's most famous work. The 1912 storefronts include the barbershop, bakery and grocery, as well as a working ice cream parlor/soda foun-

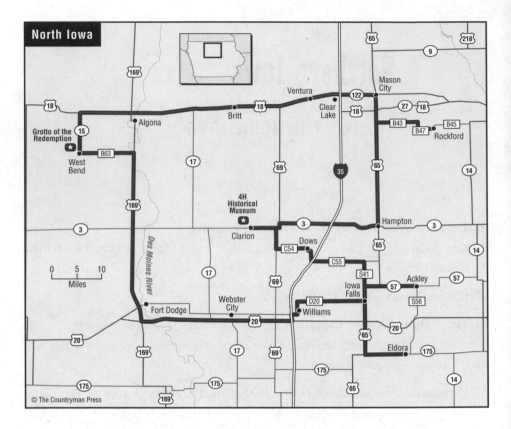

tain and a gift shop. Also on-site is a museum with lots of memorabilia and interactive exhibits related to the musical, as well as other displays on the history
of American music, including Victorian parlor music, the big band era and more
contemporary sounds.

Nearby is the **Meredith Willson Boyhood Home,** the restored 1895 Queen
Anne house where Willson was born and raised, complete with period furniture
and accessories. Tours of the home are available. You can hear plenty of trom-
bones and other instruments at the annual **North Iowa Band Festival** (www.ni-
bandfest.com), when uniformed marchers take over downtown's streets.

The Willson home is part of Mason City's **Historical Walking Tour,** which
moves through downtown and nearby residential neighborhoods (maps are available at the downtown visitors center). It passes the **Park Inn,** an extensively restored hotel designed by Frank Lloyd Wright, who also designed the adjoining
bank building. The handsome brick structure features replicas of the original light

fixtures inside and out, as well as an airy "skylight room" in the main lobby. It is the only hotel designed by Wright that still stands.

Note also the nearby **Brick and Tile Building.** In the early years of the 20th century, immigrants from eastern and southern Europe poured into Mason City to work in local brick and tile factories, whose prosperity fueled downtown development.

Wright's legacy in Mason City is also seen at the **Stockman House** (www .stockmanhouse.org), which the architect designed in 1908. The building is a fine example of Prairie School style, with broad, overhanging eaves and a cantilever roof thrusting out over the entrance. Note the strong horizontal roof lines and base, which seem to anchor the house to the earth, a Prairie School touchstone. The living room is built around a central fireplace, allowing the interior rooms to flow together opposite the impressive veranda.

The home is open to visitors and has arts and crafts furnishings inside. In addition to the Stockman House, Mason City includes numerous other examples of Prairie School architecture in the surrounding Rock Glen and Rock Crest neighborhoods, with houses from several other architects included on a separate walking tour. Guides for this walking tour are available for purchase at the Mac-Nider Art Museum on Second Street Southeast.

The tour also goes to the **Meredith Willson Music Man Footbridge,** which spans Willow Creek on the southern end of downtown. Nearby, on the edge of

---

MEREDITH WILLSON'S MUSICAL GENIUS

A musical prodigy, Meredith Willson began his professional career at age 18 after graduating from high school in Mason City, playing piccolo for John Philip Sousa's band before moving on to the New York Philharmonic and Hollywood, and finally finding his greatest success on Broadway. In addition to *The Music Man,* he wrote other musicals and symphonic works, and composed popular songs that were recorded by some of the top singers of the day.

Willson returned frequently to Mason City, often attending the North Iowa Band Festival that is still held annually, and he is buried not far from his boyhood home.

THE PRAIRIE SCHOOL: UNIQUELY AMERICAN HOMES RISE IN THE MIDWEST

One of the most enduring expressions of simple Midwestern style, the Prairie School grew out of the work of Frank Lloyd Wright and other architects, many of whom practiced their art in Chicago beginning in the late 19th century. These designers sought to create a uniquely American form and style, with lots of horizontal lines meant to evoke the wide open prairie.

While the Prairie School saw a decline in the 1920s, its legacy lives on in the many solid, well-built houses throughout the Midwest and elsewhere. These homes were designed and built according to Prairie School principles, with plenty of open space inside and overhanging eaves and hipped roofs that allow them to blend unobtrusively into the landscape. Wright himself believed in "organic architecture," with a house appearing to sprout from the land, a feature particularly well suited to the still-open spaces of the rapidly settled Midwestern states.

downtown, is the **MacNider Art Museum** (www.macniderart.org), housed in an English Tudor home that once belonged to a top executive of the Mason City Brick and Tile Company. Its collection is a fine cross-section of American art, and includes pieces by Grant Wood, Thomas Hart Benton, Andy Warhol, Alexander Calder and other artists, as well as Native American pottery and many landscape paintings. There are also frequent changing exhibitions in all sorts of media.

The museum also has a treasure trove of pop culture history to rival the local attractions devoted to Willson's musical works: it contains the original marionettes from *The Sound of Music*. Instantly recognizable to fans of the movie from the "Lonely Goatherd" scene, the marionettes were the creation of Bil Baird, who grew up in Mason City and for some 60 years presented puppet shows all over the world, entertaining with his creations. Baird and his wife operated the marionettes during the Von Trapp children's famous puppet show.

The museum has many more marionettes and other puppets from Baird's long career, and they are a hoot; you might even be excused if you skip the fine art to marvel at the many whimsical characters, including some from *Winnie the Pooh* and other classic children's tales. Keep your eyes peeled for Charlemane the Lion, who once read the news with Walter Cronkite.

For those interested in history, the **Kinney Pioneer Museum** (http://visit masoncityiowa.com/html/museums.htm) has lots of displays dedicated to frontier life, including a blacksmith shop, log cabin, jail and one-room schoolhouse. Among its many artifacts is the world's last Colby automobile, a premium vehicle that was briefly produced in Mason City until 1914. Also check out the museum's Model N Ford, antique farm and dairy wagons, a 19th-century firehouse "pumper" and the re-created studio of a local radio station. Of course, there's also a Meredith Willson display—Mason City is proud of its most famous son!

More history can be seen in the **Minneapolis & St. Louis 457 Cannonball** (www.Friendsofthe457.org), an impressive steam train engine now permanently braked in Mason City's **East Park**. It has been beautifully restored to look as it did in its heyday in the 1940s. Tours of the engine are offered on weekends from May through October.

A more bucolic experience can be found at **Lime Creek Nature Center** (www.co.cerro-gordo.ia.us/Conservation/Conservation_NatureCenter_Info.cfm) north of Mason City just off US 65. It is surrounded by nearly 10 miles of trails winding through a conservation area atop a limestone bluff overlooking the Winnebago River. Most of the trails are less than a mile long, and it's a great spot for a casual hike through forest and grasslands, with several ponds and a lake along the paths. The center has many mounted animals and aquariums holding a variety of fish, amphibians and reptiles.

Adjacent to Mason City on the west side of I-35 is **Clear Lake,** a resort community that comes alive in the summer months with boaters and fun seekers who pack into its rental cottages and condominiums. There is also a charming downtown with its centerpiece **City Park,** which has an impressive white bandstand used for musical performances. The waters of the lake shimmer in the background adjacent to the city beach.

Also downtown is the **Clear Lake Arts Center** (www.clartscenter.com), with galleries that feature area artists in changing exhibits. A few blocks away is the **Clear Lake Fire Museum** (www.clearlakefire.com), a meticulously re-created early 20th-century firehouse where guests can see an 1883 hand-drawn hose cart and a 1924 pumper truck that was used for nearly 50 years. (It's still taken out regularly for a training spin.) Kids will love the chance to ring a fire truck's bell. Historical artifacts and photos line the walls.

Another downtown attraction is **Central Gardens of North Iowa** (www .central-gardens.org), a beautifully landscaped spot with a path meandering through a variety of themed gardens that include wildflowers, woods and wet-lands. Kinetic sculptures add to the tranquility. When complete, there will be nearly 24 different gardens for visitors to explore.

Besides its attractions, downtown is also nice for a stroll. A **historic walking tour,** with maps available at the downtown visitors center, takes participants past sights such as the **Clear Lake Public Library,** a Carnegie building which dates from 1916 and is still in use; the **Lake Theater** building, which once was home to an opera house; and several Queen Anne and Gothic structures. The tour also goes by the site of the annual **ice harvests** and a pair of **amusement piers** that hosted big bands in the 1920s.

Clear Lake is most famous for a sad moment in American pop music: on the night of February 2, 1959, after playing the Winter Dance Party at the town's **Surf Ballroom** (www.surfballroom.com), teen idols Buddy Holly, Richie Valens and J. P. "The Big Bopper" Richardson boarded a small plane to fly to a gig in Moorhead, Minnesota. The plane crashed soon after takeoff, killing the three young stars as well as the pilot.

The Surf commemorates "The Day the Music Died" with a tribute every February, with entertainers and fans coming from all over to play in the ballroom. The South Pacific–themed room has been going strong since 1933 and hosts shows by all kinds of acts throughout the year. There is lots of memorabilia on the walls, and a monument to Holly, Valens and Richardson sits out front. The crash site, on farmland north of Clear Lake, is marked with a monument and a large pair of horn-rimmed glasses like those worn by Holly.

Closer to I-35 is **Fort Custer Maze** (www.fortcustermaze.com), a simulated

The Surf Ballroom in Clear Lake

western fort with lookout towers and 2 miles of trails squeezed inside the wooden walls. Prizes are awarded for the fastest times through the maze. Close by is **Iowa Trolley Park** (http://iowatrolleypark.org), a place for railroad enthusiasts where visitors can ride on a speeder railway motor car or on a hand car powered by pushing a large lever up and down. The park also hopes to restore an old steam locomotive and a historic depot.

Heading west out of Clear Lake, one passes through the small community of Ventura, home of a large **wind farm**. The massive turbines soaring over the flat fields are quite a sight, especially on clear days. Each windmill blade is 80 feet long, and the towers holding them are secured to foundations using nearly 100 anchor bolts, each more than 30 feet long and weighing more than 160 pounds.

WHAT IS A HOBO?

It may seem common knowledge that hoboes are any of the restless vagabonds spotted along the roadways and railways of America. Not so. As the folks at the Hobo Museum will probably tell you, and the attendees at the annual Hobo Convention certainly will confirm, to earn the title "hobo" one must be a person who works and wanders. On the other hand, a "tramp" is one who dreams and wanders, and a "bum" neither works nor wanders. Take care to make this distinction; true hard-traveling hoboes are a proud breed.

Also in Ventura is **McIntosh Woods**, a state park with a mile-long nature trail and a pair of yurts available for overnight accommodation. The 16-foot circular tent structures have wooden frames, windows and a clear dome looking into the sky. There are also hardwood floors salvaged from the Iowa Capitol in Des Moines. Even if you're not staying overnight, it's a pleasant spot to stop for a picnic lunch.

Another 15 or so miles down the road brings you to the small, windswept town of **Britt**, whose claim to fame is the **Hobo Museum** (www.hobo.com/museum) located in an old movie theater on the town's main drag. A small collection of hobo artifacts and photos is housed inside, but true hobo fans will want to visit in mid-August for the annual **Hobo Convention**, which the town has been hosting for more than 100 years and which includes the crowning of the hobo king and queen. Sample some fry bread or mulligan stew while you meet some

The Hobo Museum, located in Britt

veteran hoboes and learn the "code of the road," which hoboes used to send messages to fellow wanderers along the tracks. There's also a **Hobo Cemetery** in town; look for the large cross made of railroad ties. Appropriately, the railroad tracks run right through Britt, passing just a couple blocks from the museum.

Britt is also home to the **Armstrong House Museum**, an 1896 Queen Anne with many lovely details that is home to the local historical society and is open for tours. The county fairgrounds are the site of **Hancock County Agriculture Museum & Pioneer Village**, which has a collection of restored farm machinery.

The next stop, to the west, is **Algona**, which deserves attention due to a display created at a World War II POW camp. Close to 10,000 German and Italian soldiers were imprisoned at the camp on the site of the present-day Algona Airport beginning in 1944. The Germans stayed significantly longer and spent some time working on area farms. Eventually, the prisoners came up with the idea of constructing a large **nativity scene** (www.pwcamp.algona.org/nativity.html), which they did, with half-life-sized figures. It turned into quite an impressive scene, with 60 figures, including some 30 sheep, a stream that flowed into a small lake and a miniature Bethlehem in the background. The prisoners paid for all the materials used to construct the scene.

The nativity scene is now exhibited at the local fairgrounds, while a small museum downtown tells the story of the camp and the men who spent time there. Also in town is the **Kossuth Museum,** with three floors of period items arranged in historical dioramas depicting domestic life in different historical eras. Algona is also known for its annual **Band Day**, which draws marching bands from Iowa and Minnesota to compete for prizes.

Loop to the west and south on US 18 and IA 15, respectively, to reach the small town of **West Bend**, where a massive pile of sculpted rock takes up a whole city block. The **Grotto of the Redemption** (www.westbendgrotto.com) was the creation of an immigrant Roman Catholic priest who oversaw its construction in the early 20th century as a tribute to the Virgin Mary. Thousands of precious stones, including malachite, jasper, amethyst and quartz decorate the concrete walls and arches of the grotto, the largest in the world, as do pieces of petrified wood, stalactites, stalagmites and other materials. Statues stand along the paths and on the walls, with religious scenes that include Adam and Eve being driven from the Garden of Eden, the Sermon on the Mount and the Stations of the Cross. There's also a museum with displays about the building of the grotto. Chimes play on an outdoor sound system, and floodlights illuminate the grotto at night.

Head east on a farm road just south of West Bend and then turn south on US 169, which shoots straight through wide open fields for nearly 35 miles to **Fort Dodge**, a manufacturing and transportation center established in 1850 as a frontier military post at the confluence of the Des Moines River and Lizard Creek. Railroads followed not long after, as did the discovery of significant reserves of gypsum, which plays an important role in the local economy to this day.

West Bend's Grotto of the Redemption

Fort Museum & Frontier Village, Fort Dodge

The **Fort Museum & Frontier Village** (www.fortmuseum.com) commemorates those earlier days with a replica fort, based not on the original Fort Dodge but on a later stockade, with a whole street of replica historic buildings, including a school, general store, cabinet shop and livery. A nearby stockade houses exhibits of Native American, pioneer and military artifacts.

At the back of the stockade, in a small, separate pavilion, is a replica of the **Cardiff Giant,** one of the greatest hoaxes in American history. The original giant, measuring more than 10 feet tall, was quarried out of a local gypsum mine before being "discovered" on a New York farm and exhibited as a real-life fossilized giant. It soon took on a life of its own, with impresario P. T. Barnum presenting his own copy of the original (fake) giant.

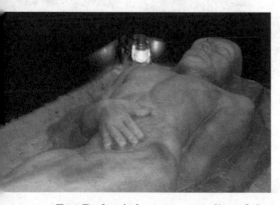

Today, the original Cardiff Giant is in the Farmer's Museum in Cooperstown, New York. Thus, the giant in Fort Dodge is a copy of a copy of a fake! (Don't think about that one too much.) Displays around the giant tell the improbable yet true story behind this all-American phenomenon and its fascinating history.

Fort Dodge is home to a replica of the Cardiff Giant

Another side of local history is seen at the **Webster County Museum** in the nearby town of Otho, with all sorts of domestic items as well as military, mining and railroad artifacts. The **Oak Hill Historic District**, south of downtown, has many impressive homes built between the Civil War and World War I. The neighborhood includes the **Blanden Memorial Art Museum** (www.blanden.org), the oldest art museum in Iowa. It has a comprehensive collection of modern art as well as a selection of other works and changing exhibitions.

Other attractions in Fort Dodge include **Oleson Park Zoo** (www.fdoleson parkzoo.bravehost.com), located in the city's largest park. The zoo has both Iowa native species and exotic specimens from around the world, including such interesting creatures as Nigerian dwarf goats, mute swans and the muntjac deer, the smallest deer in the world. Nature options include **Brushy Creek State Recreation Area** and **John F. Kennedy Memorial Park**, which is popular for fishing and hiking.

From Fort Dodge, head east along the third leg of this route. About 15 miles before reaching I-35, you'll come to **Webster City**, where you can stop off and see the **Bonebright Museum Complex**, which tells the history of Hamilton County through restored buildings, including pioneer cabins and a historic schoolhouse, courthouse and train depot.

Moving along through Hamilton County, you may want to meander onto a country road to take a look at some of the **barn quilts** that decorate farms throughout the county. Just after crossing the interstate, take side roads to the small community of **Williams**, where you can check out an impressive display of old cars at the **Hemken Collection** (www.the-hemken-collection.org). Some 65 autos are here, including several convertibles from the 1940s. Packards, Nashes and Hudsons are among the makes represented, and there's also a Stutz and a Rolls-Royce.

The next stop will probably last a little longer: continue heading east to **Iowa Falls**. A postcard-perfect small town perched on bluffs overlooking the Iowa River, Iowa Falls prospered after three railroads intersected here in the late 1800s. The town, with a population of about 5,000, managed to support a magnificent opera house, which still stands today. Several other historic structures are located downtown, including the **Princess Café,** an art deco marvel that dates to the 1930s, and a band shell located in the town's public square. The **Carnegie Ellsworth Building** is the former public library that now serves as an art gallery

The restored railroad depot in Dows now serves as a visitors center.

and visitors center. Its staff is very helpful in providing information on local attractions and events.

The **Caulkins Nature Area and Interpretive Center** (www.hardincounty conservation.com), also in Iowa Falls, features woodland, wetland and reconstructed native prairie on the Iowa River, as well as a small museum devoted to area wildlife, with displays on pheasants, raptors, waterfowl, amphibians, reptiles and other animals.

A side trip takes you south and east from Iowa Falls to **Eldora,** home to the **Hardin County Farm Museum** (www.eldoraiowa.com/farmmuseum.asp). Housed in a large white barn and open by appointment, it chronicles a century of farming from the mid-1800s to the mid-1900s. Displays include video presentations on farm life and collections of early farm equipment in the barn and outlying machine sheds. There's also a restored one-room schoolhouse with desks and other artifacts. The museum hosts events such as tractor pulls, threshing days and other displays of farming techniques.

Another side trip from Iowa Falls takes you 15 miles or so to **Ackley**, another tiny town with just as much to see. The **Ackley Heritage Center** (www.ackley heritagecenter.com) includes a museum with displays on early businesses in Ackley and other artifacts. Better yet, there's an old-fashioned soda fountain where you can savor all sorts of ice cream treats. After satisfying your sweet tooth, head on over to the **Settlement of the Prairie Site**, where several historic buildings include a school, windmill and barn along with a large prairie garden and a restored pioneer house.

From Ackley or Iowa Falls you can head west to yet another small hamlet, **Dows**, where the restored **depot**, which serves as a visitors center, sits in the shadow of grain elevators along the railroad tracks.

The depot is part of the **Dows Historic District** (www.dowsiowa.com), which also includes the **Quasdorf Museum**, where blacksmithing demonstrations are held in a historic machine shop; the **Dows Mercantile Store**, where guests can peruse antiques, folk art and other gifts or take a break in the ice cream parlor; a one-room school and a prairie home.

Next, meander over to **Clarion**, where the **4-H Schoolhouse Museum** details the history of the organization known to every farm child, with displays of rare 4-H collectibles and plenty of historic photographs. The **Heartland Museum** (www.heartlandmuseum.org) is a large structure with an impressive display of tractors and farm equipment, as well as farm toys and re-creations of some of the area's old downtowns.

Shooting back east, you'll cross I-35 yet again on your way to **Hampton**. Here, another blast from the past awaits at the **Franklin County Historical Museum**, where the usual exhibits are accompanied by unique items such as prehistoric fossils. Displays on several prominent local residents are also featured. The **REA Power Plant Museum** gives visitors a look at rural electrification, which changed farm life forever in the 1930s. Tours are available by appointment.

From Hampton it's a straight shot north back to Mason City. Before you zoom down the home stretch, however, cut over to **Rockford** to take a look at **Fossil & Prairie Park Preserve** (www.fossilcenter.com), a place where kids (and adults) can look for their own fossils by digging in a small quarry. The preserve also has an interpretive center and trails through the prairie landscape.

IN THE AREA

ACCOMMODATIONS

In addition to these lodgings, there are chain motels at the exits that line I-35, especially around Mason City.

Bed & Breakfast of Cabin Cove, 820 Indiana Avenue, Iowa Falls. Call 641-648-9571. On a quiet residential street overlooking the Iowa River, this cozy two-bedroom cabin has knotty pine walls and a gas fireplace that's perfect to curl up in front of with a good book. Or step outside for a nice view of the river. It's no rustic retreat: there's central air-conditioning and a fully equipped kitchen. Guests get a free ride on the *Scenic City Empress* as part of their stay. Moderate. Website: www.bbcabincove.com.

Decker House Bed & Breakfast, 119 Second Street Southeast, Mason City. Call 641-423-4700. This restored colonnaded mansion is within walking distance of downtown and Mason City's Meredith Willson-themed attractions. Six guest rooms are cool and airy, with antique furniture and private baths. The on-site **Sour Grapes Bistro** serves lovely lunches. Moderate to Medium. Website: www.masoncityia.com/deckerhouse.

Dickson's Landing, 1401 Main Avenue, Clear Lake. Call 641-357-8015 or 641-529-2016. A comfortable carriage house with first-rate service make this an excellent option for a weekend of resting and recharging.

The open living area includes a king-sized bed, kitchenette and dining area, with breakfast delivered to your room from the main house. A sleeping loft, reached by ladder, accommodates additional guests. It's a short walk to downtown and the lakefront. Website: www.dicksonslanding.com.

Larch Pine Inn, 401 North Third Street, Clear Lake. Call 641-357-0345. Set back on a large wooded lot, this historic Victorian home is great for a lakeside getaway, with easy access for boating, fishing and swimming. Three guest rooms have a choice of beds and private baths with clawfoot tubs. Relax on the screened porch and listen to the rippling lake waters. If you need even more of a getaway, the carriage house includes a kitchen, living room and second-level deck. Moderate (guest rooms) to Medium (carriage house). Website: www.larchpine inn.com.

Park Inn Hotel, 15 West State Street, Mason City. Call 641-422-0015 or 1-800-659-2220. A true gem, this last remaining hotel designed by Frank Lloyd Wright reopened in 2011 after an extensive renovation. The intimate boutique hotel has a lobby that is a high-ceilinged, sky-lit marvel, with art glass allowing light to tastefully stream into the open space. Guest rooms are artfully detailed, with fixtures that are replicas of some of Wright's own designs, and come equipped with modern amenities like high-definition televisions and high-speed Internet. Check out the clubby billiards room and bar for a taste of classy elegance. The hotel overlooks Central Park and is conveniently located for a stroll around the historic downtown or over to Wright's famous Stockman House. Moderate. Website: www.historicparkinn.com.

River's Bend Bed & Breakfast, 635 Park Avenue, Iowa Falls. Call 641-648-2828. An elegant, white-columned Greek Revival house overlooking the Iowa River, with high ceilings and intricate woodwork inside. Guest rooms have antique beds, private baths and plenty of light. It's an easy walk to Iowa Falls' historic downtown, and a hearty breakfast gets you fueled up for the day. Moderate. Website: www .iafalls.com/riversbendbandb.htm.

Valkommen House, 3219 370th Street, Stratford. Call 515-838-2440. Get in touch with Iowa's Scandinavian roots at this cozy guest house that sleeps up to eight guests. The simple wood-frame house was originally the home of a Swedish farm family. Both a big country breakfast and a Swedish breakfast are available. Inexpensive to Moderate.

DINING

Birdsall's Ice Cream, 518 North Federal Avenue, Mason City. Call 641-423-5365. This old-school ice cream parlor, easily recognized by its red and white decor, has been dishing out sweet homemade goodness since 1931. Don't expect gourmet flavors or fancy creations: this is the place for the basics like peppermint or chocolate and a simply divine hot fudge sundae. Crowds line up for the fresh peach ice cream in summer, and you may have to wait for a spot at the stools along the Formica counter inside the narrow interior. Inexpensive.

Camp David, 119 Main Street, Iowa Falls. Call 641-648-3221. An expansive view of the Iowa River is one of the attractions at this downtown eatery. The other is the menu, with ample portions of steaks, seafood and other all-American favorites, along with some downright excellent barbecue. It's tough to decide among the perfectly smoked chicken and ribs; that's why they offer a combo! Fish runs the gamut from Pacific-style mahimahi and tilapia tacos to blackened Cajun crab and shrimp. There are even a few pasta dishes. Daily drink specials from the bar add to the fun atmosphere. Moderate to Medium. Website: www.campdavid restaurant.com.

Cellar Restaurant & Lounge, 116 Kenyon Road (junction of US 20 and US 169), Fort Dodge. Call 515-576-2290. Adjoining the Budget Host motel, this is the place to go in Fort Dodge for steaks and seafood, with tender and tasty New York strip and rib eye among the highlights. Fish offerings are a tempting selection of salmon, orange roughy, shrimp, mahimahi and other choices. Good barbecued ribs as well. Prime rib on Friday and Saturday nights, and some salad and pasta choices for lighter eaters. Moderate to Medium.

Northwestern Steakhouse, 304 16th Street Northwest, Mason City. Call 641-423-5075. It's worth making the trek out to this inconspicuous brick building next to a large city park in a residential neighborhood: the slightly cramped restaurant serves excellent steaks, broiled to perfection and with an incredible flavor. It's a family-run business, established in 1920 by Greek immigrants to feed workers at a local cement plant. Lamb chops and Greek chicken are mouth-wateringly good as well, and there's a smaller-portion steak for the kids. Full bar. Moderate to Medium. Website: www .northwesternsteakhouse.com.

PM Park, 15297 Raney Drive, Clear Lake. Call 641-357-1991. Located just steps from the lake in a residential area a few miles from downtown, this restaurant has the feeling of a faded yet charming beach shed—the type of place where they don't mind if you come in wearing swim trunks and no shoes. Grab a stool at the counter or sit at one of the tables looking out over the lake. The menu is basic short-order fare, with a massive burger and pork tenderloin among the offerings. On summer weekends, the lawn outside heats up with a tiki bar pouring sweet, strong concoctions and a vibe that may remind you of Cancun or the Caribbean. If you stay all night, you can grab a greasy, delicious breakfast. Party on! Inexpensive. Website: www.pmpark.net /Home_Page.html.

Ralph's Garden Café, 5 South Federal Avenue, Mason City. Call 641-422-9902. Good, fresh comfort food in a modest downtown storefront. Dinner is served Thursday through Sunday and includes simple yet tasty preparations of steak, seafood and chicken. Lunch is served all week, with soups, sandwiches and a "daily special" entrée. Ralph's is also a nice spot for a good, cheap breakfast before you do some sight-seeing. Moderate. Website: www.ralphsgarden cafe.com.

RECREATION AND ENTERTAINMENT

I-35 Speedway, 3700 Fourth Street, Mason City. Call 641-424-6515. This half-mile dirt track at the North Iowa Fairgrounds features a variety of races from April through September. Website: www.i-35speedway.com.

Lady of the Lake, 1330 Buddy Holly Place, Clear Lake. Call 641-357-2243. Take a nostalgic cruise on this authentic paddle-wheeler that plies the waters of Clear Lake. The 90-minute cruise may include live entertainment. Website: www.crusieclearlake .com.

Mineral City Speedway, 2298 South River Road, Fort Dodge. Call 515-574-RACE. Motorsports fans will find races here on Friday nights, with stock cars, modifieds and other fast cars burning rubber on the track. Monster trucks occasionally hit the dirt, too. Website: www.fdspeed.com.

Rock-N-Row Adventures, 23539 First Street, Eldora. Call 641-858-5516 or 641-751-3418. Ever been tubing before? If not, this is the way to do it, with large inner tubes provided so you can float down the Iowa River. On hot days, huge clusters of tubes go floating past, many with beer cans and coolers in tow. Just lay back, look up at the sunny skies and feel the cool water. It's a relaxing way to spend a lazy summer afternoon. Website: www.rock-n-row-adventures .com.

Scenic City Empress, 1113 Union Street, Iowa Falls. Call 641-648-9517 or 1-800-873-1936. Glide down the Iowa River on a double-decker pontoon boat. Pass by striking limestone bluffs and bucolic countryside while the boat captain relates facts about local history and ecology. Cruises last about 90 minutes. Website: www.ia falls.com/empress_new/home.html.

OTHER CONTACTS

Visit Mason City, 2021 Fourth Street Southwest, Mason City, 50401. Call 641-422-1663 or 1-800-423-5724. Website: www.visitmasoncityiowa .com.

Clear Lake Area Chamber of Commerce, 205 Main Avenue, Clear Lake, 50428. Call 641-357-2159 or 1-800-285-5338. Website: www.clearlake iowa.com.

Kossuth County Economic Development Corporation, 105 North Hall Street, Algona, 50511. Call 515-295-7979. Website: www.kossuth-edc.com.

Fort Dodge Area Chamber of Commerce, 1406 Central Avenue, Box T, Fort Dodge, 50501. Call 515-955-5500. Website: www.fortdodgechamber .com.

Iowa Falls Area Development Corporation, 520 Rocksylvania Avenue, Iowa Falls, 50126. Call 641-648-5604 or 1-877-648-5549. Website: www .iowafallsdevelopment.com.

Wright County Tourism, 115 North Main Street, Clarion, 50525. Call 515-532-6422. Website: www.wrightcounty .org.

Hampton Area Chamber of Commerce and Franklin County Tourism, 5 First Street Southwest, Hampton, 50441. Call 641-456-8531. Website: www.hamptoniowa.org.

11 Central Iowa:
HEART OF THE HAWKEYE STATE

Estimated length: About 350 miles, with a circular route that corkscrews through smaller cities around Des Moines before arriving back in the state capital.

Estimated time: The entire trip, including the Des Moines sites, deserves at the very least a long weekend. However, you can also break the route up into shorter trips, using Des Moines as a base to explore surrounding communities of your choosing.

Getting there: Des Moines is conveniently located at the intersection of I-35 and I-80, and many other main highways converge on the capital, which makes it easy to hop from town to town and take in many attractions.

Highlights: A first-rate model train display in Colfax. Interesting restaurants and historic buildings in Marshalltown. An old-fashioned carousel in Story City. Interesting shopping in the charming college town of Ames. A jaw-dropping railroad trestle in Boone. The hot-air ballooning mecca of Indianola. Authentic Dutch scenery and sweet treats in Pella. A plethora of attractions in Des Moines, including an impressive state capitol tour, neat art, history and science museums, historic homes, a scenic downtown riverfront and a wide choice of dining options.

Around the state capital of Des Moines, which itself has plenty to see and do, are many undiscovered treasures for the visitor. Start off with one of the state's true gems: **Trainland** (www.trainlandusa.com), located in **Colfax**, about 20 miles east of Des Moines and just off I-80. You may think you've seen miniature train displays, but this one just about tops them all: Red Atwood has spent more than 35 years perfecting his pride and joy, which includes 4,000 feet of track

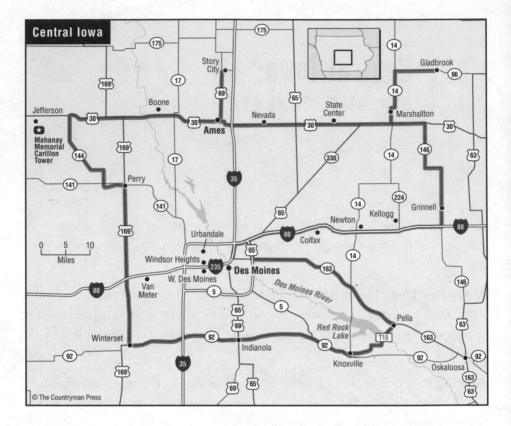

covering an area the size of two average homes. There are 20 to 25 trains run-ning at all times through three scenic areas representing different eras in Amer-ican history: frontier, steam and diesel.

Features along the tracks include landmarks Mount Rushmore, Devils Tower and the Statue of Liberty, as well as details like western gunfighters, a circus in the desert and a moonshine still. There are operating oil wells, a ski lift, a coal mine and a drive-in movie. Train whistles echo from a large sound system. The trains themselves include collectibles and rare models; look for the pink train marketed to girls by Lionel in the 1950s. You could spend hours just taking it all in. Red also sells keepsakes from an old train car adjoining the museum. He's open from Memorial Day through Labor Day.

After taking in Red's shrine to railroading, drive east to the nearby town of **Newton,** home of the **Iowa Speedway,** a stop for serious NASCAR fans. It's also a good place to stop for a quick meal or snack. Among Newton's other attractions is the **Jasper County Courthouse,** a neoclassical building with stained-glass windows in its dome, hand-painted murals and ceramic tiles laid in mosaic patterns.

The **Jasper County Historical Museum** (www.jaspercountymuseum.net), located close to I-80, has displays detailing the area's farming and mining heritage, as well as a 40-foot-long bas relief sculpture depicting the history of the county. The **Newton Arboretum and Botanical Gardens** has a walking path that weaves past native trees and plants.

Newton is perhaps most famous for being the home of **Maytag Dairy Farms** (www.maytagdairyfarms.com), which produces a famous blue cheese enjoyed on salads and burgers across Iowa. The company office sits on the edge of town in a squat building surrounded by rolling fields, home to the cows that are its lifeblood and the nearby cheese plant. A short video presents the history of the company, and guests can purchase some blue cheese of their own at the farm's cheese shop (they give free samples, too).

Just a few miles away is the tiny community of **Kellogg,** site of one of the more complete and unusual roadside attractions: eight restored historical buildings, which together compose the town's historical museum, sit on the streets of

The Newton Arboretum and Botanical Gardens

Maytag Farms, Newton

a downtown whose glory days are far in the past, ending when the railroad left. The buildings are full of artifacts, especially the old hotel, which serves as the main building of the "museum." There's also a room devoted to nativity scenes amid all the local history. Other buildings include a schoolhouse, church, bank and machine shed.

Moving on down the road brings you to **Grinnell,** which has a few things worth a look. On the campus of **Grinnell College** is the **Faulconer Gallery** (www.grinnell.edu/faulconergallery), a large, open space that displays changing exhibits by artists working in a variety of media, as well as works from the gallery's collection.

In town, you might want to stop to look at **Merchants National Bank** (www.grinnelliowa.gov/SullivanBank/History.html), whose striking exterior designed by Louis Sullivan is a fine example of "jewel box" design. Another piece of architectural history can be seen in the **Ricker House** (http://web.grinnell.edu/faulconergallery/rickerhouse), a design of the acclaimed Prairie School of the early 20th century. Grinnell's **train depot** was refurbished in 1996 and evokes the earlier age of railroading.

Turning north, head through the cornfields to **Marshalltown,** one of the larger cities in central Iowa. You can see art all around town, beginning at the **Impressionist Gallery,** located in the lobby of the city's **Convention & Visitors Bureau.** Numerous works are on display, including paintings by Degas, Matisse and Mary Cassatt. There are also sculptures scattered about the grounds, including an impressive bronze piece in the reflecting pool just outside the building's front entrance.

Next, move on to the **Ray Frederick Gallery** on the campus of Marshalltown Community College, which features regional and student artists. Outside on the campus grounds is *Seven Cubes,* a series of steel cubes that fits in with the college's architecture and design.

A handful of historic buildings line Main Street in downtown Marshalltown, including the **Marshall County Courthouse**, a striking example of Italian Renaissance style that sets it apart from other courthouses. The resemblance to the Iowa Capitol is not a coincidence; both buildings have the same architect. A statue of Marshalltown's founding father stands outside the courthouse, and tours are available by appointment.

Farther down Main Street is the **Orpheum Theater Center** (www.orpheum theatercenter.com), which retains a faded marquee, and the **Tallcorn Towers**, a former hotel that dates to the 1920s. Main Street hosts a popular **farmers' market** on Thursday nights from June through September. The **Glick-Sower Heritage Homestead** (www.marshallhistory.org) and the **Binford House** are historic homes with period furnishings; tours are available by appointment.

Marshalltown is also a nice place to experience the great outdoors: the **Big Treehouse** (www.bigtreehouse.net/treehouse.html) towers over Shady Oaks Campground, a historic sight in its own right along the old Lincoln Highway. The treehouse has 12 levels of platforms covering some 5,000 square feet. It's wired for electricity and includes a refrigerator, microwave and other modern essentials. Whimsical figures peek out around the platforms. From the top there's a splendid view of the surrounding countryside; kids will love the long climb.

More natural bliss is found at **Appleberry Farm** (www.appleberryfarm.com), a pick-your-own orchard that is particularly pleasant in the fall, when a pumpkin patch joins the apple trees. An old-fashioned country store sells jams and jellies as well as gift items.

A side trip to the northeast takes you to a most interesting attraction in the rural town of **Gladbrook. Matchstick Marvels** (www.matchstickmarvels.com), like Trainland and the Big Treehouse, is one man's hobby writ large, but in this case the owner's passion, when he's not working as a career counselor at a nearby community college, is creating large, detailed models entirely out of matchsticks. He's done everything from the U.S. Capitol to the space shuttle *Challenger* to a 13-foot-long model of the battleship USS *Iowa*. The larger pieces involve tens or even hundreds of thousands of matchsticks and take hundreds of hours to complete.

Swinging back through Marshalltown, head due west through the small community of **State Center**, the geographic heart of Iowa and home to **Watson's Grocery Store Museum**, a restored dry goods merchant from the early 1900s. State

THE LINCOLN HIGHWAY

While perhaps not as well known as Route 66, the Lincoln Highway played just as vital and colorful a role in bringing Americans across the great breadth of the United States.

The first coast-to-coast road in the U.S., the Lincoln Highway was built in 1915 to connect New York with San Francisco. The two-lane road stretched for more than 3,000 miles across 12 states, passing through some of the more evocative landscapes in the west, including a stretch in Nevada known as "the loneliest road in America."

Lincoln Highway Bridge in Tama   The Lincoln Cafe in Belle Plaine

The highway was easily recognizable due to its distinctive red, white and blue signs as well as the busts of Abraham Lincoln that were placed at 1-mile increments along the road; virtually all have disappeared since the highway was decommissioned in the late 1920s and replaced by US 30, which follows much of the original route.

Iowa has some of the best reminders of the Lincoln Highway, especially in two small towns between Marshalltown and Cedar Rapids. Tama has a bridge on the east end of town that spells out the words "Lincoln Highway," while Belle Plaine is home to both George's Filling Station, a closed gas station that retains its signage from an earlier age, and the Lincoln Cafe, one of many identically named eateries that once lined the old road.

Center is also known as the "Rose Capital of Iowa," and there is an annual parade and rose festival in the town's rose garden.

Down the road is Nevada, where the historical society maintains historic homes (www.nevadaiowahistory.org/properties.html), including the Dyer Dowell Victorian House and Evergreen Lane/Briggs Terrace, which has a barn and 19th-century schoolhouse and is home to the local historical museum. Nevada also hosts Lincoln Highway Days, an annual festival named after the historic transcontinental road.

Just on the other side of I-35 sits the lively college town of Ames, home to Iowa State University, a rival to the University of Iowa for statewide sports bragging rights. Ames also has a pleasant downtown with some nice shops and restaurants along Main Street and surrounding blocks. The university campus is home to several museums (www.museums.iastate.edu), including the Brunnier Art Museum, the Christian Petersen Art Museum, the Farm House Museum, and the Anderson Sculpture Garden. Information on campus museums can be picked up in the Scheman Building.

A more unusual display can be seen at the ISU Insect Zoo (www.ent.iastate .edu/insectzoo) in the university's entomology department, which features a collection of hundreds of bugs that guides enthusiastically show off. Cockroaches, beetles, millipedes and other crawly creatures get up close and personal with visitors. Tours must be arranged in advance. In the past, there has also been a festival of horror films featuring insects; it's not clear if it will resume.

Attractions in Ames also include Reiman Gardens (www.reiamangardens .com), a sprawling botanical wonderland with paths winding around a central lake. Displays include a rose garden and a conservatory with rare plants. The Iowa Arboretum (www.iowarboretum.org) in nearby Madrid is also worth the trip for nature lovers, with collections of hostas, herbs, daylilies, ornamental grasses and many species of trees.

From Ames, take a jog north to Story City (www.storycity.net). One of rural Iowa's better preserved towns, it has a restored antique carousel in North Park. Open from Memorial Day through Labor Day, its hand-carved wooden figures include pigs, dogs, chariots and of course horses, which whirl to the sounds of an old calliope.

A cluster of historical sites in Story City include the Bartlett Museum, the Sheldall Country Schoolhouse and the Brick Museum, all with lots of artifacts on display. The **Story Theatre/Grand Opera House** is the oldest continuously operating theater in Iowa. It shows movies as well as live performances. Story City's **Prairie Park** has trails weaving through a landscape studded with native plants. In June, the town celebrates **Scandinavian Days** to honor its Nordic heritage.

Head back to Ames and then turn west for the short drive to **Boone**. A typical small Iowa town, it is also the site of an incredible story: On the night of July 6, 1881, Kate Shelley, a 15-year-old local farm girl, heard a locomotive crash when a train trestle collapsed into Honey Creek following heavy rains and flooding. After checking on the locomotive's crew, she headed toward the railroad station in nearby Moingona to warn another approaching train, making the trip the only way she could: by crawling first across the damaged trestle and then across a nearly 700-foot bridge high over the Des Moines River in pitch darkness, as a thunderstorm raged around her and the train moved toward the bridge. After crossing, she reached the station, which sounded an alarm, and the train stopped before reaching the trestle.

A new bridge was built many years later a few miles northwest of Boone and named the **Kate Shelley High Bridge.** It's the longest double-track train trestle in the world, stretching 2,685 feet and standing an eye-popping 185 feet above the earth below. More than 60 trains cross it each day. The **Kate Shelley Railroad Museum** is in the same depot in **Moingona** where the local heroine arrived breathless with her warning. Her story is also told at the **Boone County Historical Center** (www.boonecountyhistory.org), housed in the town's original Masonic Temple; it includes other displays on local history as well.

To get a sense of what Shelley faced, take a ride on the **Boone & Scenic Valley Railroad** (www.bsvrr.com), which operates daily excursion trains that roll over the Bass Point Creek High Bridge, which stands a mere 156 feet tall. The passenger trains go to Fraser, site of coal mining beginning in the late 1800s, before heading back to Boone. There's also a railroad museum in the train's depot.

There's more history—and a lot of it—at the **Mamie Doud Eisenhower Birthplace** (http://mamiesbirthplace.homestead.com). Tons of memorabilia related to the former first lady and Boone native is displayed, including family heirlooms and exhibits related to the Eisenhowers, who visited Boone during and after Ike's presidency.

From Boone you swing west and then south, perhaps stopping off in **Jeffer-**

son for a look at the 170-foot **Mahanay Bell Tower** that sits on the courthouse lawn, before heading to **Perry.** This charming little community out past the edge of Des Moines's suburban development is dominated by the **Hotel Pattee,** which takes up an entire block of downtown. Splendidly restored inside and out, the impressive redbrick structure is worth popping into just for a look at the elegant lobby. Across the street is the **Carnegie Library Museum** (www.perryia.org /thingstodo.html) with exhibits on local history.

Moving south through Dallas County, the small town of **Van Meter** has a must-see for baseball fans: the **Bob Feller Museum** (www.bobfellermuseum .org). It's easy to spot, with the Hall of Fame pitcher's visage grinning from the side of the modest brick building. Inside are mementos from the playing days of the Cleveland Indians ace known as "Rapid Robert," who developed his skills on a nearby farm and joined the major leagues at age 17. In a career he stepped away from to serve in the Navy during World War II, Feller threw three no-hitters and became legendary for his devastating "heat," or fastball, which helped him lead the American League in strikeouts in seven seasons.

Just south of Van Meter, the road crosses into **Madison County,** setting for the famous novel *The Bridges of Madison County,* a story that became even more popular after it was adapted into a movie starring Clint Eastwood and Meryl Streep. Many sights from the movie are still standing in both the town of **Winterset** and in the surrounding countryside, where most of the famous **covered bridges** are located; a brochure and map are available from the Madison County Chamber of Commerce on Winterset's town square. (If you haven't seen the movie, it plays continuously on a monitor in the chamber.) The town's **covered bridge festival** is held every October.

Winterset's other claim to fame is the fact that it is the birthplace and childhood home of **John Wayne** (www.johnwaynebirthplace.org). The legendary actor was born in a very modest four-room home that has been restored to its original appearance. Wayne lived here until his father moved the family to California a few years later. The house contains artifacts related to Wayne's life and career. A few blocks away, "The Duke" is commemorated with a larger-than-life-sized bronze statue.

Also worth a visit is the **Madison County Historical Complex** (www.madison countyhistoricalsociety.com), which features numerous structures from the area's past, including a stone barn, log school, general store, blacksmith shop and rail-

A bronze statue of John Wayne in Winterset, the legendary actor's birthplace

road depot. There's also a park in town dedicated to famous scientist **George Washington Carver,** who lived in Winterset during some of the several years he spent in Iowa, where he first began studying and performing agricultural research. Nearby **Pammel State Park** (www.madisoncountyparks.org), named after one of Carver's mentors who also helped found the Iowa State Parks system, is notable for a unique limestone ridge called the Devil's Backbone, as well as Iowa's only highway tunnel, which leads into the park and floods during heavy rains.

The route now swings east and heads to **Indianola.** This somewhat nondescript town is nirvana for hot-air balloonists, with the **National Balloon Museum** (www.nationalballoonmuseum .com) rising in a field just off the main north-south road. Multiple displays cover everything from the history of ballooning to technical aspects of hot-air balloons to famous balloonists. In the children's area, young visitors can pilot a balloon on a simulator.

Just as impressive is the **National Balloon Classic** (www.nationalballoon classic.com), held in a nearby field every summer, when enthusiasts descend through the skies to Indianola. Competitive ballooning events are held and balloon rides are available. If you can't make it to town for the festival, you may still be able to spot a cluster of balloons soaring over the wide-open fields on a Saturday afternoon during a football game at nearby Simpson College.

From one enthusiastic subculture to another, the trip next leads east to **Knoxville,** home of the **Knoxville Raceway** (www.knoxvilleraceway.com), self-proclaimed "Sprint Car Capital of the World." The mighty midget racers, with their distinctive "wing" shadowing the car's body and engine, zoom down the dirt track in front of thousands of enthusiastic spectators, culminating every August at the **Knoxville Nationals.** The on-site **National Sprint Car Hall of Fame** (http://sprintcarhof.com) has some retired race cars as well as displays on the history and heroes of this superfast sport.

Knoxville is also the gateway to **Lake Red Rock** (www2.mvr.usace.army.mil /RedRock), Iowa's preeminent outdoor playground, with trails and boat ramps scattered around the dammed reservoir. There's also a bald eagle refuge visible from a bridge near the dam. Nearby **Cordova Park** has a 100-foot-plus observation tower with views of the lake and surrounding countryside.

On the home stretch to Des Moines, there is one more stop you really must make: **Pella,** an authentic Dutch village with old-world charm on display at **Pella Historical Village** (www.pellatuliptime.com/historical-village), a complex of about 20 buildings depicting pioneer life in the town. The village stands in the shadow of the **Vermeer Windmill** (www.pellatuliptime.com/historical-village /vermeer-mill), which rises nearly 125 feet over downtown. It was built in Holland and is the tallest working windmill in the U.S. Also check out the many tulips growing on the grounds, a small portion of the tens of thousands of the colorful bulbs that bloom every spring all over town. Note that Pella is also a fairly conservative community, and many businesses shut down on Sunday. Plan your visit accordingly.

Pella's story is told in the **Klokkenspel,** a large cuckoo clock whose stage curtain opens several times a day to reveal animatronic figures that depict scenes in the life of the village. Pella's founder, Dominic Scholte, who in 1847 led Dutch religious refugees to the frozen prairie of Iowa, baptizes a child. His wife sheds tears after her plates fall and break. A man carves wooden shoes while another heaves milk pails. Two children hold out a handful of tulips. There are plenty of other figures, most of which are engaged in some action that reflects the town's Dutch heritage. It all happens to the bells of a large carillon.

Among the bustle of the Klokkenspel show, you may notice a man holding a rifle. That's not a pioneer hunter, it's **Wyatt Earp,** who spent part of his childhood in Pella before moving west and becoming a legendary lawman. His boyhood home in Pella, located in the town's historical village, is open to visitors.

Further information about Scholte and Pella's early days can be found at the **Scholte House** (www.pellatuliptime.com/scholte-house) on the town's main drag opposite the main square. The **Pella Opera House** (www.pellaoperahouse.org) is another historical site, complete with stained-glass windows and tin ceilings.

After all this wandering, you're finally ready to take in the sights and sounds of Iowa's capital city. **Des Moines** became the state's second capital in 1857, 11 years after statehood. The capital was figuratively and literally moved from Iowa City, with furniture and safes full of records dragged across frozen terrain and brought to the hilltop spot on the east bank of the Des Moines River, where the capitol dome would rise nearly 15 years later over a rapidly growing city.

The **Iowa State Capitol** (www.legis.state.ia.us/Pubinfo/Tour) is one of the more striking state capitol buildings in the United States. Its dome stands 275 feet at its apex. Gilded in gold leaf, the white marble capitol can be seen throughout downtown and the central part of the city. Guided tours point out the many works of art inside, including a huge mural depicting pioneer settlers.

Tours also visit the old Supreme Court Chamber, the House and Senate Chambers, the Governor's Office and the law library, which has an intricate series of staircases winding through its narrow stacks and a fabulous view across the river to downtown. Perhaps most impressive is the view inside the dome, across which is stretched a large banner of a bald eagle over an American flag.

From other parts of the capitol you can look out and see the copper dome of the Supreme Court building to the south, across from a grassy plaza festooned with monuments, including a large one honoring Union soldiers in the Civil War.

From the capitol it's a short walk to the **State Historical Museum** (www.iowa history.org), a free museum which occupies a large, modern structure. The atrium interior is crowded with vintage airplanes, while the exhibit halls focus on such

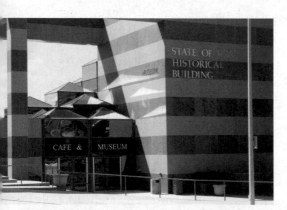

notable Iowa topics as pioneer life and the Iowa caucuses and their importance in national politics. There's also, and a unique space dedicated to items "made in Iowa." There's also a large room of detailed wildlife dioramas and a "wall of fame" of notable Iowans.

From the museum, it's a pleasant stroll or drive past the shops and restaurants of the East Village neighborhood and across the river to down-

Des Moines is home to the State Historical Museum.

TULIP TIME IN PELLA: HOLLAND ON THE PRAIRIE

Come spring, when the tulip bulbs begin to bloom, hordes descend on Pella for its long-running Tulip Time festival (www.pellatulip time.com), a full day of activities every May on downtown streets, including a parade, crowning of the Tulip Queen, traditional Dutch dancing by Pella schoolchildren and the famous "cheese races," which have to be seen to be believed. Either arrive *very* early in order to score a good spot to view the entertainment, or better yet, purchase a ticket in advance to sit in the grandstand opposite the Tulip Toren stage on the town square.

town. The Science Center of Iowa (www.sciiowa.org) has two floors of interactive displays that will thrill children, including a space room with telescopes and a planetarium theater for star shows and another room where visitors can do everything from build and fly a paper rocket to construct a miniature dam to learn about electricity. There's also an IMAX theater and visiting exhibits.

Downtown also has numerous architecturally significant buildings, with several clustered around the Polk County Courthouse. The area around the courthouse is also home to Des Moines's extremely popular farmers' market (www .desmoinesfarmersmarket.com), which spills over six blocks of Court Avenue on Saturday mornings from May through October. Also downtown is the Iowa Hall of Pride (www.iowahallofpride.com), located in the Iowa Events Center complex, with exhibits that showcase homegrown Iowa sports stars.

Farther out, the Blank Park Zoo (www.blankparkzoo.com) is home to a comprehensive collection of animals, while the Des Moines Art Center (www.des moinesartcenter.org), displays works by many contemporary artists, in a building actually composed of three separate units, each designed by a notable 20th century architect. The art center also manages the Pappajohn Sculpture Park, an

THE MEANING OF "DES MOINES"

The translation of the name of Iowa's capital city is up for debate, with some claiming it stems from any of several Native American terms for the local river that seem to mean "River of the Mounds." Yet early French fur trappers used a similar-sounding name that could mean either "the middle" or could refer to monks who once lived on the riverbank. It's a riddle that can't be solved, and residents should be thankful: a frontier military commander wanted to name the new settlement Fort Raccoon!

The Des Moines skyline

outdoor art wonderland located downtown in the area known as **Western Gateway**, which is rapidly adding some of Des Moines's most acclaimed restaurants.

Historic homes in Des Moines include **Salisbury House** (http://salisbury house.org) and **Terrace Hill**, which is the official governor's residence and offers tours. If you can't make it to a true Iowa farm, be sure to stop by **Living History Farms** (www.lhf.org), located in the suburb of Urbandale. The site gives visitors an up-close look at pioneer and Native American life in Iowa, with costumed reenactors explaining different activities. There's also a recreated town from 1875, complete with a blacksmith shop, general store and other early small-town businesses.

IN THE AREA

ACCOMMODATIONS

Aerie Glen Bed & Breakfast, 2364 First Avenue West, Newton. Call 641-792-9032. A country retreat in the woods just outside town, with nice pluses including an outdoor pool and hot tub. There are three rooms in the main house and a poolside cottage squirreled away in back, with the cottage and one of the rooms boasting a whirlpool, microwave and refrigerator. Ideal if you've come to Newton for the races at Iowa Speedway. Moderate to Medium. Website: www.aerieglen.com.

Butler House on Grand, 4507 Grand Avenue, Des Moines. Call 515-255-4096 or 1-866-455-4096. This elegant half-timbered mansion has seven guest rooms, each decorated by a local artists. All rooms have private bath, television with cable, wireless Internet and telephone. Beds are very comfortable. Hop across the street to Des Moines's fine art museum or take a stroll in Greenwood/ Ashworth Park. Moderate to Medium. Website: www.butlerhouseongrand .com.

Hotel Memorial Union, 2229 Lincoln Way, Ames. Call 515-296-6848 or 1-800-433-3449. In the heart of the Iowa State campus, looking out at the landmark campanile and Stanton Carillon, this hotel sits atop the student union and offers basic, reasonably priced rooms. The location means it's just a short walk to most university buildings and nearby businesses. Best of all, there's free parking. Inexpensive to Moderate. Website: www.mu.iastate.edu/hotel.

Hotel Pattee, 1112 Willis Avenue, Perry. Call 515-465-3511. A parade of tasteful theme suites line the corridors in this extensively restored arts and crafts building, constructed in the glory days of the railroad in Iowa. Room décor pays homage to everyone from local miners who labored long ago in the Iowa coal belt to a local circus operator to immigrants who came from all over the world

and settled on the Midwestern prairie, making for a truly unique lodging experience. A classy lounge and restaurant, fully equipped fitness center and even an on-site bowling alley add to the enjoyment. Medium to Expensive. Website: www.hotel pattee.com.

Iowa House, 405 Hayward Avenue, Ames. Call 515-292-2474. This former fraternity house (don't worry, it's been extensively renovated) has been reborn as a charming bed & breakfast with pitched gable roof. There are 13 modern and comfortable rooms with private baths, flatscreen televisions and very nice beds. Two suites include sleeping lofts

One of the unique creations in the Pappajohn Sculpture Park, Des Moines

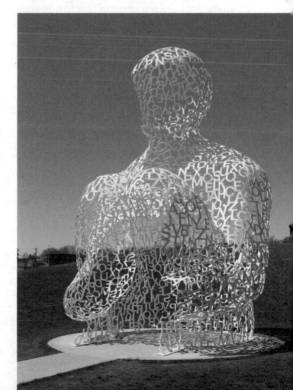

equipped with futons for additional guests. A big country breakfast starts the day off right. Moderate. Website: www.iowahouseames.com.

La Corsette Maison Inn, 629 First Avenue East, Newton. Call 641-792-6833. This large, elegant, Spanish Mission–style bed & breakfast has spacious rooms, including a upper-level penthouse with views all around. Rooms are tastefully furnished, and there are whirlpools in some bathrooms. The inn is also home to a restaurant that serves up skillfully prepared dinner classics like steaks, seafood, pork chops and poultry. Moderate. Website: www.augustbergmaninn.com.

MonteBello Bed & Breakfast Inn, 3535 530th Avenue, Ames. Call 515-296-2181. Yet another Spanish-style hacienda plopped down on the Iowa prairie, MonteBello will make you feel like a *jefe* in its Mexican-themed rooms with vaulted ceilings, king-sized beds in wrought iron frames and private baths. Light spills in through windows that give nice views of the rolling terrain and a nearby lake. Moderate. Website: www.montebellobandbinn.com.

Royal Amsterdam Hotel, 705 East First Street, Pella. Call 641-620-8400. Conveniently located at the Molengracht shopping and dining complex in downtown Pella, this smaller hotel has basic, comfortable rooms, a restaurant and a 24-hour fitness center. You may spot the town's iconic Vermeer Windmill out your window. Moderate. Website: www.royalamsterdam.com.

Suites of 800 Locust, 800 Locust Street, Des Moines. Call 515-288-5800. A luxurious lodging experience can be had at this boutique hotel in the heart of downtown. Standard rooms are available as well as suites, which come with a gas fireplace or whirlpool. Corner rooms have vaulted ceilings, and the rooms away from the street are noticeably quieter—Locust is a busy downtown thoroughfare. A cooked-to-order breakfast is included in the room rate and is served in the lounge downstairs, which come nightfall is a hip spot to grab a cocktail. An on-site spa is a great way to relax. Medium to Expensive. Website: www.800Locust.com.

Tremont's Historic Inn on Main, 24 West Main Street, Marshalltown. Call 641-752-1234. This boutique hotel has classy, spacious rooms above the storefronts of a historic downtown building. Rooms are bright and airy, with very comfortable beds. A quick walk downstairs leads guests to the Tremont's selection of restaurants. A nice spot to recharge during a getaway weekend. Moderate. Website: www.tremontonmain.com.

DINING

Alba, 524 East Sixth Street, Des Moines. Call 515-244-0261. This converted auto showroom in the East Village consistently turns out innovatively prepared dishes with a variety of fresh ingredients, giving a new spin on American comfort food with meats and seafood dressed up in extraordinarily tasty ways. There are even eclectic takes on the all-American hamburger, with toppings like pickled onions and avocado mayonnaise. Delicious deserts as well. Medium. Website: www.albadsm.com.

Baru 66, 6587 University Avenue, Windsor Heights (Des Moines). Call 515-277-6627. An intimate, authentic French bistro tucked away in a nondescript storefront in the outer reaches of Des Moines. French classics start the flavors off nicely, and the dining experience continues with enticing entrées. An extensive wine list complements the food selections. Medium to Expensive. Website: www.baru66.com.

Centro, 1011 Locust Street, Des Moines. Call 515-248-1780. This is a lively Italian joint with an extensive menu that includes pizzas baked in a coal-fired oven and big, hearty dinners like steaks and pork chops prepared with fresh, seasonal toppings and sauces. Lots of pasta choices too, as well as steaks broiled to perfection. Medium. Website: www.centrodesmoines.com.

The Continental, 428 East Locust Street, Des Moines. Call 515-244-5845. One of the city's more adventurous dining options, The Continental is located on an East Village block filled with hip boutiques and restaurants. The menu is mainly tapas, with a large selection of the small plates drawn from a wide variety of cuisines. Ask the staff for recommendations or mix and match yourself; it's hard to go wrong with any of the offerings. There are also innovative entrées and good sandwiches and salads. Moderate. Website: http://continental-lounge.com.

Drake Diner, 1111 25th Street, Des Moines. Call 515-277-1111. A classic old-school diner with a huge menu of short-order classics like burgers, fried chicken and meat loaf, as well as great greasy breakfasts served all day. There are also several salads to choose from for a lighter meal. Fills up with locals and students from nearby Drake University, who pack the booths and counter at lunchtime. Inexpensive to Moderate. Website: www.thedrakediner.com

Hickory Park, 1404 South Duff Avenue, Ames. Call 515-232-3940. *The* place to go for barbecue in Iowa, this huge, barnlike restaurant dishes up generous portions of ribs, pork, brisket, sausage and other smoky treats. Save room for one of their signature sundaes, which come with all manner of toppings that all go down just fine and help take off some of the heat from the 'cue. Even with its humongous interior, be prepared to wait, especially on a Saturday in football season when Iowa State is playing at home. Inexpensive to Moderate. Website: www.hickoryparkames.com.

La Mie, 841 42nd Street, Des Moines. Call 515-255-1625. One of Des Moines's best spots for breakfast and lunch is tucked away in a rather ordinary looking strip center. Omelets and quiches feature fresh ingredients and come out of the pan light and flavorful. Soups are hearty and delicious, and there are plenty of fresh sandwich options as well. Fills up with regulars on Saturday mornings and other days as well; come early for breakfast if you expect to find a table. Inexpensive. Website: www.lamie bakery.com.

Olde Main Brewing Company, 316 Main Street, Ames. Call 515-232-0553. This casual downtown bar and grill serves simple favorites like steaks, seafood and pasta, all of which go well with their many handcrafted beers. There's an impressive list of sandwiches and salads as well. Moderate. Website: www.oldemain brewing.com.

Taylor's Maid-Rite, 106 South Third Avenue, Marshalltown. Call 641-753-9684. This no-frills place on a slightly rundown block outside of downtown is one of the original outlets of Iowa's famous "loose meat" sandwich. Just slide onto a stool at the counter and prepare to chow down. Purists prefer mustard, pickles and onions. Inexpensive. Website: www.maidrite.com.

Tremont Grille, 26 West Main Street, Marshalltown, and **Tremont on Main,** 22 West Main Street, Marshalltown. Call 641-754-9082. A pair of restaurants on a historic downtown block. Tremont Grille is a casual lunch spot, while Tremont on Main is a formal dining room with choices like steaks, seafood and pasta. There's also the **Tremont Sports Café,** 20 West Main Street, a nice spot to kick back with a beer and watch the game. Moderate to Medium. Website: www.tremontonmain.com.

Tursi's Latin King, 2200 Hubbell Avenue, Des Moines. Call 515-266-4466. An old-school, family-run Italian place out by the state fairgrounds, its exterior evokes a Tuscan villa. There are lots of red-sauce favorites on the menu, as well as steaks, including local specialty Steak de Burgo, which comes topped with a buttery, garlicky sauce. Good chicken and veal options, too. There's a lengthy wine list and classic Italian desserts and coffee drinks. Moderate. Website: www.tur-sislatinking.com.

Zeno's Pizza, 109 East Main Street, Marshalltown. Call 641-752-1245. They've been churning out hot and delicious pies at this local favorite since 1952. The menu is straight-up and to the point: pizza with a selection of toppings. Inexpensive.

SHOPPING

Antiques Iowa, 1639 Broad Street, Story City. Call 515-733-9311. A huge antiques mall, maybe the largest in Iowa, with more than 15,000 square feet of vendors selling all sorts of collectibles and vintage items. Website: www.antiquesiowa.com.

East Village, Des Moines. This neighborhood in the shadow of the state capitol is ground zero in Des Moines for funky shopping, with lots of interesting little boutiques and gift shops, including Raygun, which specializes in Des Moines and Iowa T-shirts as well as kitschy novelty items. Stroll up and down the streets perusing the offerings. With plenty of restaurants nearby, it's easy to find a nice spot for a break as well.

Jaarsma Bakery, 727 Franklin Street, Pella. Call 641-628-2940. The inviting smell of warm pastries beckons you into this shop on Pella's main square. Lots of yummy rolls and cookies sit inside the glass display cases, but the pièce de résistance is probably the Dutch letters, light and flaky S-shaped goodies that are stuffed with a divine almond filling. You'll want a few for the road, and maybe some of their almond butter cake as well. Website: www.jaarsmabakery.com.

Shoppes on Grand, 517 Grand Avenue, Ames. Call 515-233-6010. This rambling old Victorian home has two floors of gifts, collectibles and antiques, as well as a tearoom that serves light lunches in a pleasant atmosphere. Website: http://shoppeson grand.com.

Valley Junction, West Des Moines. Like the East Village, this shopping area in West Des Moines, a separate city from Des Moines, is packed with funky boutiques, art galleries and antiques shops. Also check out the area's railroad history: this was originally the sight of an important train switching yard and there's a red caboose still standing in the neighborhood.

RECREATION AND ENTERTAINMENT

For a look at what's going on in Des Moines and surrounding areas, pick up a copy of *Juice* or *Cityview*, free weekly entertainment guides that can be found in supermarkets and other locations. Both the Court Avenue District and the East Village are good locations for bars and other nightlife, as is West Glen, a newer entertainment district near the Jordan Creek Mall in the adjoining city of West Des Moines.

If you're in Des Moines in August, you have the opportunity to indulge in the quintessential Iowa experience: the Iowa State Fair. For 10 days, the 400-acre fairgrounds come alive with an endless procession of animals from every corner of Iowa as kids put livestock through their paces in hopes of taking home a blue ribbon. The fairgrounds' sprawl of brick buildings offer a slew of exhibits that allow visitors to get up close with everything from a cow or hog giving birth to the fair's famous butter sculptures, which every year take on a different theme. The midway runs into the night, with both carnival rides and every type of greasy, sugary fair food you can imagine. Nationally famous entertainers as well as less well-known acts play the large outdoor arena. Show up the year before a presidential election and you're practically guaranteed to see candidates stumping for the Iowa caucuses. The full fair experience definitely requires a whole day, and tickets are available online as well as at local supermarkets and other merchants.

Adventureland, 305 34th Avenue, Altoona. Call 515-266-2121 or 1-800-532-1286. A wonderfully old-fashioned amusement park, located just off I-80, with rides for kids of all ages, including two roller coasters, a log plunge, a "raging river" and classics like a Ferris wheel, bumper cars and a carousel. There's an adjacent water park and an on-site hotel. Website: www.adventureland-usa.com.

Des Moines Metro Opera, 106 West Boston Avenue, Indianola. Call 515-961-6221. For close to 40 years, this regionally acclaimed company has presented a mix of classic and contemporary operas in an intimate opera house on the campus of Simpson College. The season runs from June through July and usually includes three operas. Website: www.desmoinesmetroopera.org.

Iowa Speedway, 3333 Rusty Wallace Drive, Newton. Call 641-791-8000. A stop on the NASCAR and IndyCar circuit that packs in fans for races on its tri-oval track designed by racing legend Rusty Wallace. Website: www.iowaspeedway.com.

Prairie Meadows Racetrack & Casino, 1 Prairie Meadows Drive, Altoona. Call 515-967-8544 or 1-800-325-9018. Thoroughbred and quarter horse racing takes place from April through October at this track just off I-80, in addition to simulcast racing year-round. The casino has slots and table games, and there are dining and entertainment options as well. Website: www.prairiemeadows.com.

Sleepy Hollow Sports Park, 4051 Dean Avenue, Des Moines. Call 515-262-4100. This is the place for winter fun, with skiing, snowboarding and snow tubing all available on a 15-story hill. Tubes and other equipment are available for rent, including helmets for tubers (you'll need them; it's actually a pretty fast run). A lift brings people to the top of the hill. Website: http://shspdm.com.

Valle Drive-In, 4074 County Road F48 West, Newton. Call 641-792-3558.

One of just a few drive-in theaters left in Iowa, this big screen draws viewers to a field outside of town, where first-run Hollywood hits are shown. Tickets are very reasonably priced. Website: www.valledrive-in .com.

OTHER CONTACTS

Newton Convention & Visitors Bureau, 113 First Avenue West, Newton, 50208. Call 641-792-0299 or 1-800-798-0299. Website: www.visitnewton .com.

Grinnell Area Chamber of Commerce & Tourism Group, 833 Fourth Avenue, Grinnell, 50112. Call 641-236-6555. Website: www.grinnell chamber.org.

Marshalltown Convention & Visitors Bureau, 709 South Center Street, Marshalltown, 50158. Call 641-753-6645 or 1-800-697-3155. Website: www.visitmarshalltown.com.

Ames Convention & Visitors Bureau, 1601 Golden Aspen Drive, Suite 110, Ames, 50010. Call 515-232-4032. Website: www.visitames.com.

Story City Greater Chamber Connection, 602 Broad Street, Story City, 50248. Call 515-733-4214. Website: www.storycity.net.

Boone Chamber of Commerce, 903 Story Street, Boone, 50036. Call 515-432-3342 or 1-800-266-6312. Website: www.booneiowa.us.

Greene County Chamber & Development, 220 North Chestnut Street, Jefferson, 50129. Call 515-386-2155. Website: www.greenecountyiowa.com.

Perry Chamber of Commerce, 1102 Willis Avenue, Perry, 50220. Call 515-465-4601. Website: www.perryia.org.

Madison County Chamber of Commerce, 73 Jefferson Street, Winterset, 50273. Call 1-800-298-6119; Website: www.madisoncounty.com.

Indianola Chamber of Commerce, 515 North Jefferson, Suite D, Indianola, 50125. Call 1-866-961-6269. Website: www.indianolachamber.com.

Lake Red Rock, 1105 County Road T15, Knoxville, 50138. Call 641-828-7522 or 641-628-8690. Website: www .lakeredrock.org.

Pella Convention & Visitors Bureau, 818 Washington Street, Pella, 50219. Call 1-888-746-3882. Website: www.pella.org.

Greater Des Moines Convention & Visitors Bureau, 400 Locust Street, Suite 265, Des Moines, 50309. Call 1-800-451-2625. Website: www.seedes moines.com.

12 Southern Iowa:
A LEGACY OF COAL AND THE MORMON TRAIL

Estimated length: About 150 miles, winding south from the Des Moines area and then east through many towns and small cities to Rathbun Lake.

Estimated time: Can easily be done in two days, or even as a long day trip from Des Moines or a nearby community.

Getting there: All of the places on this trip are easily accessible from both I-80 and I-35.

Highlights: A historic Mormon site at Mount Pisgah. The boyhood farm of prominent Iowan Henry Wallace. A vintage railroad station in Creston. The deep history of coal mining in this part of the state. Fun times at Honey Creek State Resort on Rathbun Lake.

Madison County or Des Moines make good jumping off or ending points for this trip, which winds among the more rugged terrain of southern Iowa. Begin in **Greenfield,** which is perhaps best known for the **Iowa Aviation Museum** (www.flyingmuseum.com). The museum, which is located at the local airport, has many vintage aircraft on display, including a 1928 Curtiss Robin, the oldest such model ever made, and a 1941 Aetna-Timm Aerocraft, the only one of its kind. There is also aviation memorabilia and the Iowa Aviation Hall of Fame.

Also in Greenfield is the **Adair County Historical Museum** (www.adairchs .org), with displays on pioneer life, the Mormon Trail and antique farm machinery, as well as a restored one-room schoolhouse. A historic home and church are located on the museum grounds. Greenfield's **E. E. Warren Opera House** (www .warrenoperahouse.com) is an impressive brick structure with a turreted tower. There are plans to extensively remodel the building and open it as a local cultural center.

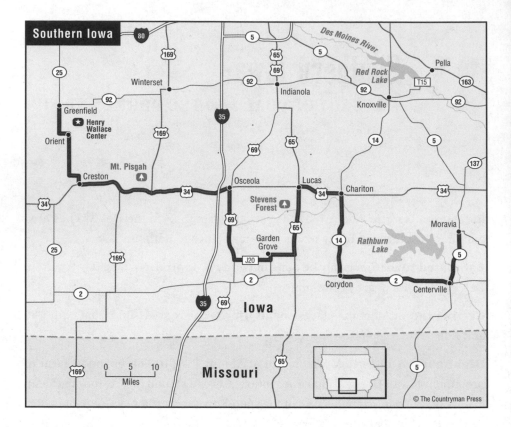

Moving into the country outside Greenfield, it's a short drive to the **Henry A. Wallace Country Life Center** (www.henryawallacecenter.com) outside the small town of **Orient,** though the last stretch of drive is down a rutted gravel road. A typical Iowa farm with a modest white farmhouse and barn surrounded by flat, windswept fields stretching to the horizon, this was the birthplace and boyhood home of Wallace, a farmer and politician who held cabinet-level posts in the 1930s and '40s. Today, the farmhouse and barn serve as a gift shop and café, respectively. There are also fruit and vegetable gardens and a sculpture garden with walking paths. The farm is owned by the **Wallace Foundation,** which sponsors agricultural and educational programs. (Wallace's family home in Des Moines is also open to visitors.) In Orient, the **Bank of Memories** museum has displays on Wallace and the Mormon pioneers who passed through the area.

The opposite of the pastoral setting surrounding the farm is found in **Creston,** an old railroad town where plenty of trains still rumble through every day, many of them hauling full coal cars. While just about every decent-sized Iowa town has an old depot, the one in Creston is particularly worth seeking out: the massive, two-story sandstone structure boasts a roof of Spanish tiles. Inside, the large waiting room is ringed with Corinthian columns and has largely been preserved from the golden age of rail travel.

One side of the waiting room features a large model train display, while

Creston's historic depot

in the hallway there's an extensive collection of presidential dolls depicting chief executives from throughout American history. The depot is especially impressive compared to the small, modern Amtrak station farther down the tracks.

The depot is just one of the area's historic attractions (www.unioncountyiowa

HENRY WALLACE: AN IOWA LEADER

From his beginnings on an Iowa farm, Henry Wallace rose to a national stage, where he dealt extensively with agricultural issues and ultimately sought the presidency.

A true son of the soil, Wallace farmed from youth onward and also edited farming publications owned by his family. Appointed by Franklin D. Roosevelt as secretary of agriculture, a position also held by his father, Wallace was elected vice president with Roosevelt in 1940. After disagreements with Harry Truman, Wallace ran for president in 1948. A strident leftist and populist, he spoke out against moneyed interests and in favor of dialogue with the Soviet Union. He won not one electoral vote in the election, in which Truman won his second term.

In his later years, Wallace farmed extensively and made advances in agricultural science. He also revised his earlier views on the Soviet Union. He died in 1965 and his ashes are interred at Glendale Cemetery in Des Moines. *The Des Moines Register* named him the "Most Influential Iowan of the 20th Century."

The Frank Phillips Visitors Center in Creston

tourism.com/html/historical.html), among them the **Union County Historical Complex,** which depicts a typical rural Iowa community from the 19th century throughout 15 buildings, including a schoolhouse, general store, blacksmith shop and depot. Creston's **Frank Phillips Visitors Center** is housed in a reconstructed Phillips 66 station, complete with period gasoline pumps and the famous "66" sign. Phillips, who grew up on a farm outside Creston, went on to found the oil company that bore his name. Nearby **Green Valley State Park** is a popular spot for fishing, boating, swimming and picnicking.

Head back out on the country roads, which lead you to the remote **Mount Pisgah National Historic Site.** Though it's an empty hillside overlooking an isolated river valley, quiet save the rustling of the wind, this was once a bustling encampment on the Mormon Trail. From 1846 to 1852, this spot, named after a passage in the Bible, was a way station for thousands of Mormon pioneers who passed through on their great trek west. Many stayed for months or even years, sheltering in nearby caves until they built log cabins to make it through the Iowa winter, and farming on the muddy slopes.

Mormon leader Brigham Young arrived at Mount Pisgah in May 1846 on his way west. Between 300 and 800 people perished here, and many are buried in a cemetery down a hillside path. There's also a replica log cabin and informative displays about the Mormon Trail. It's a very peaceful spot except for the occasional tractor crunching past on the gravel. Make sure you get accurate directions, as it's hidden down a farm road and a little tricky to find.

Passing through **Osceola,** which has a large wooden sculpture of the Native American chief outside the local bank and a large casino complex out by the highway, make your way south to **Garden Grove,** site of another important way station on the Mormon Trail. The town actually developed out of the Mormon encampment; tourists can see a display about Mormon pioneers and visit a nearby Mormon cemetery.

THE MORMON TRAIL IN IOWA: TREKKING ACROSS THE PRAIRIE

Iowa was the first challenge for Mormon pioneers after they set out from Nauvoo, Illinois, on a journey that would take tens of thousands to their new home in the valley of the Great Salt Lake, just part of the massive wave of humanity that headed west across the North American continent in the mid-1800s.

Beginning their trek in 1846, the same year the United States went to war with Mexico, the first Mormons to make the trip west crossed Iowa in just over four months, pushing through late winter storms and muddy tracks that bogged down wooden cart wheels. Led by Brigham Young, they reached the Missouri River at Council Bluffs in June of that year. At Council Bluffs they made camp at "winter quarters" until the following spring, when they crossed the Missouri and completed the trip to the Great Salt Lake in less than four months, using skills they had learned on the Iowa crossing to move more efficiently.

This first wave of Mormons left behind several semi-permanent encampments in southern Iowa, most notably at Garden Grove and Mount Pisgah. These served to welcome and fortify succeeding waves of Mormons as they prepared for the arduous crossing of the Great Plains and the Rocky Mountains. Ultimately, some 70,000 Mormons followed the trail west. Their legacy is preserved at numerous sites in Iowa.

East of Osceola you reach the Stephens State Forest, a hiking and camping paradise with trails winding into thick stands of oak and hickory. It's the largest forest in Iowa, with lots of native plants and wildlife clustered amid the trees. The forest edges up to the town of Lucas in the heart of Iowa's historic coal country. Millions of years ago, decomposing forest created carbon-rich debris that eventually became large deposits of the black mineral. Mining communities later grew up near the shafts and mines dug into the rolling hillsides.

Virtually all of the mines have been closed for more than 50 years, yet the legacy of mining still looms over the area and can be seen at the John L. Lewis Museum of Mining and Labor (www.coalmininglabormuseum.com). A large statue of the longtime labor leader, posed in full-throated oration, greets visitors in the center of the small museum.

JOHN L. LEWIS: MINING'S BIG BOSS

Born in a coal mining camp outside Lucas in 1880, John L. Lewis began mining at an early age in Iowa and Illinois. He soon became an organizer of his fellow workers in the United Mine Workers of America, becoming vice president in 1917. He became president of the union in 1920, and was also a significant figure in national labor organizations.

During his time as head of the UMWA, Lewis spearheaded strikes of millions of workers and scuffled with mine owners and the U.S. government over wages, benefits, pensions and other issues affecting workers. He had many enemies, both inside and outside the union, yet

A statue of John Lewis stands inside the museum of mining and labor that bears his name.

many workers saw him as their champion. He remained president of the UMWA for 40 years, then served as president emeritus until his death in 1969.

Displays, which cover everything from the geology of coal to labor relations throughout the 20th century, include plenty of mining tools and other artifacts. A theater room shows videos about Lewis and other mining-related topics.

Lucas County is also a mecca for outdoor enthusiasts: in addition to the Stephens State Forest, **Pin Oak Marsh** along the Chariton River, is home to wildlife like great blue herons, Canada geese, river otters and frogs. A trail through the marsh begins at **Pin Oak Lodge,** which has displays of local wildlife: aquariums with native fish, lizards and turtles, and mounted birds, waterfowl and large animals like bobcats, cougars and elk. If you're lucky, a staff naturalist may take you into the marsh to catch snakes or see other wildlife.

Not far away is **Red Haw State Park,** which offers swimming and fishing in its reservoir and is a great place to watch redbuds bloom in the spring. It also was home to one of the largest bobcat research projects in the U.S.; see if you can find a ranger to tell you all about the many bobcats that live in the area. The **Cinder Path,** Iowa's first rails-to-trails path, is also close by and is popular with bicyclists.

Several of these natural areas are clustered around **Chariton,** the largest town in the county. In a residential neighborhood you'll find the **Lucas County Museum,** an impressive complex of historic buildings, including a barn, church, schoolhouse, log cabin and circa 1907 mansion housing rooms full of historic bric-a-brac. The main museum building is located behind the mansion and has many more rooms overflowing with artifacts related to the town's history.

Before leaving Chariton, take a spin around the square to see the castlelike sandstone courthouse and a nearby restored railroad freight building. Interestingly, Chariton is home to a significant **Ukrainian** population, and has begun celebrating their heritage with a late-summer festival. There are also a few dozen **Amish** families living on farms in the area, and larger groups can make arrangements through the Chariton Chamber for an Amish meal and a tour of an Amish workshop.

Loop south through more open countryside to **Corydon,** which has an exhibit on the Mormon Trail at the **Prairie Trails Museum of Wayne County** (www .prairietrailsmuseum.org). The museum's collection also includes re-created Main Street shops, farm machinery and Native American and pioneer artifacts.

To the east is **Centerville,** which boasts of **Iowa's Largest Historic Square District,** with more than 100 historic properties, including many Italianate and Victorian designs. It's a historic coal mining area reborn as a destination for shoppers and outdoor enthusiasts. The **Appanoose County Historical & Coal Mining Museum** has two replica coal mines where visitors can stand under a seam of simulated coal, as well as lots of old mining tools and many photos from the days when mines dominated southern Iowa. There are also displays on pioneer life and the Mormon Trail, and a ton of historic artifacts. A large mining car, used to carry coal, sits outside the museum, which was once the town's post office. The nearby **old jail** is open by appointment, while the town's **railroad depot** has been converted to the local VFW headquarters. The nearby town of **Exline,** a former mining community, is home to a replica fire station featuring a fire truck from the 1920s.

You may want to time your visit to Centerville in order to arrive in late September for **Pancake Day**, which has been going strong for more than 60 years. Free gourmet pancakes are dished out to hungry eaters, and there's a parade and all sorts of entertainment.

Centerville is also well known as the gateway to **Rathbun Lake** (http://corps lakes.usace.army.mil/visitors/projects.cfm?Id=G514880), a sprawling body of water built by the U.S. Army Corps of Engineers, with many recreation areas along its shores. Several boat ramps are available, as are swim beaches and campsites. The **Rathbun Fish Hatchery** has aquariums stocked with native Iowa fish, as well as a catwalk that takes visitors through the hatchery's operations. The lake is also well known as the site of **Honey Creek Resort State Park** (see *Lodging*) near the town of **Moravia**, home of the **Moravia Wabash Depot Museum**, which has railroad artifacts, a restored train car and a model railroad.

IN THE AREA

ACCOMMODATIONS

Adams Street Country Lodge, 1412 170th Street, Creston. Call 641-344-5478. This bed & breakfast is located on a tranquil pond outside Creston. The modern home has five guest rooms, including rooms with both private and shared baths. Kick back with a book by the pond or take a stroll on the surrounding rolling hills. Moderate. Website: www.adamsstreet countrylodge.com.

Back Inn Time Bed & Breakfast, 423 Southwest Second Street, Greenfield. Call 641-743-6394. Beautiful surroundings and a scrumptious breakfast make this a wonderful spot for a weekend getaway. Well-tended paths in the garden wind past wildflowers, perennials, a fish pond and a fountain. After a stroll, retire to the front porch with a good book and a cup of coffee or tea. There are four charming bedrooms, each decorated in a different theme. Inexpensive. Website: www.backinntimebb.com.

Brass Lantern Bed & Breakfast, 2446 IA 92, Greenfield. Call 641-743-2031 or 1-888-743-2031. Sink into this hidden spot of luxury tucked away on an archetypal Iowa farm. The two bedrooms have sliding doors that open onto the terrace of a 40-foot indoor pool. Each room has a queen-sized bed and private bath. There's also a fireplace in each room and access to a shared kitchenette. Breakfast is served in an adjoining rambling historic farmhouse, or you can be truly indulgent and eat poolside. Medium. Website: www.brass lantern.com.

Continental Hotel, 217 North 13th Street, Centerville. Call 641-437-1025. Large, apartment-style suites occupy a historic building used primarily for senior housing on Centerville's main square, an easy walk to nearby shops. Rooms are basic but comfortable, with a kitchen area and separate living room. There's also free laundry service. The on-site **restaurant** has a good selection of steak, seafood and poultry dishes. Moderate. Website: www.thecontinental.info.

Honey Creek Resort State Park, 12633 Resort Drive, Moravia. Call 1-877-677-3344. This large resort on the shores of Rathbun Lake is operated by the Iowa Department of Natural Resources and features a wealth of leisure opportunities, including a large indoor water park with a slide, lazy river and several pools geared to different ages and activities. There's an 18-hole championship golf course, 50 boat slips, a fishing pier, a swim beach and nature trails through the surrounding countryside. A variety of motorized and nonmotorized watercraft rentals are available. Rooms are large and comfortable, and there's an on-site **restaurant.** There are also separate guest cottages with kitchens on the property. Moderate to Expensive. Website: www.honeycreekresort .com.

Hotel Greenfield, 110 East Iowa Street, Greenfield. Call 641-323-7323. This beautifully restored, historic redbrick hotel has stylish modern rooms with all the conveniences you'd find in a bigger city lodging, in-

cluding refrigerators and DVD players. A complimentary breakfast is provided to guests. Website: www .hotel-greenfield.com.

Inn of the Six-Toed Cat, 200 Central Avenue, Allerton. Call 641-873-4900. An authentic restored railroad hotel, this redbrick bed & breakfast near Bob White State Park has Persian rugs, tin ceilings, period furnishings and the inevitable cat-themed art. Eight cozy, comfortable guest rooms include both private and shared baths. The Presidential Suite has an antique king-sized bed and light streaming through the windows. There's an antique bar complete with cash register in the living room. Moderate. Website: www.6toedcat.com.

One of a Kind Bed & Breakfast, 314 West State Street, Centerville. Call 614-437-4540. Another stately old mansion in Centerville, with five bright and airy guest rooms with a choice of private and shared baths. It's a short walk to the central square and its charming shops, and a short drive to Rathbun Lake and all its outdoor activities. The mansion also houses a charming tearoom that serves meals and delicious desserts all day. Inexpensive to Moderate. Website: http://oneofakindbedand breakfast.com.

DINING

The Continental, 217 North 13th Street, Centerville. Call 641-437-1025.

Classic country food like pot roast and fettuccine Alfredo is served up in this modest dining room in the Continental Hotel. The menu also includes several sandwiches and salads. Inexpensive. Website: www.thecontinental .info.

Exline Old Country Store and Antique Exchange, 102 West Main Street, Exline. Call 641-658-2399. A classic country store with a menu of breakfast, burgers, sandwiches and pizza. Chow down at wooden tables beneath mounted deer heads. Afterward, take a breather on the large front porch or peruse the selection of antiques and food items for sale. Inexpensive. Website: www.exline countrystore.com.

Olive Branch Family Restaurant, 108 East Iowa Street, Greenfield. Call 641-343-7323. Homestyle favorites are served in a historic room with pressed tin ceilings and black vinyl booths next to the Hotel Greenfield. Inexpensive to Moderate.

SHOPPING

The Columns, 107 East Washington Street, Centerville. Call 641-437-1178. This grand old home a block north of Centerville's town square has all sorts of lovely accessories, handbags, furniture and decorative items in its bright, airy rooms, perfect for browsing. Website: http://thecolumns.info.

Piper's Grocery & Candy, 901 Braden Avenue, Chariton. Call 641-

774-2131. An old-fashioned candy emporium complete with a red-and-white striped awning. Feed your sweet tooth with their rich chocolates, caramels, turtles and other items. Website: www.piperscandy.com.

The Shoppes at Bradley Hall, 519 Drake Avenue, Centerville. Call 641-856-5345. More than 10,000 square feet of shopping space awaits inside a high-ceilinged, elegant historic mansion. Wander through the three floors and basement stocked with everything from antiques to candles to food and wine and so much more. Website: www.bradleyhall.info.

RECREATION AND ENTERTAINMENT

Rathbun Country Music Theater, 22053 430th Street, Moravia. Call 641-724-3505. Iowa's longest running country music show presents a mixture of songs and comedy on Saturday nights from May through October. The family-friendly, no-alcohol shows feature guest musicians sitting in with the house band on classic country tunes. They're a lot of fun. Website: www.countrymusictheater .com.

Rathbun Lake Marinas, 21646 Marina Place, Moravia. Call 641-724-3412. A full-service boat rental and service shop with marina slips and pontoon boats available for rent. Perfect for a day of fishing, cruising or tubing on the lake. There's also a small motel, the **Lakeside Inn,** on the premises, as well as **Louie's on the Lake Restaurant,** a nice spot to grab a bite before or after your time on the water. A separate marina also offers kayak rentals. Website: www .rathbunlakemarinas.com.

OTHER CONTACTS

Adair County Tourism, P.O. Box 40, Greenfield, 50841. Call 1-888-743-2031. Website: www.visitadaircounty .com.

Creston/Union County Tourism, P.O. Box 471, Creston, 50801. Call 641-782-7022. Website: www.unioncounty iowatourism.com.

Decatur County Development, 207 North Main Street, Leon, 50144. Call 641-446-4991. Website: www.decatur countydevelopment.org.

Osceola Chamber-Main Street, 115 East Washington Street, Osceola,

50213. Call 641-342-4200. Website: www.osceolachamber.com.

Tourism Lucas County/The Chariton Chamber and Development Corporation, 104 North Grand Street, Chariton, 50049. Call 641-774-4059. Website: www.lucascounty tourism.org or www.charitonchamber .com.

Wayne County Development, P.O. Box 435, Corydon, 50060. Call 641-872-1536. Website: www.waynecounty iowa.com.

Centerville-Rathbun Lake Chamber of Commerce, 128 North 12th Street, Centerville, 52544. Call 641-437-4102 or 1-800-611-3800. Website: www.centervilleia.com.

Rathbun Lake Information Center, 20112 County Road J5T, Centerville, 52544. Call 641-647-2464. Website: www.nwk.usace.army.mil/ra.

13 Iowa's Chain of Lakes:
THE OKOBOJI AREA AND STORM LAKE

Estimated length: About 150 miles round-trip.

Estimated time: From a day to a weekend to a whole week at the lake.

Getting there: Both Okoboji and Storm Lake are on US 71, which runs north-south across the western half of Iowa and is accessible from Sioux City, Des Moines and other parts of Iowa.

Highlights: The vast summer playground of Okoboji and Spirit Lake—including Arnolds Park, a great, old-fashioned amusement park—as well as boating on the lake and strolling the shore. Historical attractions and small-town charm at Storm Lake.

This narrow corridor in the northwestern part of the state is home to a scattered group of lakeside communities, each with its own unique features and attractions. Begin at **Iowa's Great Lakes** just south of the Minnesota border, a summer destination for hordes of Iowans. (Some attractions and businesses shut down from fall through spring; check ahead.)

While there are actually six lakes, created thousands of years ago by glaciers and covering more than 15,000 acres, most recreational development has focused on the duo of **West Lake Okoboji** and **East Lake Okoboji,** and is centered in the town of **Arnolds Park,** home to the popular amusement park of the same name. This is a true honky-tonk paradise, with water parks cropping up among the many lakeside resorts, boat docks and restaurants.

Start with a true gem for Iowa or anywhere else: **Historic Arnolds Park** (www.ArnoldsPark.com), an honest-to-goodness, old-fashioned amusement park that dates to 1889, on the shore of West Lake Okoboji, where you pay for rides

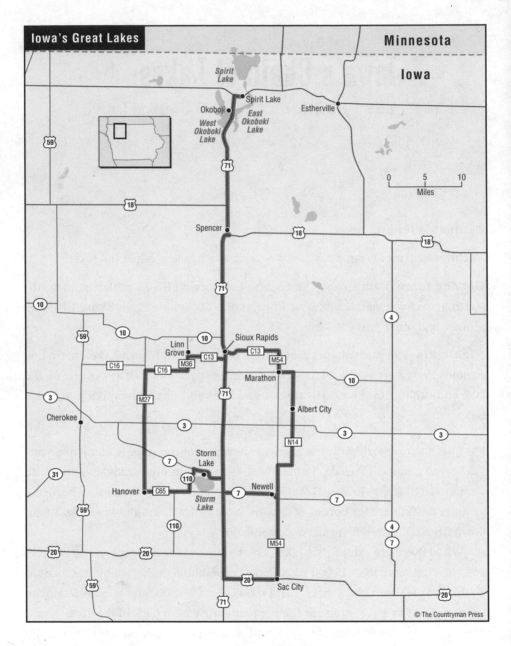

with individual tickets (day passes are also available) and can find easy free parking just a short walk away. A red-and-white roller coaster, the Legend, encircles the compact park, which is small enough that even little kids won't get tired walking around. The park actually closed down in 1987, but reopened two years later.

The Legend whips around curves and down some fast, steep drops, including an initial drop of 63 feet, passing by the park's classic Ferris wheel, carousel and other rides and giving riders a quick view of the lake. In operation since 1927, it's one of the oldest roller coasters still standing anywhere. The park also has bumper cars, a log flume and rides for smaller children, as well as an adjacent go-cart track and miniature golf course. (Okoboji is also a major golf area; several courses are sprinkled throughout local towns.)

A lakefront boardwalk runs past the outside of the park, passing by the **State Pier** and *Queen II,* an excursion boat that offers relaxing cruises on the lake. There are some museums nearby, including the **Iowa Great Lakes Maritime Museum** (www.okobojimuseum.org), which tells the long history of pleasure boating on Iowa's Great Lakes through displays of everything from a restored boathouse to a 30-foot boat salvaged from the lake bottom. There are lots of historical photographs and maps, and the museum also has a gift shop and an information center that provides details about local attractions.

Closer to the park, the **Iowa Rock 'N Roll Museum** (www.iowarocknroll.com) showcases music acts from Iowa as well as internationally famous groups like the Beatles through displays of records, concert posters and other memorabilia. At the other end of the museum spectrum, the **Higgins Museum of National Banking** (www.thehigginsmuseum.org), also known as the Museum of Money and located away from the lakeshore in the town of **Okoboji**, has the largest collection of national bank issues on display. The museum provides a look back at the days when local communities printed their own currency and Iowa had more "hometown cash," or banks issuing their own currency, than any other state.

A more relaxed lakeside experience awaits in the town of **Spirit Lake**, with charming shops and restaurants clustered along Hill Avenue in the heart of "Olde Town." The town sits on **Big Spirit Lake**, which is more about fishing than tearing across the water in a motorized craft, with abundant walleye, perch, panfish and bass.

The **Abbie Gardner Historic Museum** is a modest cabin that was home

Downtown Spirit Lake

to a woman who authored a memoir of her time in captivity following an 1856 confrontation between settlers and Native Americans known as the Spirit Lake Massacre. The event helped spark the Dakota War of 1862, a major engagement between Sioux warriors and U.S. troops that was one of the largest Indian Wars in American history, culminating in a mass execution of Sioux. The cabin has historic artifacts on display.

History is also on display at the **Clark Museum of Okoboji Area and Iowa History** (www.okoboji.com/attractions/museums), located in nearby **Milford**, with a large number of historical photographs and other displays, and at the **Dickinson County Museum**, located in an old train depot in Spirit Lake, where it chronicles the railroad, resorts and industry around the Great Lakes.

Heading south from the lakes soon brings you back into the more familiar Iowa landscape of flat farm fields. After about 20 miles you come to **Spencer**, a good-sized county seat where you can take a break before heading back out into the open countryside. It's another 30 miles to **Storm Lake**, a relaxing getaway spot like Iowa's Great Lakes, but with a flavor all its own.

Anchored by three lighthouses, including a 30-foot-tall brick octagonal light that stands lakeside in Scout Park and illuminates the waters with a rotating beacon, Storm Lake is a natural lake with pristine, powdery beaches interspersed with boat marinas, lodgings and a large water park resort. Bronze statues stand in lakeside parkland.

Storm Lake's downtown, on the north shore of the lake, retains a small-town Iowa charm, with an old railroad depot and some good restaurants. **Harker House** (www.harkerhouse.com) is a restored 1875 French mansard-style home full of period furniture and artifacts. The **Buena Vista County Historical Museum** (www.stormlake-ia.com/bvchs), located in an old auto plant west of downtown, has a re-created pioneer Main Street complete with a board sidewalk and a bank, general store, doctor's office and barbershop among the structures. The museum also features exhibits of farm machinery and military items. A log house and country school, both refurbished and open for display, can be found closer to the railroad tracks.

A change of pace from exhibits focused on the past can be found at **Santa's Castle**, a tribute to all things Christmas in Storm Lake's old Carnegie Library building. The castle is home to a large model railroad and the country's largest collection of antique Christmas figures. Unfortunately, the museum is usually open only in December; call and try to make an appointment to see it at other times of the year. Art lovers will want to take a look at the town's **Witter Gallery**, next to the Storm Lake Public Library, which displays works in a variety of media.

Down on the lakefront, take a break from swimming or boating to visit the **Living Heritage Tree Museum** (www.heritagetreemuseum.com) in **Sunset Park**. There are close to 50 trees here, with most named after famous people, like the George Washington sycamore (not a cherry tree, interestingly), the Isaac Newton apple tree and at least two trees dedicated to Ulysses S. Grant. The walking path is a peaceful place to take a stroll.

The tree museum isn't the only place in Storm Lake that honors trees: the parkland along the lake is studded with **tree sculptures**. Keep your eyes peeled for the bear catching a fish (you have to see it to believe it), the pelican, totem pole, eagles and troll family, among many others. New sculptures are added regularly, and you may even see the artist carving his newest creation.

A ring of outlying towns preserve the past in old buildings, making for a nice country drive starting in **Newell**, home to the well-preserved **Allee Mansion** (www.newellhistorical.org), an 1891 Queen Anne Victorian with a striking tower and a colorful history that includes the self-proclaimed checkers champion of Iowa. Your guide can tell you all about him and some of the mansion's other residents, as well as details of the house like the secret passageways that lead to outbuildings. There are also beautiful stained-glass windows, an oak staircase and pocket doors.

From Newell move on to **Albert City**, where a complex of five buildings includes a historic depot that was the site of a shootout during a 1901 bank robbery that left three people dead. There are still bullet holes in the depot walls, and a gun used by one of the robbers is on display. There are also collections of china, glassware, Hummel figurines and restored antique cars in the baggage room, including a 1910 Model T Ford and Stanley Steamer.

The other buildings are one of Albert City's earliest homes, a 19th-century schoolhouse, an old general store with antique household items and the **Heritage House,** which exhibits tractors and farm machinery as well as historical artifacts. Come August, the **Threshermen and Collectors Show** (www.albertcity threshermen.com) includes demonstrations of antique farm machinery, blacksmithing and other old-time skills.

Nearby **Marathon** is home to the **Marathon Area Historical Society**, where visitors can see a restored railroad depot and caboose. Guests can take a ride around the old train yard, too. Down farm roads is **Sioux Rapids,** site of the cabin of the county's first white settler, Abner Bell, as well as a schoolhouse and a vintage movie theater.

Next, swing over to **Linn Grove,** the "Catfish Capital of Iowa," located on the **Old O'Brien Glacial Trail Scenic Byway,** a compact rural route that encircles the "four corners" junction of Buena Vista, Clay, O'Brien and Cherokee Counties, moving through rolling rural scenery shaped by Ice Age glaciers and crisscrossing the Little Sioux River several times. As part of the 130-mile **Inkpaduta Canoe Trail,** Linn Grove is a good base for canoeing and fishing on the river. You may spot bald eagles soaring over the dam close to town.

Perhaps the most complete historic site on the trip comes on the home stretch, in the town of **Hanover,** home to **Hanover Historical Village,** a celebration of the area's German pioneer heritage. The village includes a general store, sawmill, machine shed, millhouse and settler's home furnished with period domestic items. True polka aficionados will want to show up in August for the annual polka festival, which also features demonstrations of pioneer skills like rope making and apple pressing, as well as tours of the historic buildings.

The Chautauqua Building in Sac City

During your travels you will undoubtedly spot colorful **barn quilts** on farms all over the backroads, but the really breathtaking sight comes just before you arrive in Hanover: massive windmills rise from the flat Iowa landscape, their gargantuan towers seeming to blot out the sun. The blades are nearly 80 feet long, while the concrete foundations weigh 200 tons each.

At this point you can either head back to Storm Lake or take a side trip to **Sac City,** which has some fine Victorian architecture as well as the only stoplights in the entire county. A city park on the east side of town is home to a vintage **Chautauqua Building**—one of only two remaining in Iowa—which once hosted lectures and today is used for musical performances.

Closer to downtown, the **Sac City Museum** has the usual collection of artifacts and historic structures, but there's a true oddity as well: the **world's largest popcorn ball,** which is made of nearly 1,000 pounds of popcorn glued together with sugar and syrup and sits in a shed on Main Street (Sac City has a popcorn factory in town). If you want more strange sights, cruise on over to **Ida Grove,** which has several structures built in the shape of castles, including the local newspaper office, a shopping mall and a skating rink. The castles were built by a wealthy former resident who also constructed a scale model of the HMS *Bounty* on a private lake. Ida Grove is a small town and the castles aren't hard to find, although most are private property and not open to visitors. Still, go ahead and stare at all this medieval architecture plunked down among the Iowa cornfields.

IN THE AREA

ACCOMMODATIONS

There are numerous resorts and hotels scattered across the Okoboji and Spirit Lake area with a variety of activities and amenities. Many fill up for long stretches of the summer; contact resorts well in advance to ensure rooms are available.

Hannah Marie Country Inn, 4070 US 71, Spencer. Call 712-262-1286. A relaxing escape away from the hustle and bustle of both the Great Lakes and Storm Lake, with five comfortable rooms, delicious breakfasts and gardens that are perfect for strolling. Inexpensive. Website: www.hannah mariecountryinn.com.

Kingman Place Bed & Breakfast, 13710 240th Avenue, Spirit Lake. Call 712-336-6865 or 507-236-2183. A charming Colonial home on a lawn studded with mature oaks and maples right on the lakeshore. Comfortable feather beds and a delicious breakfast make it easy to forget your worries as you settle in for a relaxing weekend at the quieter end of the Great Lakes. Gaze out over the waters as you sit on the dock. There are three rooms, all with private bath. Moderate. Website: www.kingman place.com.

Okoboji Country Inn, 1704 Terrace Park Boulevard, West Okoboji. Call 712-332-2358. This bed & breakfast within walking distance of West Lake Okoboji is a simple farmhouse on the outside, but step through the door and you're in the middle of a luxurious getaway, with rooms that feature comfortable beds and plenty of sunlight. Each of the six guest rooms is decked out in a different color scheme. Both shared and private baths are available. Moderate to Expensive. Website: www.okoboji countryinn.com.

Wild Rose Inn of Okoboji, 2625 41st Street, Spirit Lake. Call 712-332-9986. A bed & breakfast in an impressively large home set on wooded acreage, with suites that offer a choice of Jacuzzi or veranda; all come with private bath. Great breakfasts, gourmet snacks and a downstairs game room. The inn also hosts wine dinners. Moderate to Medium. Website: www .wildroseresort.com.

DINING

Boathouse Bar and Grill, 502 Lake Avenue, Storm Lake. Call 712-732-1462. The nautical theme of this casual restaurant continues on the

menu, where the specials include Alaskan king crab, lobster and oysters either fried or on the half shell. They also do a good steak, as well as prime rib, smoked pork and burgers with all sorts of toppings. Fun atmosphere and kids' menu. Moderate. Website: www.stormlake-ia.com /boathouse.

Boz Wellz, 507 Erie Street, Storm Lake. Call 712-732-3616. Hearty, well-prepared meals are served at this cozy downtown storefront. Hand-cut steaks are well broiled and tasty. Other options include Iowa favorite grilled pork loin or a big, juicy burger. Boz Wellz is particularly proud of its Reuben sandwich, piled high with tasty corned beef. Dessert is a slice of the cheesecake prepared on the premises, but it might be tough choosing from the many varieties offered. Moderate. Website: www.boz wellz.com.

Bracco Okoboji, 317 240th Avenue, Arnolds Park. Call 712-332-7900. Located at the large Bridges Bay resort, this bustling, deckside, open-air joint will transport you to the Caribbean, especially when warn breezes are blowing off the lake just past the railing. The feeling of the islands continues with the menu, which features dishes like Jamaican jerk chicken, fish tacos and other seafood options. Plenty of other menu selections range from burgers to steaks, pasta to flatbread pizzas and even sushi. To complete the fantasy, order one of the powerful daiquiris or other tropical drinks (you can refill it later at the beach bar). Website: www.bracco restaurant.com/okoboji.

Family Diner, 1604 Hill Avenue, Spirit Lake. Call 712-336-5422. A cute little diner in the heart of Spirit Lake's strolling and shopping. Friendly service and good food make this a perfect place to fuel up on standard breakfast and lunch items. The menu also includes some delicious soups and sandwiches. Inexpensive.

Global Deli at the Market, 1610 Hill Avenue, Spirit Lake. Call 712-336-2520. This gourmet grocery on downtown's main drag has a café with tasty sandwiches, including tasty gyros with fresh fixings. There's also a salad bar, yummy soups and choices like falafel and pasta. It's also a perfect spot to pick up items for a lakeside picnic lunch. Inexpensive.

Honey Kissed Pizza, 701 Lake Avenue, Storm Lake. Call 712-732-7222. A fun, laid-back joint in downtown Storm Lake with plenty of loyal regulars who swear by the pizza, which includes specialty pies like bacon cheeseburger, barbecued chicken or a carnivore's delight with five different kinds of meat. Lighter fare can be found on the salad bar. There's also pinball and video games, and the walls are covered with a collection of rock 'n' roll album covers. Inexpensive to Moderate.

Rabab's Neighborhood Bistro, 1621 Hill Avenue, Spirit Lake. Call 712-336-3400. The interior of this popular eatery is stylish and tasteful, with exposed brick and ductwork and soft jazz playing in the background. The kitchen is just as smooth, turning out plenty of fresh, tasty dishes off a limited menu of steak, seafood and pasta. Appetizers have an international flair, like Jamaican jerk shrimp or a Lebanese *mezza,* or sample plate of Middle Eastern goodies. Moderate to Medium. Website: www.rababs bistro.com.

Smokin' Jakes, 117 Broadway, Arnolds Park. Call 712-332-5152. Dive into a huge platter of hickory-smoked baby back ribs at this no-frills barbecue pit in the Old Town district. All sorts of other smoked meats are available too, as are steaks, burgers and a full slate of sandwiches. A long list of beer and mixed drinks gives you plenty of options to wash down all the meat. If you still have room after tackling your meal, the Granny's Corner portion of the menu offers delectable desserts like ice cream cones, sundaes and root beer floats. Stays open late, which is perfect if you've got a hankering for some 'cue in the wee hours, or for that matter breakfast, which is served late into the night. Moderate. Website: http://smokinjakes.com.

Table 316 Steakhouse, 316 North US 71, Arnolds Park. Call 712-332-6090. Char-grilled slabs of prime steak sizzle on the grill at this rambling, casual restaurant that draws crowds. Jumbo shrimp and chicken Alfredo are other menu standouts, as is prime rib served au jus. In addition to various cuts of steak grilled as you like them, there are specialty steaks marinated in sauces like red chili and teriyaki. Also serves Sunday breakfast. Moderate. Website: www.table 316.com.

SHOPPING

Barn Swallow, 1212 US 71 North, Okoboji. Call 712-332-7752. This inviting shop in a rambling old house has all sorts of housewares, decorative items, locally themed gifts, and children's books and clothing.

Bay View Gifts & Garden, 3202 US 71 South, Spirit Lake. Call 712-336-8948. A treasure-trove of gifts is found at this shop between the three main Great Lakes. New merchandise arrives frequently and includes wine accessories, handbags, rugs, lamps and other home items. Carries antiques and kids' stuff, too.

Bungalow 29, 29 Dam Road, Arnolds Park. Call 712-332-2903. Just a block from the famous amusement park, this upscale women's clothing shop has outfits from many different designers, with stylish attire in denim, cashmere and other fabrics. Take

time to browse through the selection; you may find a hidden treasure.

Central Emporium, 144 Lake Shore Drive, Arnolds Park. Call 712-332-5293. This building resembles an old armory from the outside, but it's actually a fun local mall with close to 20 merchants who sell everything under the sun. Pick up clothing, swimwear and sunglasses as well as jewelry and home decor items. There's a bookstore and candy shop, as well as a café, bar and restaurant for taking a break. Website: http://central emporium.com.

Country Garden, 1603 Hill Avenue, Spirit Lake. Call 712-336-4889. Gifts and crafts from all over the world can be found in this converted gas station that now sports a Colonial facade. Silk and fresh cut flowers are also among the enticing offerings. Website: www.lakescountrygarden.com.

Hill Avenue Book Company, 1711 Hill Avenue, Spirit Lake. Call 712-336-5672. A cubbyhole of an independent bookshop with plenty of selections across a variety of genres. The staff is well versed in many authors and can help guide you to a particular title or make recommendations you might enjoy.

A Piece of Work, 1619 Hill Avenue, Spirit Lake. Call 712-336-1077. This converted automobile showroom features artists working in a wide variety of media, everything from painting and sculpture to glass, wood, jewelry, photography and more. Take a look inside just to see the impressive setup and peruse the art. Website: www.apieceofworkinc.com.

This 'N That Eclectics, 1618 Hill Avenue, Spirit Lake. Call 712-336-4411. Unique furniture and housewares at this funky Olde Town shop. The shelves and aisles contain a potpourri of clothing and knickknacks, including many items with a nautical theme. Much of the furniture is custom-made by one of the proprietors.

Wash House, 1704 Terrace Park Boulevard, Milford (West Okoboji). Call 712-332-2358. Located in the Okoboji Country Inn, this gift shop has three floors of home bric-a-brac and decorative items. Check out the selection of jewelry, French milled soaps and various wine-related items. Handbags and wall art are just some of the many other goodies you'll find. Website: www.okoboji countryinn.com.

OTHER CONTACTS

Okoboji Tourism, P.O. Box 215, Okoboji, 51355. Call 712-332-2209 or 1-800-270-2574. Website: www .vacationokoboji.com.

Spencer Chamber of Commerce, 122 West Fifth Street, P.O. Box 7937, Spencer, 51301. Call 712-262-5680. Website: www.spenceriowachamber .org.

Storm Lake United, 119 West Sixth Street, P.O. Box 584, Storm Lake, 50588. Call 712-732-3780 or 1-888-752-4692. Website: www.visitstorm lake.com.

Sac Economic and Tourism Development, 615 West Main Street, Sac City, 50583. Call 712-662-7383. Website: http://saccountyiowa.com.

14 Northwest Iowa:
LEWIS AND CLARK COUNTRY, DUTCH WINDMILLS AND ICE CREAM!

Estimated length: About 200 miles, looping from Sioux City north to the Minnesota border, then back to Sioux City.

Estimated time: Weekend, or even as a day trip from Sioux City.

Getting there: Sioux City, the starting point, is at the intersection of I-29, US 20 and US 75.

Highlights: Lots of historic spots and other sights in Sioux City. A unique small-town museum and planetarium in Cherokee. The highest point in Iowa (such as it is) just south of the Minnesota border. Windmills and Dutch culture in Orange City. A fabulous ice cream parlor and museum in Le Mars.

This part of Iowa feels like a remnant of the open frontier, with *long* distances between towns across flat, empty fields. The overwhelmingly rural character of this wide-open and sparsely populated part of the state makes it a bit more difficult to find overnight lodging; really the only urban area is **Sioux City**, a metropolitan area of 150,000 residents that sits on the Missouri River at the three-way junction of Iowa, Nebraska and South Dakota.

Sioux City is rich in history, dating back to the eponymous Native American tribe that once hunted for buffalo on the surrounding open plains. French fur trappers later moved into the area, and in 1804 the Lewis and Clark expedition stopped here, where they lost a member of the team—the only one to die during their trek west. The area eventually became a key junction for both steamboats and railroads.

Along with being a transportation center, Sioux City built massive stockyards that grew to rival those in Chicago and Omaha, as well as adjoining meatpacking

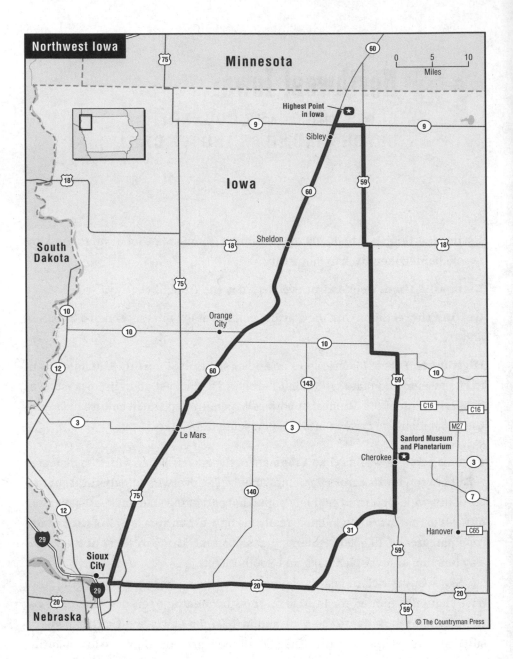

facilities; these have since closed. An effort to spruce up downtown and residential neighborhoods around the turn of the 20th century led to many art deco and Prairie School buildings going up around the city. More recently, immigrant populations from Africa, Southeast Asia, and Latin America have brought diversity to the area.

Note: Sioux City and other communities along the Missouri River suffered extensive damage from Missouri River flooding in 2011; the riverfront area, where several of Sioux City's tourist attractions are located, was especially hard hit. Check in advance to see if attractions and other destinations have reopened.

Much of the area's history is on display at the downtown **Sioux City Public Museum**, which reopened in 2011 after an extensive renovation. All kinds of historical items are displayed in the huge museum, including vintage airplanes, cars and a steamboat paddle-wheeler in an area devoted to transportation. Other exhibits examine the importance of the stockyards and meatpacking industry to Sioux City's development and a Native American gallery focusing on the tribes that lived along the Missouri River. There are plenty of interactive exhibits that kids will enjoy as well.

The museum even has an exhibit devoted to tragedies that have befallen the area, notably the spectacular 1989 crash landing of an airliner that skidded off a runway at Sioux City's airport before plowing into a cornfield and was incorporated into the 1993 film *Fearless*. The crash, in which 111 people died, is also commemorated at the **Flight 232 Memorial**, which includes a statue based on a famous photograph. It's located by the **Anderson Dance Pavilion** on Sioux City's **riverfront**.

The riverfront also features extensive parkland crisscrossed by walking trails in the shadow of the arching **Veteran's Memorial Bridge**, which carries traffic between Iowa and Nebraska. The **Lewis & Clark Interpretive Center** (www .siouxcitylcic.com), just steps from the waters traveled by the pair and their party and marked by a large statue out front, is a free museum with one of the most extensive collections devoted to the two great explorers. Animatronic robots tell the story of their journey up the Missouri River and into the West, and there are numerous interactive exhibits and displays on Native American and pioneer history. It's a perfect spot for both adults and kids to learn about a fascinating event in America's past and its impact on the country.

Close by, the **Sergeant Floyd River Museum** (www.siouxcitymuseum.org), housed on a boat permanently anchored on the riverfront, is a showcase of the Missouri River and efforts to harness it by earlier generations of Sioux City residents. Learn about fur trapping and the wide variety of river craft that plied local waterways during the steamboat era. There's also a restored engineer's quarters, radio room and officers' room.

LEWIS AND CLARK: A VOYAGE OF DISCOVERY

The iconic expedition of Meriwether Lewis and William Clark was a signature moment in American history. With a team of just over 30, the two traveled by canoe, keelboat and on foot through a vast swath of territory virtually unseen by Europeans or other immigrants.

Setting out in 1804 following the Louisiana Purchase—which doubled the size of the United States at the time, and is equivalent to nearly a quarter of current U.S. territory, including all or part of 15 states—the expedition, commissioned by President Thomas Jefferson, spent more than two years traveling from St. Louis to the Pacific Ocean coast in present-day Oregon.

The significant transcontinental crossing was both commercial and scientific in scope. Lewis and Clark mapped the areas in which they traveled, providing a guide to future travelers and laying the eventual foundation for trade routes through the West. They also collected and cataloged a wealth of flora and fauna, which kept naturalists busy for many years examining a whole new assortment of plant and animal life.

Along with their Native American companion Sacagawea, the pair interacted with tribes along the way. While there was conflict with some, many assisted the two explorers in their travels.

Towns and cities along the Missouri have erected legacies to the two explorers, perhaps none more extensively than Sioux City, with its riverfront museum and impressive monument to the fallen member of the expedition, Sergeant Floyd, as well as a series of Lewis and Clark murals at a local mall and Lewis and Clark Park, home to the local minor league baseball team.

An even greater tribute to the unfortunate member of the Lewis and Clark party who perished in Sioux City is found at the **Sergeant Floyd Monument** (www.nps.gov/nr/travel/lewisandclark/ser.htm), a towering obelisk on the southern outskirts of town. It's even visible from the nearby interstate. Floyd, who is believed to have died as a result of a ruptured appendix, was not only the lone member of the Lewis and Clark expedition to die on the three-year trip, but was also the first American soldier to die west of the Mississippi. The monument is located on the spot where he was buried.

At the other end of the city, the **War Eagle Monument** commemorates the Native American chief who served as a guide on the Mississippi and Missouri Rivers and as a messenger for American troops in the War of 1812. He was renowned for his skill at peacefully resolving disputes between native tribes and settlers. Later, he joined with a fur trader who settled near the junction of the Missouri and Big Sioux Rivers. Their settlement eventually grew into Sioux City.

The monument stands in a blufftop park also named for War Eagle, near where the chief was buried, as were several members of his family. There are very nice views over the confluence of the rivers that made Sioux City. The trader's settlement, **Bruguier's Cabin,** has since been moved to the riverfront, where it is open to visitors.

Back downtown, a stroll around the streets takes you past some fine architectural edifices, including the **Woodbury County Courthouse,** a Prairie School–style structure with intricate terra cotta features and a stained-glass dome. The **Historic Fourth Street District** is marked by old, weathered commercial buildings and warehouses reborn as nice restaurants, shops and entertainment options.

Even more history is found at **Milwaukee Railroad Shops Historic District** (www.milwaukeerailroadshops.org) on the site of a former large complex of rail-

Woodbury County Courthouse, Sioux City

THE LOESS HILLS: IOWA'S NATURAL SPLENDOR

Winding across the western edge of Iowa like an old clothesline, the Loess ("Luss") Hills make up a narrow belt of mostly forested slopes, a welcome break from the endless swaths of open fields that otherwise dominate the landscape.

Created during the last Ice Age, the hills are the result of windblown silt, or loess, piling up into hills during glacial activity. The hills stand several hundred feet in some places, with a layer of topsoil covering the loess. Erosion of the silty soil has led to the hills having something of a terraced appearance. Western Iowa shares this unique landscape with the Yellow River Valley of China, the only other place on Earth where loess reaches such heights.

Prior to European settlement, the hills were largely covered with prairie landscape, but the introduction of agriculture and settled communities discouraged the wildfires that maintained the prairie. Today, the hills are largely covered with trees, although swatches of prairie can be seen as well, serving as a habitat for wildlife.

The Loess Hills National Scenic Byway runs from the northern edge of the hills on the Iowa-South Dakota border through remote areas all the way to south of Council Bluffs, paralleling the Missouri River, and is divided into a series of shorter routes.

Along the byway are numerous spots for hiking and exploring the Loess Hills, including Stone State Park by Sioux City (see *Entertainment* and *Recreation*), as well as Loess Hills Wildlife Area, Turin Loess Hills Nature Preserve and the Sylvan Runkel State Preserve, all located between Sioux City and Council Bluffs, and all good places to see the hills' native prairie landscape. Close by are Preparation Canyon State Park and Loess Hills Pioneer Forest, both located near the town of Moorhead, home of the Loess Hills Hospitality Association, which can provide maps and guides. In Onawa is Lewis and Clark State Park, which has replicas of the boats used on the explorers' expedition, as well as *three* local museums and an arboretum. More information can be found at www.visitloesshills.com and www.loesshillsalliance.org. There are also Loess Hills attractions in the Council Bluffs area; see that chapter for details.

road maintenance buildings that showcases the importance of the railroad in Sioux City. Take a walking tour and visit the roundhouse and a historic steam engine. There are other old rail cars to see as well. Meanwhile, **Trinity Heights** (www.trinityheights.com) has religious statues that stand strikingly against the skyline, including a 33-foot-tall statue of Christ and a 30-foot-tall Virgin Mary. A life-sized Last Supper is also on display. Native plants and flowers complement strolling paths that wind through the grounds.

If you need a break from history, check out the **Sioux City Art Center** (www.siouxcityartcenter.org), a free museum notable for a striking glass tower at the center of its building. Open for more than 70 years, the museum has a fine collection of creations by regional, national and international artists. There are unique works like Grant Wood's *Corn Room* mural, which takes up an entire gallery. Thomas Hart Benton's works are also well represented among the many Midwestern artists on display.

Heading east from Sioux City, cross the Little Sioux and Sioux Rivers as you veer northeast on your way to **Cherokee**. A typical small Iowa town, it is also home to a unique local treasure: the **Sanford Museum & Planetarium** (http://sanfordmuseum.org), which was the first planetarium in Iowa. The modest round building sits on the lawn in front of the museum and still gives monthly sky and star shows, as well as special presentations. The museum features exhibits on area geology and prehistoric cultures, including fossils recovered from local digs. There are also animal skins and furs on display.

From Cherokee, head west if you just can't wait to get to the ice cream mecca of Le Mars (see below). Or, continue driving north through a long, lonely corridor of fields and farms, with the landscape getting emptier the closer you get to Minnesota.

Before you reach the border, head west on the road heading to **Sibley**. A few miles outside of town, just off the road and down a small farm road is **Hawkeye Point** (www.osceolacountyia.org/explore/hawkeye). This is the highest point in the state. At 1,670 feet it's not much compared to other high points, but it's ap-

Hawkeye Point, the highest point in Iowa

propriate: the small rise looks out over endless cornfields, an Iowa vista if there ever was one, with a silo towering overhead. There's also a small monument at the site.

Nearby in Sibley is the **McCallum Museum** (www.sibleyiowa.net/leisure /museum), a showcase of pioneer and Civil War artifacts as well as oddities like a two-headed calf. The biggest oddity of all is that the museum was built around the first wooden house in the county in order to protect the house. The local fairgrounds are home to the **Otter Valley Model Railroad,** open by appointment, with more than 5,000 feet of track extensively landscaped for the tiny trains.

The outlying small town of **Ashton** has **DeBoer's Grocery Store,** with mercantile effects from several small-town shops, while **Harris,** on the way to Okoboji Lake, is the site of a **mini grotto** made of rocks from many states.

Heading south, it's a drive through the vacant countryside to **Orange City,** a town of less than 6,000 residents. Like Pella in central Iowa, it revels in its Dutch heritage, with a tulip festival every May (www.octulipfestival.com). There's a Dutch bakery, meat market and wooden shoe factory, and many buildings have Dutch details in their architecture. The town's **visitors center** is housed in a replica windmill, one of several in town. Another, the **Old Mill,** is located in the parking lot of a local paint factory. It demonstrates wind power and is furnished inside like a typical Dutch craftsman's home.

Across the street is a trailhead for the **Puddle Jumper Trail,** a hiking and bicycling path that runs a few miles to the community of **Alton.** In the center of town, **Windmill Park** could be transplanted from Holland, with a model windmill and wooden shoe and lots of tulip beds. There's also a nice little bandstand. The **Century Home** is an impressive Victorian mansion that once belonged to Orange City's first mayor and is open to visitors.

From here, you drive through another stretch of lonely, rolling countryside to reach a true oasis: **Le Mars,** the self-proclaimed "Ice Cream Capital of the World." The town makes a good case: not only is it the headquarters of Blue Bunny Ice

Cream, which churns out more than 100 million gallons of luscious goodness every year, utilizing a storage freezer that is 12 stories tall and a city block long (vanilla is their most popular flavor), not only does it celebrate "Ice Cream Days" every summer, it also has a fabulous downtown pilgrimage site for those with a sweet tooth: an **ice cream parlor** (www.wellsenterprisesinc.com/Parlor-Museum /Default.aspx) run by the company.

The large, old-fashioned sweet shop is easy to spot, with a giant sundae dish sculpture on the sidewalk. Inside, friendly servers dish up any one of several flavors as well as decadent treats covered with syrup and toppings. Go ahead, try the Goliath, with its six (or is it seven?) scoops, or one of the many other yummy sundaes, shakes, floats or innumerable other gut-busting specials. Walk it off afterward with a visit to the small museum up-

Blue Bunny Ice Cream Parlor and Museum in Le Mars

stairs, where you can view interesting photographs and memorabilia from company history, then stroll over to the **Plymouth County Historical Museum** (http: //plymouthcountymuseum.homestead.com/museum.html), which has three floors of exhibits in the town's former high school.

After loading up on ice cream and maybe even dining in one of Le Mars's good restaurants, it's a fairly quick drive back to Sioux City and northwest Iowa's one taste of urbanity.

IN THE AREA

ACCOMMODATIONS

Many chain hotels and motels can be found along the highways that converge in Sioux City, including several just over the state line in Nebraska and South Dakota.

Marina Inn, 385 East Fourth Street, South Sioux City, Nebraska. Call 402-

494-4000. This large hotel on the banks of the Missouri River has splendid views of the nearby Siouxland Veterans Memorial Bridge and the lights of Sioux City. Upscale rooms have plenty of space and floor-to-ceiling windows for taking in the surrounding landscape. There are plenty of amenities, including a fitness center and pool. The in-house restaurant, Kahill's, is good for digging into the local cuisine, with a focus on big portions of red meat. Moderate. Website: http://marina-inn.com.

Stoney Creek Inn, 300 Third Street, Sioux City. Call 712-234-1100. Like its other outposts in Iowa and across the Midwest, this large, northwoods-themed hotel has rustic decor that gives it the look of a hunting lodge. Rooms, however, are modern and comfortable, and all have a refrigerator, microwave and flat-screen television. There's an indoor/outdoor pool, an on-site lounge with food and complimentary breakfast. Moderate. Website: http://stoneycreekinn.com/locations/index.cfm/SiouxCity.

DINING

Archie's Waeside, 224 Fourth Avenue Northeast, Le Mars. Call 712-546-7011. Wonderful tastes in Le Mars are not confined to the Blue Bunny Ice Cream Parlor. This temple for carnivores in the heart of beef country, a multigenerational family enterprise that has won national acclaim, serves up wonderful steaks, dry-aged and then grilled until juicy and flavorful. While the porterhouse earns most of the accolades, there's also rib eye, T-bone and several other cuts. Most of the seafood dishes are deep-fried; in general, this isn't the place for subtlety or small portions. A good-size wine list provides a nice complement to the big cuts of beef. Moderate. Website: www.waesdie.com.

Bob's Drive-Inn, Fifth Avenue Northwest and Plymouth Street West, Le Mars. Call 712-546-5445. At the opposite end of the culinary spectrum from other local favorite Archie's, this low-slung joint at the intersection of two highways on the edge of Le Mars is the place to wolf down a "loose meat" sandwich, a spicy pile of ground beef, with or without a hot dog thrown in. Add some fries and a milkshake if you really want the full experience. (Just don't forget to save room for the Blue Bunny Ice Cream Parlor later.) Inexpensive.

Buffalo Alice, 1022 Fourth Street, Sioux City. Call 712-255-4822. Tasty nachos, chicken wings and pizza at this no-frills bar and grill whose walls are covered with a collection of interesting memorabilia. Located in the heart of Sioux City's downtown entertainment district, it's a favorite with a younger, beer-drinking crowd, who pack in after work and on weekends for the impressive selection of brews. Inexpensive. Website: www.buffaloalice.com.

De Koffiehoek, 819 Lincoln Place Southeast, Orange City. Call 712-707-9399. Basic breakfast and lunch at this coffee shop in a newer development on the outskirts of town. Nothing fancy, but the egg plates and coffee will get you started in the morning, while simple sandwiches make for a nice, light lunch or break from sight-seeing. Inexpensive. Website: www.koffiehoek.bizjubon.biz /home.

Eldon's, 3322 Singing Hills Boulevard, Sioux City. Call 712-224-3332. This sleek, upscale eatery is reflective of big city restaurants, with decor that features mahogany and granite. Beef is the mainstay, as one would expect in a town that once boasted sprawling stockyards. The menu features juicy and tender steaks and prime rib, as well as delicious hamburgers, including one topped with blue cheese. Sandwiches, soup and salads are good lighter choices, and there's a nice wine list. Medium. Website: http://eldonsrestaurant.com.

Green Gables, 1800 Pierce Street, Sioux City. Call 712-258-4246. A homestyle restaurant in a funky little building north of downtown. Old-fashioned favorites like chicken and burgers keep regulars coming back, but the biggest draw is probably the scrumptious hot fudge sundaes, which come with a little pitcher of the chocolate goodness to pour over the ice cream at your own discretion. Inexpensive to Moderate.

Habitue Coffeehouse & Creperie, 108 Central Avenue Northeast, Le Mars. Call 712-546-4424. An antidote to the more indulgent eating choices around Le Mars (steaks at Archie's, fried fare at Bob's, ice cream at Blue Bunny), this sleek and stylish café has crêpes that make a nice light meal, with many fillings inspired by Mexican and Italian cuisine. Of course, you can also get sweet crêpes like peach Amaretto and strawberries and cream. There are soups and sandwiches and a full slate of coffee drinks and baked goods, too. Inexpensive to Moderate. Website: www .habituecoffee.com.

Hatchery, 121 Third Street Northwest, Orange City. Call 712-737-2889. This modest brick building across from Orange City's downtown Dutch-themed park was, in fact, a chicken hatchery for many years. Though there are several chicken dishes available, the menu runs the gamut from all-American favorites like burgers, steaks and seafood to numerous Mexican items. Overall, it's a low-key dining experience with some good food. Inexpensive to Moderate.

Kahill's, 385 East Fourth Street, South Sioux City, Nebraska. Call 402-494-4000. Across the river from Sioux City in the Marina Inn, this riverside restaurant serves up well-prepared steaks along with classic upscale favorites like duck, blackened redfish and rack of lamb. There are also more exotic choice like bison sausage and Asian sea bass. The bar has small plates as well as an impressive drink selection, and the restaurant provides room service in the hotel. Medium. Website: http://marina-inn.com/taste.

Luciano's, 1019 Fourth Street, Sioux City. Call 712-258-5174. Classy Italian dining in a historic building makes this a popular spot. A large selection of pasta dishes, from old favorites like manicotti and fettuccine Alfredo to pesto and butternut squash ravioli highlight the menu, as do osso buco, veal parmigiana and some tasty steaks. Start off with one of the many colorful martinis from the bar, or choose from the lengthy beer and wine list. Finish with one of their sweet desserts. Moderate. Website: www.italiandiningsiouxcity.com.

Minerva's, 2945 Hamilton Boulevard, Sioux City. Call 712-277-0800. Another of Sioux City's many steakhouses (though part of a chain based in South Dakota), Minerva's has ribs and chops on the menu alongside the rib eye, New York strip and other steak choices. Interesting steak toppings include a sauce of horseradish, blue cheese and peppercorns, as well as standbys like onions and mushrooms. Seafood offerings include several enticing salmon options. Pizza and burgers round out the menu. Extensive wine list. Moderate to Medium. Website: www.minervas.net /minervas-restaurant-sioux-city-ia .php.

Nederlander's Grill, 604 Eighth Street Southeast, Orange City. Call 712-737-3900. A somewhat formal yet relaxed dining room with deep roots in Orange City. Lots of delicious comfort food like smothered chicken, barbecued ribs and bacon-wrapped pork chops, as well as steaks and seafood. The food is fresh and tasty. Moderate. Website: http://nederalndersgrill .com.

Rebo's, 1101 Fourth Street, Sioux City. Call 712-258-0395. A restaurant with a funky interior and a flair for exotic cooking. Mexican and Caribbean choices share space on the menu, with some tempting small plates like a salsa sampler and Jamaican chicken wings. Tasty sandwiches and salads, too. Inexpensive to Moderate. Website: http://eatrebos .com.

SHOPPING

Galley Gift Shop, 1000 Larsen Park Road, Sioux City. Call 712-279-0198. With two locations, one at the Sergeant Floyd Welcome Center on the Sioux City riverfront and the other at the Sioux City Public Museum, this is a nice spot to pick up gifts and souvenirs with a local twist, including T-shirts, postcards and children's toys. Also check out the gift shop at the Sioux City Public Museum. Website: www.siouxcitymuseum.org/store.asp.

The Old Factory, 110 Fourth Street Southwest, Orange City. Call 712-737-4242. Wooden shoes as fine as you'll find in Holland are still made and sold at this historic storefront outside downtown. Peruse the many *klompen* hanging from the ceiling inside, some painted with artistic designs. Also for sale are Dutch imports like blue and white Delft earthenware, antiques and food items. There's also a small coffee area where you can relax and marvel even more at the wooden shoes.

Palmer's Old Tyme Candy Shoppe, 405 Wesley Parkway, Sioux City. Call 712-258-7790. This shop in a historic building sells the offerings of a local, family-owned candy factory that has been cranking out yummy goodies for well over a century. It's best known for the Twin Bing bar, a confection of cherry-flavored nougat covered with chocolate and peanuts. Plenty of other tastes of heavenly chocolate are also for sale here. Website: www.palmercandy.com.

RECREATION AND ENTERTAINMENT

Argosy Casino, 100 Larsen Park Road, Sioux City. Call 712-294-5600 or 1-800-424-0080. Slots and table games can be found in this 35,000-square-foot gambling palace on the Sioux City riverfront. There's an on-site restaurant, too. Website: www .argosysiouxcity.com.

Orpheum, 528 Pierce Street, Sioux City. Call 1-800-745-3000. The impressive marquee leads to an elegant lobby in this restored downtown theater, home to numerous live events, including musical entertainment and stage productions. Website: http://orpheumlive.com.

Stone State Park, 5001 North Talbot Road. Call 712-255-4698. This park at the north edge of Sioux City is an easy way to experience the landscape of the Loess Hills. There are hiking trails with great views of the hills and surrounding valleys, prairie and rivers. Within the park, the **Dorothy Pecaut Nature Center** (www.wood buryparks.com/naturecenter.html) has interpretive displays, wildlife dioramas, a 400-gallon aquarium with native fish and river life, and a children's area where visitors can handle natural artifacts and fossils.

OTHER CONTACTS

Sioux City Convention & Tourism Bureau, 801 Fourth Street, Sioux City, 51101. Call 712-279-4800. Website: www.visitsiouxcity.org.

Cherokee Chamber of Commerce, 416 West Main Street, Cherokee, 51012. Call 712-225-6414. Website: www.cherokeeiowachamber.com.

Osceola County Economic Development Commission, 300 Seventh Street, Sibley, 51249. Call 712-754-2523. Website: www.osceolacountyia .com.

Orange City Chamber of Commerce, 509 Eighth Street Southeast, P.O. Box 36, Orange City, 51041. Call 712-707-4510. Website: www.orange cityiowa.com.

Le Mars Convention & Visitors Bureau, 40 Central Avenue Southeast, Le Mars, 51031. Call 712-548-4971. Website: www.lemarsiowa.com/cvb /cvb.htm.

15 Southwest Iowa:
FROM COUNCIL BLUFFS TO
THE COLD WAR IN COON RAPIDS

Estimated length: About 250 miles, running from Council Bluffs northeast to Denison, Carroll and Coon Rapids, then south to Atlantic and Clarinda before returning to Council Bluffs.

Estimated time: Two to three days.

Getting there: Council Bluffs is at the intersection of Interstates 80 and 29.

Highlights: Railroad sites in Council Bluffs, including one of the best train museums anywhere. An amazing collection of religious art. A typical Iowa farm that once was the scene of a historic rapprochement between the United States and the Soviet Union. A giant windmill *and* a giant statue of a bull just a few miles from each other.

Small towns sprinkled in the farm belt between Des Moines and Omaha are home to some interesting attractions, including the legacy of Iowa's Old World immigrants visible in several rural communities. This trip may be split into two legs, with Council Bluffs as a base and I-80 serving as a dividing line between the legs.

A major crossroads and way station since Lewis and Clark passed through on the Missouri River, **Council Bluffs** earned its name after it was the site of a meeting between the two explorers and a local Native American tribe. Within a few decades, the strategically located spot on the edge of the Great Plains became a jumping-off point for pioneers seeking a new life on the frontier, its streets bustling with wagon trains and suppliers peddling all manner of goods for the trek west.

Mormon families were among those who passed through, and today the city

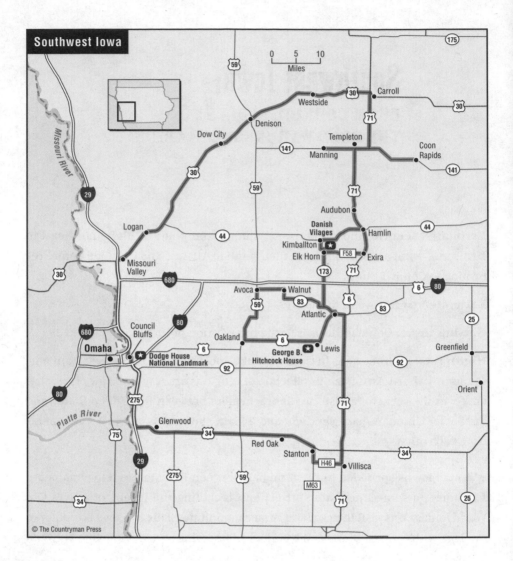

has several Mormon-related sites. Later, railroads moved in and the city became a major railroading center, the eastern end of the first transcontinental railroad, with trains clanking through day and night. While a knot of railroad tracks is still visible from the nearby interstate that zips cars to and from Omaha, whose sky-line looms just across the river, Council Bluffs today is known more for gambling than railroads, with casinos looming near the riverfront.

Note: Areas around Council Bluffs were hit by Missouri River flooding in 2011, and many visitor destinations faced a long road to recovery; check ahead of

One of the featured trains at the Union Pacific Railroad Museum

time to see if a place you wish to visit is open for business.

Begin your visit to Council Bluffs in the charming downtown. **Bayliss Park** (http://parksandrec .councilbluffs-ia.gov/bayliss.asp) is a delightful patch of green amid blocks of old commercial buildings, with a spectacular fountain at its center. It's a wonderful spot to sit and rest on a sunny day. There are also several monuments, including one to the Mormon Trail pioneers. Another impressive fountain sits a couple blocks away at Main Street and Broadway.

Across the street from Bayliss Park is the **Union Pacific Railroad Museum** (www.uprrmuseum.org). Housed in a historic beaux-arts building that was once a Carnegie Library, the museum has multiple floors displaying a vast trove of railroad artifacts and exhibits, with some items that date to the mid-1800s.

The picturesque fountain in Bayliss Park

COUNCIL BLUFFS:
GENESIS OF THE TRANSCONTINENTAL RAILROAD

Facing the frontier from its vantage point on the Missouri River, Council Bluffs became a natural starting point for settlers making their way west in the mid-1800s. The march west soon involved railroads, and future Civil War General Grenville Dodge spent the 1850s surveying the area for the Union Pacific and other railroad lines.

In 1859, Abraham Lincoln came to Council Bluffs and decided that one end of a transcontinental railroad stretching to the Pacific Coast would be located right there in the city on the banks of the Missouri River. Council Bluffs commemorates its significant place in railroad history with a giant golden spike monument as well as an obelisk monument to Lincoln that supposedly stands at the spot where the future president surveyed the area.

Kids will be enthralled by the many interactive displays showing how trains work, as well as those that bring visitors inside railroad cars from the golden age of train travel; check out the comparison between train and plane passenger seats to see what we've given up in making the switch from traveling by rail to air!

Just down the block is the historic **Squirrel Cage Jail** (www.thehistorical society.org/jail.htm). No, it's not a jail for squirrels, although the black squirrel is the city's mascot (look for them at Bayliss Park and around town). Rather, it's an old town jail built with its cells grouped inside a large cylinder, which could be rotated by turning a crank. This enabled just one jailer to watch the jailed inmates.

One of just three such jails in the U.S. (and the only one that stands three stories tall), it served as the city jail until the late 1960s.

The exterior of the unique Squirrel Cage Jail in Council Bluffs

Stop by the **Pottawattamie County Courthouse** downtown for a look at part of one of Grant Wood's **Corn Room Murals**. Several panels of the iconic Iowa artist's study of his native landscape hang on the walls.

Train buffs can get even more railroad history by making their way south toward the main rail yards, next to which sits the **RailsWest Railroad Museum** (www.thehistoricalsociety.org/depot.htm) in the city's restored 1899 depot. Inside are railroad artifacts and an impressive model railroad. Outside are several rail cars visitors can tour, including a steam locomotive. The **Golden Spike Monument** (parksandrec.councilbluffs-ia.gov/historical.asp?page=3) sits in a nearby park, thrusting skyward. The 56-foot-tall gold-painted concrete spike was actually built as part of a 1930s movie promotion, but the city embraces it as part of its long legacy of railroading and the building of the transcontinental railroad, of which Council Bluffs served as a key terminus.

The **Historic General Dodge House** (www.dodgehouse.org), home of the man who was instrumental in making Council Bluffs a major railroading center, sits

The Golden Spike Monument in Council Bluffs

halfway up a bluff in a neighborhood lined with brick streets and overlooking downtown. The impressive brick Victorian, which is open to visitors, has been meticulously maintained and includes period furnishings.

The Historic General Dodge House in Council Bluffs

An unusual related attraction is found looking out from nearby Fairview Cemetery: the **Ruth Anne Dodge Memorial** (parksandrec.councilbluffs-ia.gov/historical.asp?page=2), a large statue of an angel offering

up a vessel of flowing water. Known as the "black angel" and sculpted of solid bronze by Daniel Chester French, known for his sculpture of Lincoln at the Lincoln Memorial and other works, the angel was inspired by a dream that came to the widow of Grenville Dodge, Civil War general and noted railroad builder. Also in the cemetery is the **Kinsman Monument,** which honors Civil War veterans.

From here, you may wish to head up a steep bluff to the **Lewis and Clark Monument** (parksandrec.councilbluffs-ia.gov/historical.asp?page=5), which sits in a pleasant park to commemorate the meeting of the explorers with tribal leaders, a meeting that eventually gave Council Bluffs its name. The park commands stunning views of the surrounding Missouri River Valley. It's a nice place for a picnic.

Prior to the railroad, pioneers headed west using more simple conveyances, some of which you can learn about at the **Western Historic Trails Center** (www.iowahistory.org/historic-sites/western-historic-trails) just off I-80. Exhibits take a look at the four historic trails that converged here in the 1800s: the Lewis and Clark Trail, the Oregon Trail, the Mormon Trail and the California Trail. Learn about the hardships of the journey west through maps, films and interpretive displays.

Outside, a nature trail winds around some additional exhibits, including markers to Lewis and Clark and other trekkers and trail followers, and connects

to a longer trail that leads to a nearby state park. The surrounding terrain is tallgrass prairie, where the wind blows through large, open fields. If you stand on a rise behind the museum and look west toward the Missouri River, imagining that the skyline of Omaha isn't there, you get a sense of the vast landscape that earlier migrants saw when they lit out on the trail in search of land, gold or something else.

One of the larger groups of trail followers were the Mormons who headed west in the mid-1800s. Iowa was the first length of their trek after setting out from Nauvoo, Illinois, and

Sculpture at the Western Historic Trails Center, Council Bluffs

A statue of Brigham Young and two counselors at the Kanesville Tabernacle

Council Bluffs became an important way station along the way to their ultimate home on the shores of the Great Salt Lake. In June 1846, the first band of Mormon pioneers reached the Missouri River, where they built camps on both the east and west banks. Settling into semi-permanent farming communities, Mormons stayed in the area through the winter, laying in supplies and making preparations for the next leg of the trip, which they began in the spring of 1847, heading away from the river and into the Great Plains.

The Mormon settlement in Council Bluffs, known as the **Grand Encampment,** was located near the current site of the Iowa School for the Deaf and is noted with a historic marker. Closer to downtown, **Kanesville Tabernacle** is a replica of a modest log cabin where Mormons once met and where Brigham Young was sustained as president of the church. A bronze statue depicts Young with two of his counselors, and there are displays on Mormon history. (There is also a **Mormon Trail Center** across the river in Omaha, where many Mormons also had winter quarters.)

If you're more interested in planes than trains or trails, check out the **Commemorative Air Force Museum** (www.greatplainswing.org), whose hangars

OMAHA: BRIGHT LIGHTS ACROSS THE RIVER

Though it was actually founded after Council Bluffs, Omaha grew to be the larger of the two cities, gaining important stockyards and railroads and becoming a center of the insurance industry. There's plenty to see here, including a first-rate zoo and a baseball stadium that hosts the College World Series every year.

Visitors may actually find it more convenient to stay across the river in Omaha; there is a greater selection of hotels, as well as interesting restaurants in the Old Market area near downtown.

hold combat aircraft, military vehicles and a treasure trove of military memorabilia, including plenty of historic weapons and uniforms.

Leaving Council Bluffs, swing onto I-80, moving away from the river, then cutting onto US 30 and crossing the Loess Hills to reach the town of Logan. There's just one attraction here, but it's a unique one: the Museum of Religious Arts (www.mrarts.org). Brought together in the vast exhibition space are nine wax-figure depictions of the life of Christ, including Palm Sunday, the Last Supper and the Crucifixion, and other examples of Judeo-Christian art, all displayed in a building that features stained-glass windows and an intricately decorated chapel. Many pieces were brought here from small-town and rural churches. There is also an area dedicated to Holocaust survivor art. Three large crosses that stand on a hill outside the museum are impressive in the sunset.

Follow US 30 another 35 miles to Dow City, home to the historic Dow House, then on to Denison, home of the late actress Donna Reed, who has a local performing arts center named after her and whose Oscar statuette for *From Here to Eternity* is displayed at the historic McHenry House. Denison has many historic homes that lie along a walking tour; some of the homes have been converted into bed & breakfasts, making the town a pleasant spot to spend the night in what is otherwise wide open countryside, with virtually nothing but farms as far as the eye can see.

Proceed east on US 30 from Denison to Carroll, a good place for a pit stop and maybe a walk around the historic Victorian Romanesque depot. After you've filled up your tank and your tummy, hop onto US 71 heading south to Templeton. This unassuming farming hamlet has an association with whiskey dating back to Prohibition, and some enterprising individuals have begun selling bottled whiskey they have christened **Templeton Rye** (www.templetonrye.com), distributed out of a building on the edge of a cornfield. Tours may be available; call ahead to check.

There isn't much else in Templeton, so take a little detour east on IA 141 to **Coon Rapids**. Outside of town is the **Garst Farm**, a stretch of cornfields that has been largely converted to **Whiterock Conservancy** (www.whiterockconserv

---

THE LOESS HILLS:
NATURE JUST NORTH OF COUNCIL BLUFFS

While most people heading north from Council Bluffs to Sioux City rush along on I-29, you're missing out if you don't swing off onto a side road leading to one of Iowa's more scenic landscapes: the Loess Hills, dunes of blowing silt, created by glaciers, that settled into hills hundreds of feet high and offer scenic vistas over the surrounding valleys and fields.

Note: The area around the Loess Hills was significantly damaged in 2011 by Missouri River floods; call ahead to see if attractions have reopened.

The **Loess Hills Scenic Byway**, a collection of roads winding through the hills, gives a taste of the scenic vistas, while sites like the **De Soto National Wildlife Refuge** (www.fws.gov/midwest/desoto) and **Wilson Island State Park** get you closer to both the hills and the nearby river, with a chance to spot birds and wildlife, including bald eagles. There's also a salvaged steamboat at De Soto's visitors center.

Both De Soto and Wilson Island are located outside the town of **Missouri Valley**, which is also home to the **Wisecup Farm Museum** and its collection of antique farm machinery, as well as the **Harrison County Historical Village**, which has a country store, blacksmith shop and old country school. Nearby **Hitchcock Nature Center** (www.pottcoconservation.com/html/hitchcock.html) has interpretive exhibits on the Loess Hills as well as numerous hiking trails.

The farmhouse at Garst Farm, Coon Rapids

ancy.org), a natural paradise with miles of hiking trails and fishing and paddling opportunities. It's also worth touring the farmhouse to see a well-preserved Iowa farm and mementos from a visit by Nikita Khrushchev.

Loop back on IA 141, continuing west of Templeton to **Manning.** This town is proud of its German heritage and is home to an authentic 1660 **Hausbarn** (www.germanhausbarn.com) from a village in the Schleswig-Holstein region of Germany. The combination home and barn has a thatched roof made of reeds grown near the Baltic Sea, giving the roof an estimated life span of 75 years.

In Manning's **Heritage Park,** where the Hausbarn is located, visitors also will find the **Leet/Hassler Farmstead,** which includes a bungalow with Mission-style furnishings dating from its construction in 1915. The grounds also contain a car-

KHRUSHCHEV IN IOWA: THE COLD WAR THAWS IN THE CORNFIELDS

Amazingly enough, Garst Farm was the site of one of the most incredible scenes during the Cold War. When Soviet premier Nikita Khrushchev made plans for a 1959 visit to the U.S., the two people he specifically asked to see were President Dwight Eisenhower and Roswell Garst, an Iowa farmer who had developed a form of seed corn he had earlier brought to the Soviet Union, and who favored more open dialogue between the U.S. and the Soviets.

During his visit to Garst's farm, Khrushchev and his family shared a picnic lunch with the Garst family and toured the farm. The easygoing visit may have helped smooth the way for Khrushchev's talks with Eisenhower later in his trip. He and Garst remained in touch for many years afterward, as did their families.

riage house and several other out-buildings. **Kinderfest** is celebrated every June in Manning.

The sights keep popping up as you retrace IA 141 back toward Templeton, then hang south on US 71 to **Audubon**. A large statue of **Albert the Bull** greets guests in a park on the south side of town. A Hereford who stands in the historic heart of beef country, Albert stands 30 feet tall and weighs 45 tons, with much of his interior steel framework salvaged from old farm windmills.

Audubon also pays homage to its namesake, noted naturalist **John James Audubon**, with a statue, murals in the town post office and library, and a "bird walk" made up of sidewalk tiles featuring different birds from Audubon's book, *Birds of America*.

South of Audubon you can visit **Nathaniel Hamlin Park**, with displays on cornhusking and historical buildings, as well as a long row of windmills and a herd of elk grazing in a field. Farther south is the **Courthouse Museum**, which examines local history.

Double back on US 71 and veer west on IA 44 at the town of **Hamlin** (not to be confused with the park) so you can move on to more European heritage: the towns of **Kimballton** and **Elk Horn**. Both have strong Danish roots; a park on Kimballton's main drag even has a statue of the **Little Mermaid**.

Swing south onto IA 173 and drive the few miles to the bigger town of Elk Horn, which is proudly known as the largest rural Danish settlement in the U.S. Several sights in town evoke Denmark, including a large **Danish windmill** (www.danishwindmill.com) and the **Danish Immigrant Museum** (www.danish-museum.org), whose exhibits and buildings include a homesteader's log cabin and the house of a *bedstemor* (grandmother). To top it all off, a **Tivoli Fest** is held around Memorial Day every year.

At this point you are less than 10 miles north of an onramp to I-80, which

Danish influences like this windmill can be seen throughout Elk Horn.

you can either take west to Council Bluffs or east to Des Moines, or else cross the interstate and continue with the trip.

About 8 miles after crossing the interstate you reach the somewhat larger town of **Atlantic,** which has some decent overnight accommodations. From Atlantic, the trip loops into the country and then returns, beginning by following US 6 south to nearby **Lewis.** Sitting on a promontory overlooking the East Nishnabotna River, **Hitchcock House** (www.hitchcockhouse.org) is a brown sandstone structure that served as a stop on the Underground Railroad. Escaping slaves would hide in a secret room in the basement as they moved stealthily on their trek to freedom. Iowa was close to the front lines of the Underground Railroad, as some slaves crossed the border from nearby Missouri, although many came from what is now Kansas and eventually passed into Iowa from nearby Nebraska City on the Missouri River. Volunteers give tours and provide information about the Underground Railroad.

From Lewis, the loop route stays on US 6 to **Oakland,** where it hooks north on US 59 to **Avoca.** Here there's a tractor lover's paradise: **Farmall-Land USA** (www.farmall-land-usa.com), which has more than 150 tractors ranging from full-size behemoths to pedal and toy tractors. Each is accompanied by an informative display explaining its history and uses.

A little east of Avoca on IA 83 is **Walnut,** where there's a profusion of **antiques shops** (www.iowasantiquecity.com), lending it the nickname "The Antique City." There are some 20 shops in town, and the main commercial street, appropriately named Antique City Drive, has shops lining both sides in addition to restaurants and cafés that are nice places to take a break from hunting for the perfect finds. You may also want to check out the **Walnut Creek Historical Museum** while you're in town.

It's about 15 miles back to Atlantic, following IA 83 East as it jogs through the countryside. Once again, you may wish to jump on the interstate or take one more loop tour through small towns and rural areas.

This last loop begins by shooting due south on US 71 and following it for more than 30 miles to **Villisca,** whose main attraction is a house that was the site in 1912 of a horrific unsolved murder of eight individuals as they slept. Today, tours are given of both the **Villisca Ax Murder House** (www.villiscaiowa.com) and the local cemetery, describing the events and the mystery surrounding the murder; call in advance to arrange a tour. Some visitors even arrange to stay overnight in the house; does that sound like a good idea to you?

South of Villisca is **Clarinda,** birthplace of both 4-H and Glenn Miller, both of which are commemorated in the town's **Nodaway Valley Museum** (http://nod awayvalleymuseum.org). Next, head west on US 34 to **Stanton,** where you can complete the tour of Scandinavian heritage in southwest Iowa at the **Swedish Heritage and Cultural Center** (www.stantoniowa.com), which has lots of artifacts and other displays. You can also operate an old telephone switchboard, work a 19th-century loom and even slide down a retro school fire escape. An old country school sits on the grounds of the center, and the town's water towers, which can be seen from the center, are shaped like a Swedish coffeepot and cup.

Less than 10 miles west of Stanton on US 34 is **Red Oak,** whose historic neighborhood of **Heritage Hill** has homes of several architectural styles from the turn of the 20th century. The **Montgomery County Courthouse** is an interesting Missouri limestone structure in Richardsonian Romanesque design. Stop in at the **Montgomery County History Center** to see displays of everything from prehistoric cultures to modern times.

Finally, head west on US 34 to the town of **Glenwood,** which sits at the southern end of the Loess Hills, not far from the Missouri River, to see how some of the original inhabitants of the area lived at **Glenwood American Indian Earth Lodge,** a replica of the type of dwelling used by an area Plains Indian culture.

From here, you're even closer to I-29 and a short drive back to Council Bluffs.

IN THE AREA

ACCOMMODATIONS

Many of the listed accommodations are found in small country towns. Located at a crossroads of two interstates, Council Bluffs has numerous franchise hotels, as well as rooms available at local casino hotels (see *Entertainment and Recreation*).

Adams Street Bed & Breakfast, 726 North Adams Street, Carroll. Call 712-792-5198 or 1-866-792-0726. This restored historic home has five guest rooms, including three suites with a king-sized bed, gas fireplace and whirlpool tub. All rooms have modern amenities like cable television service and a DVD player. It's just a short walk to downtown. Inexpensive to Moderate. Website: www.adams streetbandb.com.

Big Grove Country Inn, 18807 450th Street, Oakland. Call 712-482-6840. One of the more unique accommodations you'll stay in anywhere: an authentic log cabin reassembled at this rural bed & breakfast. It's comfortable inside, with a modern bathroom and bed along with a stone fireplace. There are also more contemporary rooms available and a restaurant that serves hearty meals. Moderate. Website: www.biggrove.com.

Cabin by the Creek, 1938 G Avenue, Red Oak. Call 712-623-4757. This bed & breakfast sits alongside a restored dairy barn and a relaxing pond in the rolling countryside outside Red Oak. It's large and fully modernized, with two guest rooms festooned with quilts and antiques. The breakfast is a nice start to the day. Moderate. Website: www.cabinbythecreek.net.

Clark's Country Inn, 701 Walnut Street, Walnut. Call 712-784-3010. An antique-filled home (naturally, in Iowa's self-proclaimed antiques capital) with three very reasonably priced guest rooms with private baths. The front porch swing and outdoor pond invite relaxation, and fall leaf colors on the trees around the house are especially pretty. Walk a few blocks to the antiques shops. Inexpensive. Website: http://clarkscountryinn.com.

Conner's Corner Bed & Breakfast, 104 South 15th Street, Denison. Call 712-263-8826. A converted turreted mansion with stained glass and hardwood floors. Pleasant, nicely accessorized rooms include private baths and individual details like canopy or antique beds. The inn was for sale as of 2011 and at last check was accepting reservations only for groups who book the whole house for two or more consecutive nights; call to see about its current status. Moderate. Website: www.connerscorner.com.

Crescent View Bed & Breakfast, 1200 Walnut Street, Crescent. Call 712-227-0051. Magnificent views await guests of this B&B perched on a bluff above the Missouri River. Two guest rooms are well appointed with both fireplaces and high-definition television sets; one has a canopy bed. Both have private baths with Jacuzzi tubs. Take a seat on the outdoor patio and breathe in the fresh country air as you take in the rolling hills. Breakfast is a classy affair, with eggs Benedict and quiche among the offerings. Moderate. Website: www.crescentview bnb.com.

Deb's Bed & Breakfast, 305 Park Street, Westside. Call 712-663-4285 or 1-866-433-9209. Country and small-town living is the thing at this modest home just off US 30 between Denison and Carroll. Sip coffee or tea on the porch as you gaze out at the neighborhood. There are three guest rooms, each with amenities like a king-sized or four-poster queen-sized bed. Very reasonably priced. Inexpensive.

Gin's Inn, 216 South Main Street, Templeton. Call 712-669-9200. This small farming hamlet seems an odd place for a bed & breakfast, but visitors to Templeton Rye Distillery or nearby attractions in Coon Rapids or Manning may want to spend a night in one of the four themed rooms. The large front porch is a nice spot to kick back with a favorite beverage. Inexpensive to Moderate. Website: www .ginsinn.com.

Glidden House Bed & Breakfast, 2640 Donna Reed Road, Denison. Call 712-263-2238. This modern home in the countryside beyond Denison has

four modestly priced guest rooms along with a game room and two fireplaces that are nice to gather around in winter. A delicious breakfast makes for a good start to the morning. Inexpensive to Moderate.

Harrisdale Homestead, 60182 Dallas Road, Atlantic. Call 712-254-2254. Situated on a working farm, this bed & breakfast features a real country breakfast and four simple, modestly priced guest rooms. This is about as remote as it gets: the home sits on a narrow farm road surrounded by a sea of green fields. A real look at rural life in Iowa. Inexpensive. Website: www.harrisdale.com.

Hartwig House Inn, 407 North Main Street, Denison. Call 712-263-2540. A large, impressive home surrounded by a wide lawn, with three guest rooms that retain their original furniture but have been upgraded with modern conveniences. All have private baths. There are two sitting areas and a guest-only kitchen where breakfast is served. Inexpensive to Moderate. Website: www.hartwig house.com.

Providence Inn, 1517 First Avenue South, Denison. Call 712-263-5548. A beautiful remodeled Victorian with a huge front porch and a homey feel, this bed & breakfast has six cozy rooms with both shared and private baths as well as space to kick back with a favorite book. Linger in the breakfast nook before taking a stroll around the neighborhood. Inexpensive to Moderate. Website: www.providenceinnbnb.com.

SF Martin House Bed & Breakfast, 419 Poplar Street, Atlantic. Call 712-243-5589. Known as much for its restaurant as its accommodations, this Victorian home is a true step back in time, complete with vintage chandeliers and a player piano. There are three guest rooms, with touches of shabby charm. Inexpensive.

Whiterock Resort, 1390 IA 141, Coon Rapids. Call 712-684-2964. Just off a main road cutting through the cornfields, this farm turned sylvan paradise has a choice of lodgings: the **Garst Home Farm Lodge** is a bed & breakfast in the main farmhouse, site of a famous visit by Soviet premier Nikita Khrushchev, with five rooms ranging in size and with amenities like televisions and DVD players. Other accommodations are available in cottages located deeper in the conservancy. No other food service is available, but you can arrange catering in advance. Moderate. Website: www.whiterockconservancy.org/whiterock-resort.html.

DINING

There isn't much upscale dining in this largely rural area; it's a meat-and-potatoes, small-town café kind of place.

Bloomer's Bar-N-Grill, 1235 Plaza Drive, Carroll. Call 712-792-9101. A classic sports bar with some fine pub grub like burgers, chili, chicken strips, nachos, wings and other tasty finger food. There are booths, tables and of course seats at the bar, where you can closely watch any of the many games playing on the televisions overhead. Inexpensive. Website: www.bloomersbar.com.

Cronk's Café, 812 Fourth Avenue South, Denison. Call 712-263-4191. Fill up on an Iowa classic, the breaded pork tenderloin sandwich, at this unassuming restaurant. Other meat sandwiches are available, but go with the tenderloin, pounded until tender and fried to a delicious crispiness. Inexpensive.

Danish Inn, 4116 Main Street, Elk Horn. Call 712-764-4251. This nondescript, low-slung building on Elk Horn's largely quiet main drag hides a restaurant positively overflowing with delicious American and Danish food. Prime rib, shrimp and crab legs share the bill with Danish meatballs, sausage and stuffed pork loin. You may also want to try a *smorrebrod,* or open-faced Danish sandwich. The weeknight buffet is a popular choice, as is the Sunday lunch/brunch buffet. Website: www.danishinnrestaurant.com.

Darrell's Place, 4010 First Street, Hamlin. Call 712-563-3922. Another purveyor of the famous Iowa pork tenderloin sandwich; this one is a contender for the best tenderloin in the state, with an especially tasty hunk of breaded pork. There are also good hamburgers and chicken nuggets. The standard accompaniment is a mug of frosty root beer. Inexpensive.

Duncan's Café, 501 South Main Street, Council Bluffs. Call 712-328-3360. Nothing fancy here, just good comfort food at a downtown breakfast and lunch spot that draws a crowd of longtime, loyal regulars. You can chow down on a burger or barbecued pork sandwich while wedged into a booth or seated at a table. Duncan's is also known for its chicken plates. Inexpensive.

Main Street Café, 102 South Main Street, Council Bluffs. Call 712-328-3801. Another all-American diner in downtown Council Bluffs, Main Street Café serves decent if unexciting burgers, sandwiches and lunch plates, as well as good homestyle breakfasts. Be sure to try a slice of pie for dessert. Inexpensive.

SHOPPING

Kanesville Kollectibles, 530 South Fourth Street, Council Bluffs. Call 712-328-8731. *Tons* of old vinyl records and other pop culture treasures line the floors and walls of this wonderfully dusty shop in a historic building just outside downtown. You could spend hours just flicking through the platters, probably recognizing ones you once owned. Website: http://kanesville.tripod.com/kanesville.

Olive Branch Country Store, 19278 Conifer Lane, Council Bluffs. Call 712-322-2669. All kinds of neat stuff can be found at this old school–style store, everything from jewelry to gifts to personal care products. Poke around the shelves in search of unique knickknacks. Website: http://olivebranchcountrystore.blogspot.com.

RECREATION AND ENTERTAINMENT

Ameristar Casino, 2200 River Road, Council Bluffs. Call 712-328-8888. Slots, video poker and table games. Website: www.ameristar.com/Council_Bluffs.aspx.

Harrah's Casino, 1 Harrah's Boulevard (I-29 Exit 53A), Council Bluffs. Call 712-329-6000. Slots, video poker and table games as well as restaurants and hotels with amenities like spas and children's programs. Website: www.harrahscouncilbluffs.com.

Horseshoe Casino Council Bluffs and Bluffs Run Greyhound Racing, 2701 23rd Avenue, Council Bluffs. Call 712-323-2500. A combination casino with slots and table games as well as regular greyhound racing. Website: www.horseshoecouncilbluffs.com.

OTHER CONTACTS

Council Bluffs Convention & Visitors Bureau, 149 West Broadway,

Council Bluffs, 51501. Call 712-325-1000 or 1-800-228-6878. Website: www.councilbluffscvb.com.

Missouri Valley Chamber of Commerce, 100 South Fourth Street, Missouri Valley, 51555. Call 712-642-2553. Website: www.missourivalleychamber.com.

City of Denison, 111 North Main Street, Denison, 51442. Call 712-263-3143. Website: www.denisonia.com.

Carroll Chamber of Commerce, 407 West Sixth Street, Carroll, 51401. Call 712-792-4383. Website: www.carrolliowa.com.

Audubon County Tourism, 800 Market Street, Audubon, 50025. Call 712-563-2742. Website: www.audubon county.com.

Atlantic Area Chamber of Commerce, 102 Chestnut Street, Atlantic, 50022. Call 712-243-3017 or 1-877-283-2124. Website: www.Atlantic Iowa.com.

Red Oak Chamber and Industry Association, 307 East Reed Street, Red Oak, 51566. Call 712-623-4821. Website: www.redoakiowa.com.

Glenwood Area Chamber of Commerce, 32½ North Walnut Street, Glenwood, 51534. Call 712-527-3298. Website: www.glenwoodia.com.